T0294266

Foreign devils and other journalists

Foreign devils and other journalists

Edited by
Damien Kingsbury, Eric Loo and Patricia Payne

Monash Asia Institute
Clayton

Monash Asia Institute
Monash University
Victoria 3800
Australia

www.monash.edu.au/mai
monash.asia.institute@adm.monash.edu.au

© Monash Asia Institute 2000

National Library of Australia cataloguing-in-publication data:

Foreign devils and other journalists

Bibliography
ISBN 0 7326 1183 0

1. Journalism - Australia - Objectivity. 2. Journalism - Australia - Political aspects. 3. Journalism - Asia, Southeastern - Objectivity. 4. Journalism - Asia, Southeastern - Political aspects. 5. Asia, Southeastern - Foreign relations - Australia. 6. Australia - Foreign relations - Asia, Southeastern. I. Kingsbury, Damien. II. Loo, Eric Giap-seng. III. Payne, Trish. (Series : Monash papers on Southeast Asia ; no. 52).

070.449959

Designed and edited by Emma Hegarty
Typeset by Emma Barling
Cover design by Bernard Romerona
Printed by Brown Prior Anderson

Contents

Introduction

Damien Kingsbury, Eric Loo and Patricia Payne

It is a truism that the world has entered an era dominated by mass communication, in which the flow of information increasingly shapes or contributes to the lives and world views of the citizens of the global community. Within that flow of information and for all its shortcomings, the news media stand out as the primary source of mass communication, for Australia, for the states of Southeast Asia and elsewhere.

Acknowledging the fundamental role of the news media in mass communication, this collection of essays looks at some of the more prominent issues concerning both the news media in Southeast Asia and, as Australia has moved to enmesh itself in the region, between Australia and the states of Southeast Asia. We have brought together essays from some of Australia's leading observers of and commentators on the news media in Southeast Asia and on Australia's regional media relations. Each of the contributions offers its own insights and perspectives, but together we believe they begin to offer an overarching assessment of the issues.

Some of the essays here were first presented, in their original form, in July 1996 at the 20th annual conference of the Asian Studies Association of Australia, which was entitled 'Communicating with/in Asia'. It was believed that these papers addressed critical issues in the field of the news media's communication both with and in Southeast Asia in particular. There was also thought to be sufficient congruence between the original papers for them to be presented as a collection. As we discussed this group of essays the editors were drawn to work by other scholars in the field, and subsequently took the liberty of also including some further relevant essays.

The respective analyses offered here provide a variety of perspectives that should assist discussion and critical assessment of the role of the news media within the region. Some of the perspectives also have potential for application in principle within debates about the news media in other regional contexts.

Having noted that, the role of the news media across a range of political, economic, cultural and technological settings is complex and often problematic. Though initially an invention of the West and finding its most conducive home within a liberal pluralist framework, it cannot automatically be assumed that the news media can or want to identify themselves with such an ideological position. It may be that liberal pluralist news media form a type that is idealised by some observers, but which may not reflect the reality of its purpose or function or may, in some cases, be inappropriate.

The news media's traditionally accepted role was that they acted as a watchdog over public affairs, to scrutinise governments and other official institutions and to offer a voice to the general public. They were the means by which people learned of relevant events, through which grievances could be aired and, not least, a source of entertainment. A more critical approach to the news media also had them as essentially reflecting the views of controlling elites, providing a voice for dominant social interests while excluding those considered threatening, difficult, unworthy or irrelevant. Yet another view suggested that the news media had a central role in the enhancement and development of the lives of ordinary people, that they should be educational and constructive and act as positive team members in achieving socially worthwhile goals.

Only a step away from this, some governments, seeing themselves as the embodiment of the state, have often attempted to harness the news media as a tool not only for social and economic development, but also as a means of enhancing their political well being. There is perhaps no government that has not tried to at least influence the news media in this respect, and in a market place of competing ideas this is perhaps as legitimate a contribution to the information process as any other. Everyone has agendas—even the news media themselves.

The role of the news media in Southeast Asia did not just begin, but is located within its history of reporting significant events from the region. One of the most notable events that made news in Southeast Asia, and which could be said to have marked the greatest intensity of foreign interest in the region, was the Vietnam War. As an event that involved Australian and other allied troops and, at least initially, was considered to reflect the international tensions associated with the Cold War, the Vietnam conflict was a primary source of news, and the reporting of it helped shape public perceptions of the purpose and efficacy of foreign involvement there.

Perhaps more than any other conflict, the Vietnam War was considered to be the first 'reporters' war', in which reports and often graphic images were relayed outside of the country within hours of taking place. In the period immediately following the war the news media were accused of having unravelled the allied effort in Vietnam. This view has been successfully challenged by the emergence of information which clearly notes that the war was already unravelling, and fails to note that throughout the conflict the news media was largely 'on side'. Nevertheless, the power of the myth of news media manipulation articulated after the Vietnam War heralded an era of consistent railing against the purported power, accuracy and intent of news media coverage and commentary. This practice of abuse of the news media continues from political leader, who have built on the foundation of the myth largely created in their own interests.

Another significant aspect of reporting of the Vietnam War was the development of Australian public awareness of the complexities of Southeast Asia. Reporting of the war accentuated the reality of Australia's geographic proximity to the region, as well as highlighting Australian ignorance of it. Much contemporary interest in Southeast Asia can be traced back to the Vietnam War and the issues it raised.

Since these tumultuous events of the 1960s and 70s, the news media have developed and their processes of communication are far more immediate than even the quick turn around of information from the Vietnam conflict. Rather than typing hard copy and transmitting it by telex, crudely transmitting photographic images over telephone lines or flying film from news bureaux back to television stations 'at home', the news media employ new technological developments.

Portable computers feed stories via modem direct to sub-editors on news desks, photographs are scanned and similarly filed direct to sub-editors' terminal screens ready for pagination, and satellites now ensure that video images are transmitted almost immediately from bureaux to television, cable and satellite networks, while reports live from the field have become almost commonplace, giving audiences both immediate and intimate access to events.

New media technologies are also beginning to make an impact on the flow of information, both as conventional news and in forms that as yet defy categorisation. The most popularly discussed new media form is the internet, which allows individuals to communicate directly with increasingly large audiences via 'news pages' or 'websites' on the world wide web—a network of personal computers connected to each other via modem/telephone through 'service providers'.

Similarly, satellite technology does not formally acknowledge terrestrial boundaries and the flow of information across borders is increasing. In societies where there are restrictions on the style or content of information that may be made available, this would appear to offer scope for a freer access to information. Yet limitations can apply here too. In a field as diverse and complex as that of the news media, the hopes invested in these new technological forms for increasing the free flow of information may yet bear fruit, but they may also have confused enthusiastic desire for cold reality.

In any case, the free flow of information implies a certain universality of such desire, which is not always universally endorsed. In the first instance, a greater quantity of information does not imply a greater quality of information, and audiences may simply turn away from the growing avalanche of trivia and irrelevance. Changes to technology could imply a need to rethink how information is communicated, and perhaps what is being communicated. Certainly, if the current revolution in communications technology is as profound as some of its proponents claim, existing communications styles could become as displaced as oral traditions after the invention of the printing press and consequent mass literacy.

Further, in a world which is increasingly 'globalised'—in which ideas and the media that carry them have the potential to transcend borders—there is also a move towards a greater sense of identification with the local. There may be aspects of social identification that can be considered to apply to all people all of the time (or most people most of the time), but faced with such often overwhelming and sometimes unpalatable universality many people also find comfort in retreating into the familiar, or calling on familiar cues to construct (or reconstruct) their sense of self in opposition to this communicated 'other'. Culture, in this sense, has become more self-conscious.

This self-consciousness of culture and the shared identify of communities challenges what could be seen to be the hegemonic implications of an information process that is still dominated, in world terms, by news media primarily located in the major Western capitals. Not only is the information supplied by these outlets not value-free, but it often carries the types of messages that can be considered offensive, confrontational and possibly dangerous or in just plain poor taste.

By presenting a particular world view as universal, the news media can be said to be imposing a set of values that do not find consonance with the local experience. The perceived imposition of such a world view can be almost too readily understood as a form of cultural imperialism, perhaps more insidious than conventional imperialism because, inadvertently perhaps, it attempts to colonise people's minds rather than their homes. Yet this implies a certain premeditation, which news practitioners tend to argue against almost regardless of their own cultural location.

In this sense, it will be instructive to watch the growth of the news media in Southeast Asian societies, where a range of different agendas is contributing to the development of a potential and probable challenge to the existing Western news media giants. It may be that the Western model of the news media is not the only one that is viable, and a model that is more appropriate to emerging Southeast Asian states better reflects a non-Western cultural framework.

This issue of culture and its construction then begs the question of the construction of the nation-state, which is a particularly difficult area in a region, the states where are almost entirely defined by the colonial experience. For the state to be viable, there must be a shared sense of common purpose, a standardisation of the 'local' world view. Yet no state in the Southeast Asian regional can claim cultural homogeneity, even in broad terms, so the construction of a 'national' culture is beset by difficulties even before it begins. Add to this sometimes the competing claims to cultural identification, or simply different world views, and the edifice of the post-colonial state can start to look shaky.

To include in this potentially volatile mixture external cultural influence, such as the news media, bringing with them not just a competing world view but sometimes one that can be viewed as intentionally divisive, there is a recipe not just for conflict but, potentially, for a challenge to the state itself. For this reason, and that of 'development', it is not surprising that many state leaders have attempted to co-opt the news media to assist in this purpose. In some states the news media only allowed to operate within certain guidelines, or more or less under direct government control.

However, particularly in states where there is an infrequent change of government, the state and its government tend to become conflated and the interests of protecting the state soon become those of protecting the interests of the government. Further, government appeals to controlling the news media on cultural or developmental grounds sometimes reflect the construction of an official culture or the development of a particularly cosy economy, which may suit the interests of a ruling elite but which may or may not reflect the aspirations or world views of the people who comprise the state.

Hence, there is potential for conflict between governments and the news media, within states and between states. It is these areas of culture and politics, conflict and contestation, of controlling or using the media or being controlled or used by it, or of driving or being driven by news media agendas, upon which the material in this book rests.

Fact or Friction?
The collision of journalism values in Asia

Alan Knight

The media play a key role in the life of every country, but it is a role which differs from one country to another. When these differences are misunderstood or ignored; as frequently happens in the Western media operating in developing countries, the result is friction.

Lee Kuan Yew, then Singapore's Prime Minister, speaking to the American Society of Newspaper Editors, 14 April 1988. (Lee 1989:117)

Journalists can no longer hide behind national boundaries, ignoring the impact of their reporting on neighbouring countries. Satellite television, interactive news services, improved telephone and fax services and the internet do not acknowledge border checkpoints, challenging politicians' attempts to censor or direct news. But these new technologies, spread by rising affluence, also allow wrong or insensitive reports to bounce rapidly around the region's media, encouraging disharmony and discrimination.

Reports of a racist politician receiving support in Australia can be transmitted instantly to audiences across the ASEAN nations, threatening negotiated trade and diplomatic arrangements. Asian governments, which may not themselves espouse media freedoms, can choose to interpret such reports as evidence to support caricatures of Australians as ignorant, ill-educated white supremacists. Australian reporters, meanwhile, can be characterised as dishonest by Asian politicians seeking to bolster sagging domestic political support. Reports detailing ruling family corruption in Jakarta during the Suharto period were likewise regarded as a direct insult to the national interest and international diplomacy.

Australia, which has the longest tradition of a free press in the region, is in danger of being unfairly castigated for its journalists' robust approach to reporting, if not their insensitivities to non-Western cultures. Australian working journalists' lack of self-analysis means that many assume that value systems they learn in Australia are universal. When foreign correspondents with such views arrive in Southeast Asia, this ignorance of 'other' media procedures can be interpreted as cultural arrogance. The collision between differing journalism value systems can result in what Singapore's Senior Minister, Lee Kuan Yew, calls 'friction'. Australian journalists' long held identification with what they call Western interests, and what many Asians identify as the old colonial powers, make them easy targets for increasingly well connected and articulate Asian critics.

Even conservative news organisations recognise the need for change. The former Editor in Chief of *The Australian*, Paul Kelly, said that Australian journalists should try to be sensitive to cultural differences as a matter of professionalism. Kelly said that Western journalists should be particularly aware of the tone they used when reporting Asia:

> I think that we still find it difficult in as much as our cultural predilections are to the United States and to the UK, and we must continue to cover those parts of the world because they're important in their own right and their certainly very much the areas of interest for a lot of our readers. But by the same token it's enormously important for us to expand and improve our coverage of Asia far more than what we've been able to do. I think this is going to be an ongoing and difficult challenge for the Australian media. (Kelly 1996)

Australians are coming to understand what many Asians have long recognised: negative and stereotypical reporting is not only inaccurate and ethically wrong, it can have a direct impact on national economies and international relations. Singaporean consumers can easily choose other than 'racist' Aussie beef. Malaysians can send their children to someone else's universities. Wealthy Indonesians can do their Christmas shopping in Hong Kong instead of Sydney.

Competing ideologies

There are at least three broadly defined news theories that can be identified in reports on the Southeast Asian region. As a result, notions of 'truth' should be considered as not only being created by differing perceptions but as also resulting within different theoretical frames.

Hong Kong, Thailand, the Philippines and, during UNTAC's administration, Cambodia[1], allowed what Fred Siebert called 'libertarian' journalism. With the introduction of satellite television such liberal Western news values, as practised and promoted by the Atlanta based CNN network, or the London based BBC World Service, penetrated previously isolated audiences from Korea to Pakistan.[2] Meanwhile, Indonesia, Malaysia and Singapore officially encouraged what the ASEAN secretariat described as 'development' journalism. China, Laos and Vietnam applied what Malaysia's Prime Minister, Mahathir Mohamad, called 'the authoritarian and communist models'.

---

[1] Cambodia's 1993 constitution guaranteed a free press. However, the Minister for Information, Ieng Mouly, was quoted in the *South China Morning Post* (24 November 1993): 13, as saying that any journalist who criticised King Sihanouk would be arrested. The Ministry had banned the printing of photographs of 'scantily clad women'.

[2] The author observed a small cable system running across the rooftops in Phnom Penh, which allowed local families to tune into Hong Kong television via Star TV.

Mahathir, who takes a close personal interest in international media reporting, defined the three approaches in the following ways. He said the authoritarian or communist model required the journalist to act not only as a voice but also as an arm of the state:

> Under the communist model there can be only one truth—the truth as defined by the party—the media must work assiduously to mould opinion to ensure a oneness of perception and thought. The existence of one view, 'the correct view' is ideal. (Mahatir 1989:110)

Under the 'development' journalism model, favoured by Mahathir:

> ...the media must be allowed to compete in the economic market place and curry the favour of their target customers, but they must do so within the bounds of decency and responsibility. Contrary to what is thought in many of even the best journalism institutions, the deadline is not sacred. In my view, and I state this without any reservation or apology, the public good is always sacred. (Mahatir 1989:116)

According to Mahathir, libertarian theory stated that:

> man [sic] is a supremely rational animal with an insatiable desire for truth; the only method by which truth can be grasped is by the free competition of opinion in the open market place of ideas. (Mahatir 1989:111)

With the virtual disappearance of the Australian communist presses following the collapse of the Soviet Union,[3] it can now be said that nearly all Australian journalists work within the libertarian theory of the media defined by Fred Siebert in 1956. The concept of 'freedom of the press' is rooted in Western concepts of liberalism, where government is believed to serve individuals who are regarded as rational beings. Siebert argued that, in theory at least, the libertarian media aimed to serve the public.

> Under the libertarian concept, the functions of the mass media are to inform and entertain. A third function was developed as a necessary correlate to the others to provide a basis of economic support and thus to assure financial independence. Basically the underlying purpose of the media was to help discover truth, to assist in the process of solving political and social problems by presenting all manner of evidence and opinion for the basis of opinions. (Siebert et al 1963:51)

Western paradigms

Australian journalists learn industry practices and priorities within a Western professional culture that tolerates if not encourages criticism of

---

[3] The Australian Communist Party weekly, *Tribune*, ceased publication in 1992. The former Trotskyist weekly, *Direct Action*, was reconstituted in 1991 as *Green Left Weekly*, which continues to published with a part-time staff. However, the newspaper is no longer an expression of a party line, with articles being produced by a wider group.

governments, corporations and prominent personalities. They usually endorse the first article of the code of professional conduct for the International Federation of Journalists, which states that 'Respect for the truth and for the right of the public to the truth is the first duty of the journalist'.

Within Australia , the pursuit of the 'truth' can be delayed and diverted by near monopolies of media ownership, and state and federal government interventions as well as defamation, contempt of court and security legislation imposing 'D' notices. But, as local media organisations are absorbed into transnational media entertainment corporations, commercial considerations can also be seen to influence international news coverage. Hugh Menzies told *Intersections with Asia* that a growing number of today's media empires are owned by companies whose managements were not all that interested in the truth-seeking aspect of journalism:

> The new owners want their empires to have a piece of the Asian business action and are not about to let their news operations, which contribute little or no profits, mess things up by revealing too many naked emperors.

> The full ramifications of this development are yet to play out. But there has been at least one straw in the wind. During the opening ceremonies of the Atlantic Olympics, NBC commentator Bob Costas make a passing remark about China's less-than-scintillating human rights record. Other commentators subsequently discussed charges of drug-taking by Chinese swimmers, observing that their performances at the Games fell far below previous efforts when drug-testing was less strict. Beijing complained and NBC subsequently apologized. (Menzies 1996)

Menzies said that NBC was now owned by General Electric, which had a massive investment stake in China. 'News coverage does not contribute much to GE's bottom line and, today, bottom lines matter more than prestige,' Menzies said.

This conservative view of news can be seen to coincide with the sort of development journalism defined by some Asian governments who see the 'bottom line' of nation building as more important than truth seeking. In countries where the business affairs of the ruling elite have become intertwined with government privilege, it can be only a short step from censoring in the national interest to adjusting news agendas to benefit profits.

Development journalism

The governments of Malaysia, Singapore and, before the fall of Suharto, Indonesia, endorsed the concept of 'development journalism', which placed the role of journalists within the task of nation building. Whitney R Mundt, writing in *Global Journalism*, stated that proponents of development journalism believed that the mass media should assist in economic development, eradication of illiteracy, and political education. Under this system, a predominately privately owned press is expected to help the government be seen to seek social justice (Mundt 1991:21).

While the 'libertarian' media may seek to inform, entertain and perhaps make money, many journalists in Asia were expected to inform, interpret and promote (Chalkley 1983:94). Juan F Jamias argued that the difference between 'libertarian style' and 'development' journalism is purposiveness:

> In its strict sense, conventional journalism, rooted in the West, is non purposive. The task of the objective or non-purposive journalist is to report the facts as they are , or more realistically put, how they appear to him. These facts or vents may be interpreted but no more than this is sought in deference to the reader who is envisaged to be a customer in the free market of ideas.
>
> In contrast, the task of the development journalist is not only to inform ie to report the facts, or to interpret, but also to do promotion, to elicit action or some other behavioural change. To illustrate, an economics story about family planning, is not written for its own sake but to set an agenda for action. In short, development journalism is purposive. (Jamias 1983:99)

It follows that an Australian critique of an Asian head of state, such as Indonesia's former President Suharto, was seen in Jakarta as an offensive overstepping of normal journalism practices. Indeed, such reporting could be interpreted as an intentional insult, with implicit Australian government support. Suharto himself defined journalism in terms of Indonesian education and social development:

> Since it occupies such an important position, the press has an enormous impact in all sectors such as politics, the economy, the socia-cultural environment whether it does or does not fulfil its role and responsibilities. A successful press will accelerate efforts to achieve national targets while a press which does not fulfil its role will no doubt delay the attainment of identified targets. It is precisely this realisation on the part of the press that has caused it to urge us to support the slogan : 'positive interaction between the press, the government and the people', as stated in the Main Guidelines of State Policy (GBHN—Garis-Garis Besar Haluan Negara). (Soeharto 1989:132)

In theory, the Indonesian government demanded support for its policies from a predominantly privately-owned yet government licensed media. In practice, this meant censorship of issues dear to government hearts, but relative freedom to discuss issues further afield. Prior to the pro-democracry riots in 1998, reports on Suharto family corruption did not appear. References to Australian corruption or incompetence continue to do so. Australian journalists often saw this as a journalistic double standard.[4]

---

[4] Indonesia's former Ambassador to Australia, Sabam Siagian, himself a former journalist, dismissed such complaints as an inability to analyse the subtleties of Indonesian journalism

Singapore

Singapore, according to Lee Kuan Yew, was 'unique'. The Republic boasted of a literate and highly educated population that the government hoped would service a communications centre rivalling Hong Kong. Meanwhile, it enforced a ban on satellite television and imposed rigorous censorship. Singapore's small size and population, as well as its policy of teaching English as a national working language, allowed the *Straits Times* group to dominate the local media. The *Straits Times*, which itself lost an uncompromising editor in a tussle with the government in 1959, emerged as the republic's only English language newspaper after government pressure forced the closure of its two competitors, the *Eastern Sun* and the *Singapore Herald*.

The Code of Professional Conduct of the Singapore National Union of Journalists outlined strict guides for behaviour by journalists. Point one of the Singaporean code could just as easily apply to a carpenter or a plumber: 'Every member shall maintain good quality of workmanship and high standard of conduct' (Razak 1985:454).

Point two seemed more concerned about how journalists were seen rather than how they acted: 'No member shall do anything that will bring discredit on himself, his union, his newspaper or other news media or his profession' (Razak 1985:454).

In contrast to the Australian, Filipino, Thai, Hong Kong and even Indonesian codes, point three of the Singaporean code provided only a qualified support for freedom of expression: 'Every member shall defend the principles of freedom in the honest collection and dissemination of news and the right of fair comment and criticism' (Razak 1985:454).

Under this code, journalists should be allowed freedom to collect and disseminate news, provided that it was done honestly and fairly. Unlike the Australian code , it is implied that someone other than journalists should be the judge of what is honest and fair. In practice, this arbiter may be the Singaporean government.

In the past, Singapore has restricted circulation of foreign newspapers, including *Time*, *Asian Wall Street Journal*, *Asiaweek* and *Far Eastern*

---

practices. He suggested that while Indonesian journalists supported their own national development, this does not mean that they necessarily have to be kind to Australia. He told an ACIJ Conference on Foreign Reporting in 1992 that 'the Indonesian press, usually dubbed a docile press by their foreign colleagues, although somewhat limited in their straight news reporting, particularly of an investigative nature—though that is not always the case—does in fact have the capability to bring about a long term impact on the political dynamics of the country'.

Economic Review. Lee Kuan Yew claimed those foreign journalists, who published their stories beyond the direct control of the Singaporean authorities, were trying to interfere with Singapore's domestic politics:

> Singapore's domestic debate is a matter for Singaporeans. We allow their [certain foreign] papers to sell in Singapore so that we can know what foreigners are reading about us. But we cannot allow them to assume a role in Singapore that the American media play in America, that of invigilator, adversary, and inquisition of the administration. If allowed to do so they will radically change the nature of Singapore society, and I doubt whether out social glue is strong enough to stand such treatment. (Lee 1988:121–122)

Lee, like Mahathir, inherited substantial powers over the press, an established system of censorship and active Special Branch from the British colonial government, which sought to limit 'free speech' during the Malayan 'emergency'. (Barber 1971:189; 216)

In the post colonial era, continuing restrictions were paraded as a virtue, an indigenous counter to the dangers associated with development.[5] In recent years, this argument has been refined with a claim that Western campaigns for human rights, including freedom of the press, should not necessarily apply to Asians. In the context of journalism, this approach was described as 'Asian' news values, where responsibility to national cohesion superseded liberal notions of a marketplace of ideas.

Indeed, the Singapore *Straits Times* Training Manager, Shiva Arasu, recently argued that free speech may be more fiction than reality, even in Western countries whose own press criticise Singapore's media controls. Ms Arasu said that freedom of the press was already moderated by government intervention and entirely contained by the self interests of media owners:

> The degree of freedom enjoyed is determined by political and commercial considerations. Every newspaper and TV station determines for itself how much freedom it can possibly enjoy. This tradition and practice is universal, both in the east as well as the west. In recent years commercial considerations have become more prominent. Journalism is a business. (Arasu 1996)

Ms Arasu may be correct, insofar as journalists everywhere are under pressure to self censor what they learn. Yet stark differences remain in practice between countries where freedom of speech is given at least lip service and more authoritarian regimes where it is questioned or suppressed. Dissident journalists may find it difficult to find a job in Australian

---

[5] At the 1978 Commonwealth Heads of Government Conference in Sydney, which I covered, Lee deflected Australian media questions about Singapore's authoritarianism by suggesting that the oppression of Australian Aborigines indicated that Australians' attitude to Asia was characterised by racism. Foreshadowing the rise of the developing economies and Australia's relative decline, he predicted Australians would become 'the poor white trash of Asia'.

mainstream media obsessed with economic rationalism, contemptuous of non-parliamentary political debate and infatuated with infotainment. But in Singapore, journalists have been forced to write theatrical reviews to skirt the official censors and avoid the threat of criminal libel.[6] In Suharto's Indonesia, the Independent Journalist Union was disbanded, activists jailed and critical magazines banned.[7] China, meanwhile may have been making a transition to a mixed economy, but there are few signs that its aging clique of rulers is ready to consider mixed opinions among the wider population. According to Reporters sans Frontiers, China had 26 journalists in jail in 1994 (Reporters sans Frontiers 1995:72).

The 'socialist' ideal

Despite its drive for economic rationalisation, China in the late 1990s maintained tight control of information received by the population. Radio and television stations were state controlled; their executives belonged to the relevant government Propaganda Department, bulletins were still being censored on air, and armed guards with machine pistols and drawn bayonets were still on sentry duty outside studios and master control rooms. Newspapers, particularly those in the wealthy provinces or those who reported business rather than strictly political affairs, were able to exercise more degrees of independence. They were all still state-owned and bound to the idea of socialist journalism.[8] Under this journalistic philosophy, newspapers were integrated with the policies of the party and government. Articulating this theory in 1901, V I Lenin said that the press should disseminate ideas for political education, and enlist political allies, acting as a collective propagandist, agitator and collective organiser. Lenin likened newspapers to the scaffolding around a building under construction: a scaffolding that not only marked the contours of the work and that facilitated communication, but also one that allowed the builders to distribute the work and view the results. Lenin saw newspapers playing a critical role in the development and training of the 'revolutionary' party itself. Communist journalists would become more

---

[6] The play 'The Lady Soul and Her Ultimate 'S' Machine' was written by *Straits Times* journalist Tan Tarn How and performed in January and February 1993 by the Theatreworks Ltd, Singapore. It challenged censorship regulations to criticise corruption and abuse of power by Singaporean politicians.
[7] In 1995, I attended a meeting held in Jakarta to mark the first anniversary of the closure of the magazine *Tempo*. Organised as an art showing of *Tempo* cartoons as a way to circumvent a ban on un-lincensed political meetings, the event was attended by about 150 former journalists, editors and readers as well as a large number of Indonesian intelligence operatives.
[8] The *South China Morning Post* reported on 26 November 1993:
The Communist Party's mouthpiece, the *People's Daily*, has called for absolute loyalty so the party can push forward another round of reforms. In a commentary published yesterday, the paper said party members must submit to the leadership…

than a voice of the communist state, they would be perceived as an arm of the ruling party.

In his comparative study of mainland Chinese and Hong Kong press coverage of world news, Li Tsze Sun cited the *People's Daily* as a prime example of a newspaper committed to communist journalism.

> Since 1949, when the CCP [Chinese Communist Party] took over China, it has become the Central Committee's official organ. The integration of the paper into the party and the government is clearly indicated by the fact that the newspaper's leaders are the CCP's top elites. The Chinese government's intolerance of the *People's Daily* staff joining the 1989 Beijing pro democracy movement can be seen as an inevitable outcome for a newspaper of such nature. (Li 1993:4–5)

On 28 November 1989, Jiang Zemin, who had just become Party Secretary, declared that the media should operate as 'the mouthpiece of the party' as well as of 'the people'. He claimed that some Chinese journalists' support for the pro-democracy movement was linked to bourgeois liberalisation, a product of a deviation from Marxism, which he said had created confusion among the masses. Chinese journalists were subsequently required to educate the people in the spirit of patriotism, socialism, collectivism and confidence in the struggle, to overcome difficulties in China's way of reconstruction and reform. According to Jiang, journalism was an important part of the party's work, and had to keep in close contact with the masses and fight persistently against bourgeois liberalisation (Jiang 1993:214).

Gunter Lehrke, a former Deputy Secretary-General of the Singapore based Asia Media Information Research Centre, claimed this enforced politicisation caused disillusionment among mainland journalists and created disaffection among audiences:

> Demotivation and political suppression of those involved in program production are taken as tools to 'improve' the output. The officials obviously give credence to the continuous repetition of slogans that brainwash and form the new socialist individual, neglecting the desire of the audience. However, the people seem to know better and listen to foreign broadcasts. Today even farmers in remote rural areas buy short-wave receivers in order to get more reliable information. In the southern province of Guandong, peasants purchase satellite dishes to get access to foreign TV. The future beneficiaries of such systems are already identified; commercial channels and their international media tycoons. (Lehrke 1993:218)

Hong Kong

In the closing days of British colonialism, Cantonese-speaking Hong Kong-based reporters regularly went into China to record incidents otherwise ignored by the mainlaind media. Their stories about strikes, industrial accidents and police corruption provided new insights for viewers receiving broadcasts in Guandong. They also attracted criticism from Chinese officials acutely embarassed by evidence of widespread *laissez faire* exploitation in what the official Chinese media still promoted as a workers' state.

Hong Kong, while still a British Crown colony, was unquestionably the most consistent base for 'libertarian' journalism in East Asia. Freedom of expression, combined with excellent transport and communications, helped attract the largest and perhaps the most important concentration of media in the region. Hong Kong's journalistic influence was felt through its 600 strong corps of foreign correspondents, many with region-wide responsibilities, as well as through the international news magazines, news agencies and satellite television operations centred there.[9]

Hong Kong journalists making the transition to Beijing control were keenly aware of what it could mean for their work. Before the handover, there was concern that China might be more ready than Britain to enforce moribund but still repressive colonial legislation that was never erased from the Hong Kong statute books. Hong Kong Journalists Association Chair Mak YT said journalists were under subtle pressure to conform:

> While the clandestine nature of self-censorship means that it is difficult to pin down actual examples, there has at the same time been little evidence to suggest that the situation has improved. Television documentaries vilified by the Chinese government have been bought and then never broadcast, popular but critical TV programs have been axed, and critical newspaper columns and cartoons suddenly dropped. There are many reasons for self-censorship. Proprietors might wish to maintain good relations with the Chinese government to ensure post-1997 survival and a stake in the huge China market. Front-line journalists may exercise self-censorship to maintain a harmonious relationship with their contacts...Given the close relations between China and Hong Kong, Beijing is unlikely to allow Hong Kong a free hand if the political situation on the mainland becomes more tense. The media tends to become the first casualty in any such situation. (Mak 1996)

---

[9] Hong Kong has a particularly diverse and competitive media. As a 1991 Australian Department of Foreign Affairs and Trade's economic briefing paper on the colony reported:
Hong Kong has a flourishing mass media, including 69 newspapers (39 Chinese and two English dailies) and 610 periodicals at the end of 1990, two private TV companies and one government Radio/TV network...Hong Kong is a base for about 600 foreign correspondents and major regional publications such as the *Far Eastern Economic Review*, the *Asian Wall Street Journal* and *Asiaweek*. It also has a flourishing film and TV program production industry and a major printing and publishing industry.

Lands of the free

Authoritarian governments promoting 'Asian' news values attract strong and consistent criticism from journalists based in Asian countries where freedom of speech is accepted as part of the political process. Much of the opposition is centred in the Philippines and Thailand, which have themselves oscillated many times this century between authoritarianism and libertarianism.

Thailand means 'land of the free'. However, media freedoms have been qualified during swings between democracy and what have been in effect military dictatorships. The Australian news cameraman Neil Davis died there while recording once such exchange of government (Bowden 1987).

Christian missionaries introduced the first printing press to Thailand in 1835. Throughout the 19th century, publishing was mainly confined to the royal court and missionaries, advocating either Buddhism or Christianity respectively. However, the tradition of using the press to allow public debate of contending ideas was established during this period, with members of the Thai royal family submitting articles for publication under pseudonyms. The *Royal Gazette*—founded in 1858—is still used for official announcements. Daily newspapers came into their own in the early 20th century under the reign of King Vajiravudh. During his reign, some 20 dailies (among them one in Chinese and two in English) were printed (Thongbai 1990:123–124).

The first point of the Thai journalists code of ethics affirmed that the main task of all journalists was 'to promote, preserve and uphold the freedom of the press' (Razak 1985:455). The Thai press was seen to be obliged not only to report news, facts and opinions as well as help people understand the events of the day, but was also expected to look after social well being, act as a medium for social organisations, and promote and clarify social beliefs values and views. However, to perform such duties, the press demanded freedom.

Such beliefs helped create a press that ranged from 'blood, bodies and scandal' Thai language tabloid newspapers to quality English language broadsheets. Thai journalists were perceived to be more tenacious and less willing to buckle under to authorities than most of their Asian counterparts. Their freewheeling, daredevil attitudes made it more difficult for authorities to bring them to heel. During the 1992 demonstrations that brought down the military backed government in Bangkok, many newspaper journalists simply ignored threats of a crackdown (Heuvel and Dennis 1993:166–173).

The Publisher of the *Nation* newspaper, Suthichai Yoon, said that freedom of the press should not be thought of as a Western value, but rather an international one. To think otherwise would patronise Asian people in developing economies. He claimed that Thai journalists were prepared to confront the authorities to expand such freedoms:

> We fought very bravely. We really had to show the governments, both military and democratically elected, that the only way the readers, the public and international business would see Thailand in a proper way was through a free press. We tried to write credible stories which could be verified. If we continued to write stories which were true, based on facts, taking a clear position, we got the public support. And when we got the public support, it was very difficult for a military regime to stop us. (Yoon 1994)

Mr Yoon said that his newspaper did not subscribe to what some Asian leaders expounded as Asian values. He was quite sceptical, feeling that such terms were used as a prelude to censorship and for protecting powers that be. 'Asian news values and Western news values, to us, they are basically the same', he said.

> In Singapore, government propaganda may be treated as a page one lead. So we decided instead that news should be what is of interest to the readers; that which will be useful them in making decisions and judgement of political and economic issues. This is not necessarily what the government would want us to present to the readers. In Singapore, most of the stories are based on what the government thinks the readers should get. We couldn't sell our papers like that. (Yoon 1994)

Mr Yoon said that Thai journalists were 'pragmatic' about Asian values—they applied them when it seemed appropriate and discarded them when necessary.

Paisal Sricharatchanya, the Managing Director of the *Siam Post*, believes that the Thai audience is becoming more sophisticated as it becomes more affluent. Thailand's growing international trade links helped create a demand for quality journalism, which he defined as 'fast and accurate' reporting:

> The Thai press has come to be respected as the freest institution in the whole of south east Asia. Perhaps the only comparable example would be the Filipino press. But the freedom of the Filipino press is a little artificial because I think the Filipino press has been suppressed for a long time under the Marcos regime. So once the lid was lifted with the advent of people's power, press freedom exploded. In that situation, whoever had the money, tried to publish their own papers...Freedom was not built gradually over the years. Whereas in the case of Thailand freedom has been developing over the last century, so that it is more solid, more resilient and more mature. Because of that a quality press was able to develop. (Sricharatchanya 1994)

Following the overthrow of Philippines President Ferdinand Marcos in February 1986, and the abolition of martial law, the Marcos 'crony' press was ιιplaccd by a liboratod and effectively 'libertarian' media.[10] The sudden burst of freedom after 14 years of repression brought with it a surge of enthusiasm about the power of the media to improve society. In most Asian countries, political liberalisation created a gradual liberalisation of editorial policies at established newspapers. In the Philippines, change came like an avalanche, which swept many of the discredited 'crony' newspapers away (Heuvel and Dennis 1993:95). By 1993, two of the three top selling Manila daily newspapers were operated by journalists who had been banned or goaled during the Marcos years (Soliven 1994).

Maximo V Soliven, the publisher of the Philippines *Star*, believed that journalists should confront authoritarian governments. He claimed his 'banner year' was 1960, when he was ejected from Singapore, Vietnam and Burma. He was subsequently jailed by Ferdinand Marcos, and shared a cell with Ninoy Aquino, whose wife was later to launch a criminal libel action against him. Soliven said that the Filipino press should reject the 'streak of Confuciansm' that resulted in many Asians believing 'father knows best'. He described the press as 'our last best hope', providing a braking mechanism on the system of government, even though he claimed Filipino journalists were still too 'meek and cowed' (Soliven 1994).

Dr Doreen G Fernandez, Chair of the Department of Communications at the Ateno de Manila University, said that the press should act as a critic, checker and conscience of government as well as an educator of the people. The press should be sworn to tell the whole truth and nothing but the truth:

> It is the medium through which the people receive the information that they must have in order to make decisions that run the democracy. As witness, it stands as watchdog of the government on the people's behalf—not necessarily an adversary (unless the government is abusive), but ally and partner in the cause of democracy. (Mehra 1989:81)

Dr Fernandez said, however, that with this freedom came responsibility; the Filipino press had the duty to formulate and enforce its own codes.

The National Press Club of the Philippines Code of Ethics called on journalists to scrupulously report and interpret the news, taking care not to supress essential facts, nor to distort the truth by omission or by improper emphasis. Filipino journalists were asked to refain from writing reports which would adversely affect a private reputation, unless 'the interest' justified it.

---

[10] John Mills, Australian Embassy, advised by fax on 12 February 1993 that there were 14 English language newspapers in Manila, including the *Manila Bulletin* and *Philippines Daily Inquirer*. Mills described the press as 'freewheeling'. It is backed by American-style commercial television stations and privately owned radio networks, including the influential, Catholic church-owned Veritas network. According to Richard Shafer (1990) there were also 157 predominantly Tagalog language provincial newspapers.

FOREIGN DEVILS AND OTHER JOURNALISTS

- 14

FOREIGN DEVILS AND OTHER JOURNALISTS

When in doubt, dignity should the watchword of Filipino journalists, according to this code (Razak 455).

Conclusion

Australian and other Western journalists must recognise that they can longer insult Asian sensibilities by intention or just plain ignorance. They should accept and seek more Asian sources to broaden the context of stories that must reflect the region's changing economic and political realities. However, they should also recognise that some calls for more acceptable reporting of Asia are politically as well as culturally loaded.

It still may be that the public interest is not the same as the interests of governments or indeed corporations which seek to entertain and only incidentally inform. Journalists may have to consider the needs and welfare of their audiences. They might remember that the views of the elites and their demands for preferential reporting will not necessarily be globally beneficial. Hard experience may suggest quite the reverse. As Filipino publisher Teodoro Locsin pointed out, Western journalists should guard against confusing Asian sensitivities with the demands of Asian rulers. Journalists who abandone their ethics and concede to such censorship are not doing ordinary people any favours:

> There are things uniquely Asian, distinctive ways of living and coping. But rather than being opposed to such values as free speech, open assembly and democratic elections, these things find purer expression under such values. I want to know what my Indonesian brother and Malaysian sister really think about his country, my country, the rest of the world. I do not care to know what the President's daughter-in-law, stepping out of a Paris boutique, says the people of her country believe. How would she know? (Locsin 1996)

Journalism codes of ethics in Australia, New Zealand, Britain, the United States, Thailand, the Philippines Hong Kong and even Malaysia endorse professional practice that seeks to inform and educate the public. Yet their independence can be hedged by what the Hong Kong Journalists Association called economic censorship. Meanwhile, the 'journalism is a business' approach directly undercuts some of the radical founding notions of development journalism, that a journalism theory which sought to take reporters and editors beyond liberal rhetoric and make them agents of genuine social reform.

Kunda Dixit, Asia Pacific Director of the Interpress News service, eschews both approaches. He no longer calls himself a development journalist. But he argues consistently for an interventionist role by journalists seeking social justice:

Poverty, population growth, climate change and the loss of cultural and biological diversity are such serious challenges to future life on the planet that reporting them calls for a new breed of journalists—journalists without mental borders who have the energy and vision to move beyond the traditional classroom concepts of reporting and writing. Reporters who do not just report, but look behind the headlines to examine cause and effect. They must be reporters with wider horizons who constantly explore regional or international linkages to national problems. Journalists shouldn't just hold a mirror to society, but be a part of its reflection. And most importantly, journalists must feel part of the societies and the planet that they write about and care for it. (Dixit 1996)

References

Arasu, A 1996, *Intersections with Asia* conference, Sydney.

Barber, N 1971, *The War of the Running Dogs: How Malaya defeated the Communist Guerillas 1948–60*, Fontana, London.

Bowden, T 1987, *One Crowded Hour*, Collins, Sydney.

Chalkley, A 1983, 'Reporting the Development Story' in Generoso, Gil Jnr, *The Asian Reporter : A Manual on Reporting Techniques*, Press Foundation of Asia, Manila.

Dixit, K 1996, *Intersections with Asia* conference, Sydney.

Heuvel, J and Dennis, E 1994, *The Unfolding Lotus: East Asia's Changing Media*, Freedom Forum, New York.

Jamias, J 1983, 'Third World Perspectives' in Generoso, Gil Jnr, *The Asian Reporter: A Manual on Reporting Technique*, Press Foundation of Asia, Manila.

Jiang Zemin, cited by Lehrke, Gunter 1993, 'Radio and Television in the People's Republic of China', *Media Asia*, Singapore.

Kelly, P 1996, *Intersections with Asia* conference, Sydney.

Lenin, V I 1901, *Collected works*, Vol 5, cited in the International Organisation of Journalists, *Lenin about the press*, Prague.

Li Tsze Sun 1993, *The World Outside When the War Broke Out: A Comparative study of two Chinese Newspapers of Different Systems*, Hong Kong Institute of Asia–Pacific Studies, Hong Kong.

Locsin, T 1996, *Intersections with Asia* conference, Sydney.

Mahathir, Mohamad 1989, 'The social responsibility of the Press' in Mehra, A, *Press Systems in the ASEAN States*, Asian Mass Communication Research and Information Centre, Singapore.

Mak YT 1996, *Intersections with Asia* conference, Sydney.

Mehra, A 1989, *Press Systems in the ASEAN States*, Asian Mass Communication Research and Information Centre, Singapore.

Menzies, H 1996, *Intersections with Asia* conference, Sydney.

Mundt, W 1991, 'Global Media Philosophies' in Merrill, John C (ed), *Global Journalism: a survey of international communication*, Longman, New York.

Razak, A 1985, *Press Laws and Systems in ASEAN States*, Confederation of ASEAN Journalists, Jakarta.

Reporters sans Frontiers 1995, *1995 Report*, John Libbey and Company, London.

Shafer, Richard 1990, 'Provincial Journalists in Third World development', *Media Asia* 17:3.

Siebert, Fred 1956, 'The Libertarian Theory of the Press' in Schramm, Wilbur, Siebert, Fred S, and Petersen, Theodore (eds), *Four Theories of the Press: the authoritarian, libertarian, social responsibility and Soviet Communist concepts of what the press should be and do*, University of Illinois Press, Urbana.

Soeharto, 1989, National Press Day speech in Mehra, A, *Press Systems in the ASEAN States*, Asian Mass Communication Research and Information Centre, Singapore.

Soliven, M V 1994, personal interview, Hong Kong.

Thongbai Thongpao/Hamelink, Cees. J. Mehra, Achal 1990, *Communication, Development and Human Rights in Asia*, Asian Media, Information and Communication Centre, Singapore.

Constraints on reporting Australia's near neighbours

Damien Kingsbury

For the last 20 or so years, Australian journalism on or from Singapore, Malaysia and Indonesia has been claimed as a considerable source of friction between the governments of these countries and Australia. Indeed, the issue of Australian journalism has been cited by Indonesia as being the primary bilateral difficulty in its relations with Australia (Alatas, 1994). Malaysia's Prime Minister, Dr Mahatir bin Mohammad, has also complained about Australian journalism, particularly when it has raised issues of the environment and human rights (for example, Malaysian High Commission 2/1988; Murdoch 1991; see also Searle 1994). Singapore's former Prime Minister, Lee Kuan Yew, has criticised the Australian news media for what he has called 'preaching'. According to Lee's successor, Goh Chock Tong, Australia talked too much and did too little (Byrnes 1994:168).

This paper touches on some of the issues in this regional criticism of Australian journalism, including those of culture and politics. Here culture is intended to mean the processes of social organisation, value systems and world views that prevail within a particular social group, which may or may not correspond with the idea of the state. Politics overlaps with culture in the area of social organisation and may (or may not) reflect common value systems or world views, but does include conceptions of the state and the achievement, use and maintenance of power. In particular, the issue of cultural difference, or different 'values', has been claimed by a number of regional leaders to be at the heart of their concerns about the Australian news media.

In broad terms, the Australian news media have, according to regional leaders, behaved with insensitivity, ignorance and an overriding sense of cultural chauvinism in their reporting of Australia's near neighbours. They have, according to this view, offended cultural sensibilities, interfered in domestic affairs, imposed a set of values that are not only alien to the region but which have imperialist or neo-imperialist overtones and are, implicitly, racist. By extension, this perspective presents Australia as a remnant of the colonial past, an imperial outpost clinging to an unfounded sense of superiority and cast adrift in a rising sea of post-colonial states, the attempted assuaging activities of former Australian Prime Minister Paul Keating not withstanding. Australia's journalists have been, according to this criticism, their country's most vociferous, uncultured and uncouth proponents. This is the broad view most often presented when the Australian news media is discussed in public by regional leaders.

Further, it should be noted that sometimes even members of Australia's domestic elite align themselves with this perspective of, regional leader for reasons of belief, personal advancement or political advantage. Examples of this Australian support for a regional leaders' perspective of Australia could be said to include the 'Indonesia lobby' of former Australian ambassadors to Jakarta and some academics, the former Minister for Foreign Affairs, Senator Gareth Evans, and some senior business people with investments in Southeast Asia.

This post-colonial 'anti-imperialist' criticism has been directed not just against Australia's media but against Australia more generally. For example, in 1986 criticism was directed both at Australia's media and at Australia more generally by the Indonesian military newspaper *Angkatan Bersenjata*, as well as the Indonesian publications *Kompas, Sinar Harapan, Prioritas, Merdeka* and *Suara Pembaruan*. Similar criticism came from Malaysia, for example over the ABC's *Embassy* television series in 1990 and from Indonesia over the broadcast on SBS television of the BBC program *Slow Boat to Surabaya* in 1991, among many others. The *Far Eastern Economic Review* and Malaysia's *New Straits Times* also ran a series of letters highly critical of both Australia and its media, and the *NST* ran a critical commentary and a cartoon depicting ABC television as a garbage truck carrying rubbish bins loaded with 'TV Specials' and 'Stop Press' items for the 'Fair Dinkum Network', with an Australian reporter saying into a microphone: 'And now...our crew is back with the latest' (*New Straits Times* 5 August 1991:5). There is little doubt that the Australian news media is a favourite target of regional criticism.

This regional criticism addressed the expression of Australian concerns for regional issues as diverse as the marginalising and sometimes repressive treatment of ethnic minorities, environmental degradation, political participation and, more generally, issues such as the separation of the judiciary and the legislature, adequate legal representation, treatment of refugees and those of freedom of expression, association and political participation, which comprise the basis of civil and political rights.

If these are the types of issues that attract such regional ire, the criticism then begs the question of who could potentially benefit from such criticism. It is the contention of this paper that such criticism of Australian journalism less often reflects genuine (socially based) cultural difference than political difference and that this, on the part of regional leaders, is self-serving.

A significant division between the perspectives put by regional leaders and the Australian news media concerns distinctions between society and the individual. According to what is claimed as a broadly based regional conception, Asian societies have greater concern for the welfare of the group rather than the individual. According to this conception, Western societies such as Australia are primarily concerned about the individual, which, in turn, is claimed to be at the expense of the wider society. 'Society' in the case of the three countries identified is embodied in the state and the state, in turn, is embodied in the government, which, in these three cases, has not been open to political change and has held power for a minimum of three decades. The state in each case is embodied in the ruling party—Golkar in Indonesia, (until May 1998), the People's Action Party (PAP) in Singapore and the United Malay National Organisation (UMNO) in Malaysia and the party was in each case dominated by its leader: Suharto, Lee and Mahatir.

This Asian conception, such as it is presented, places particular emphasis on notions of hierarchy, respect for authority, loyalty and a disinclination to openly debate (the preferred mode of settlement of difference being consensus—the negotiated removal of points of greatest objection). Such values have been described by, Lee Kuan Yew, amongst others, as constituting 'Asian values' or an 'Asian way'. This is claimed to reflect a contemporary interpretation of traditional Confucian values of self-control, duty and the pre-ordained order of things. Such values can perhaps be claimed to find a cultural echo in predominantly ethnic Chinese societies[1] such as Singapore and perhaps in the ethnic Chinese part of the Malaysian state, but are less easy to rationalise amongst Malaysia's majority Muslim ethnic Malays, or in the predominantly Muslim Indonesian state (which is in turn largely syncretic and to a considerable extent nominal in its Islamic belief). Further, there is an inconsistency in interpreting how 'Asians' actually behave, with Philippine and Thai political society, for instance, being robust, often internally confrontational and relatively free, as Indonesian political society was from 1949 until about 1957. This in large part reflects the idea of 'Asia' being of Western origin (Said 1991) and being culturally heterogeneous.

However, such 'Asian' values have been claimed by Lee and others to be at the heart of the economic success of Singapore[2] and the growing prosperity of other regional societies (and could therefore explain the Philippines' lack

---

[1] It is worth noting that while a cultural characteristic may be 'authentic', its formation does reflect the real, material circumstances in which it was founded. Hence, formalised respect for authority could be suggested to reflect the long-standing context of a feudal authoritarian state.

[2] A reflection of Singapore's economic success under Lee, and its public sense of social organisation, is its train system, which is arguably the most efficient, clean and well ordered in the world. It is a little more than just playful to recall similar public transport efficiencies introduced to Italy between 1922 and 1945.

of economic success, although they are less easy to rationalise in Thailand). According to such 'Asian' values, journalism should maintain social cohesion, should not be controversial or 'sensationalist', and should promote the wellbeing of the state by avoiding conflict or confrontation and enhancing economic development. This approach to journalism applies to the governments' perceived role for the media in Indonesia, Singapore and Malaysia.

According to Subrata, the Director-General of Press and Graphics in Indonesia's Department of Information, there were five aspects to the role of the news media in Indonesian society:

> The first is we have to make social understanding, where we are going to and what kind of aspects we are going to do and such...Of course, [the second point is] we have social confidence, to convince our people that they do understand where we are going to about our developmental structure. Then number three is the social responsibility, the sense of belonging to our nation's spirit. Again,...that sense of belonging means that social responsibility is the most important thing for our nation, for our people here. Number four, of course, is social control, must be there. This is one of the main parts of the press, to make social control. This social control must be constructive and must be responsible to the kinds of examples I just mentioned, of unity, of all of our main tasks. And then number five, of course, social participation. So all the media, including the press, have to be aware of this and have to motivate our people how to make participation in the developmental project (Subrata 1993).

By contrast, Australia's pluralism and the expression of dissenting views is interpreted as constituting internal divisions and as therefore responsible for Australia's inability to compete with the new industrialising economies of Southeast Asia and its relative economic decline. According to Suharto, democracy represents 'the tyranny of the majority', while Lee and Mahatir have been similarly critical of the Westminster two-party system. Australia's pluralism has not done it any favours, according to Lee, and if Australia was not careful Australians would become the 'white trash of Asia' (Byrnes 1994:xi).

Yet the criticisms of Australia's economic performance, especially by Lee Kuan Yew, were always exaggerated, ignored some of the more attractive characteristics of Australia's liberal political culture, and conveniently failed to acknowledge the significant changes that have been implemented at both macro- and micro-economic levels. It has been claimed, in large part, that these criticisms of Australia's economic performance were self-serving, intending to locate Australia exclusively as a supplier of raw materials to the newly industrialised economies of Asia (Byrnes 1994:172). Similarly, the political criticisms of Australia by the Indonesian armed forces newspaper,

Angkatan Bersenjata—that Australia could not be trusted, that communists influenced the Labor government and so on—also reflected less Australia's political reality than a desire on the part of Indonesia's armed forces, ABRI, to impose its own extremely narrow and regimented view of political order.

By any international standard—and for all the remaining faults, of which there are not a few—Australia is a remarkably tolerant society, not just accepting ethnic diversity but actively encouraging it. Australia does have a history of institutionalised racism, in particular through its 'White Australia' policy and in treatment of its indigenous peoples. There was also some discomfort amongst many Australians about the arrival in Australia of migrants from non-English speaking European backgrounds in the wake of the Second World War, and again in the late 1970s and early 1980s as the 'boat people' fleeing the aftermath of the Indochina wars came to Australia in sudden and large numbers. There are still traces of this in Australian society, notably expressed by the One Nation party, though not endorsed by its media.

But the Australian government and most pre-existing Australians have largely accepted these people, particularly once it was understood that they tended to embrace rather than reject the liberal pluralism on which Australia's political society is founded. Such liberal pluralism is at fundamental odds with Indonesia's government generally and its influential armed forces in particular, and has been explicitly rejected by both the Singaporean and Malaysian governments.

By contrast, Malaysia has institutionalised its own form of racism—positive discrimination in favour of ethnic Malays—intended to bolster their economic standing but which tends to act more as tokenism. Malaysia has also been critical of Singapore for its treatment of minority ethnic Malays, while Filipinos have been critical of the treatment of their 'guest workers' at the hands of Singaporeans. Many non-Javanese Indonesians regard the Javanese as cultural (and sometimes political) imperialists, which was reflected in a series of regional rebellions against the Jakarta government in the 1940s and 50s,[3] and is still frequently (though cautiously) expressed by many contemporary non-Javanese Indonesians. Many Javanese in turn regard non-Javanese Indonesians as less than fully civilised. 'In Java...the people say quite flatly, "To be human is to be Javanese"' (Geertz 1993:52). So, if there is intolerance of others by

---

[3] Prominent examples of radical dissent included the failed Tan Malaka coup of 1946, the Madiun Affair in 1948, in which sections of the PKI staged a rebellion against the Sukarno–Hatta government then fighting the Dutch, armed revolt in Makassar and Ambon in 1950, the Darul Islam Rebellions from the early 1950s in West Java, South Sulawesi and Aceh, and the Permesta-PRRI (Revolutionary Government of the Republic of Indonesia) rebellion in 1957–58 in Sumatra and Sulawesi.

Australia's regional neighbours, Australians are not the sole target of that intolerance.

Having noted a generalised tolerance of others, Australia's historical record of treatment of its indigenous peoples *is* appalling. But it is a false logic to claim—as some regional leaders have—that Australians have therefore forfeited their right to express concern over human rights issues, especially given that there has been an active and genuine program within Australia to redress often much earlier indigenous grievances. While containing many flaws and having many problems, Australia does not generally seek to resolve such problems through stifling expression of concerns about them. Indeed, it is a normative quality of a relatively open political society that social (and political) wrongs can best be addressed through open discussion.

In trying to defend Australia more generally from some of the more scurrilous attacks upon it by regional leaders, it would be very easy here to slip into what Edward Said has referred to as the 'politics of self-congratulation' (Said 1981). This paper is not intended to be 'self-congratulatory', although it would be disingenuous to deny that it is polemical. Rather, it is intended to point out a basic distinction between Australia and its political culture and that of some neighbouring governments that from time to time express disapproval of Australia.

That is, for all its faults, Australia tends to allow a considerable degree of personal freedom, particularly where politics is concerned, while maintaining a healthy separation between the state and the judiciary. This 'separation of the powers' is fundamental to the consistent application of justice and the rule of law. The three states of Indonesia, Singapore and Malaysia are to a lesser or greater degree authoritarian and have very circumscribed political participation. In Indonesia the state and the judiciary are fused, in Malaysia the judiciary is significantly compromised (Burger and Bogert 1988) and in Singapore it is used to achieve political ends, such as silencing critics.

Similarly, while regional criticism of Australia appears to be less based on reality and more on questionable interpretation or self-serving rhetoric, criticism of Australian journalists in particular often appears at best a failure to recognise as a very real part of Australian political culture the normative quality of a relatively unfettered 'watchdog' role for the news media. The news media are partners in the Australian political structure—the so-called 'fourth estate'—and they are, or at least should be, independent and sometimes critical of the government of the day. Through this relative independence and potential for criticism, the news media help ensure that government performs in the more broad public interest, rather than its own sectional interest.

It might be going too far to suggest that the news media should 'afflict the comfortable and comfort the afflicted', as some journalists say, given the ideological implications of the term. But it is far more reasonable to suggest that the news media have a right and indeed a responsibility in a democratic society to provide a voice for the views and concerns of ordinary citizens, in many cases in regard to government policy or practice. This is one of the 'checks and balances' that can limit the authoritarian leanings of government, scrutinise its administration and expose its tendencies towards inefficiency, misconceived policy or corruption. In this respect, Australian journalists tend to make a distinction between the government of their own country and that of others (Swancott, in Milne 1989:3). Nor, in a sense, do Australian journalists make a distinction between the nationality of the citizens whose interests they might implicitly represent.

I acknowledge here that this might tend towards a somewhat idealistic view of Australian journalism generally and Australian foreign journalism in particular. Most overseas stories are more prosaic than of struggles between authority and the individual. But many stories *are* of this type and in most cases it is these types of stories that call forth the greatest negative responses from regional governments. For example, stories that focus on issue of human rights, which are most often perpetrated by governments seeking to quell political opposition or the expression of an independent political will, are amongst those most frequently targeted for criticism. It is this role of providing a voice to the concerns of ordinary people, in societies where the political process is at best constrained and sometimes little more than a sham, to which some regional leaders object most strongly. I might cite here the general examples of reporting on the displacement of indigenous peoples in logging areas in Kalimantan, Sabah and Sarawak, the efforts of factory workers to claim better pay and conditions—and their suppression (such as Indonesia's Marsina case), the effective suppression of political oppositions, the compromising of the judiciary and rebellions against the central government (such as in East Timor and Irian Jaya).

There is also the criticism by regional governments that many Australian journalists do not act professionally, or that they would be more welcome in the region if they behaved in a professional manner (Alatas 1994). The two definitions of the term professional that come to mind are, on the one hand that a person is paid for their work, and on the other hand, more specifically, that they are a part of a recognised self-regulating profession that has particular rules of conduct. Journalism has long been recognised as not being a profession in this latter sense, in that it is not self-regulating, but is rather a craft, though with particular legal and ethical guidelines (and for union members self-imposed rules of conduct).

Having identified journalism not as a profession but as a craft, Australian journalists have not actually become worse at their craft over the period of the last couple of decades (and in many cases they were often already very skilled). Rather, on balance, Australian journalists have become noticeably better.

Australian journalists are, on the whole, better educated, more articulate and more socially engaged than their forebears often were. They are broadly less inclined to the boozy stereotypes that characterised the 'old school' and, interestingly, they are increasingly likely to be female. Australian journalism, once a blokes' club for long lunches and drunken nights, is more these days a meritocracy. This more thoughtful journalism is reflected in their approach to reporting regional affairs. In the region, rather than simply report bald facts, Australian journalists are more inclined to look at the context of those facts, to understand their history and to consider their local implications. The problem is not so much that Australian journalists are not sufficiently professional, rather it is that they are simply journalists just doing the job of journalism, and perhaps they are doing it better. The term 'professional' therefore means, in this regional context, a willingness to bow to the desires of politicians. As a matter of principle, Australian journalists tend not to do this.

So, if there is a distinction between the political landscape of Australia and some of its neighbouring states and, on balance, the standards of Australian journalism have not declined, perhaps the real issues lie in other than the rhetoric of offence taken by neighbouring governments. It could be suggested that the sensitivity on the part of Australia's neighbours reflects more the direction of their own developments.

Some internal developments

The period of a generally increasing intolerance of Australian journalism in Southeast Asia parallels a more general intolerance of Western journalism (or of journalism as such) in developing countries, as outlined by UNESCO's call in 1978 for a New World Information and Communications Order (UNESCO 1978). At least initially, the NWICO reflected some very genuine concerns about the pace of post-colonial development and the role information played in that.

The economic benefits it was believed should have followed the end of colonial exploitation in many, perhaps most, cases did not materialise. In part, this was attributed by the leaders of many developing countries to unfair or excessively negative reporting of their affairs by the international—read Western—news media. When the only news to come out of many places concerned natural or human disasters, there was little encouragement to trade and even less to invest. When such disasters included war, corruption, oppression and dissent, sometimes that disinclination was justified

In the first instance, the criticism of excessively negative reporting was levelled against the major international news organisations, which do wield enormous influence in shaping global perceptions of international events. Such organisations include the American-based news agency Associated Press (AP), United Press International (UPI), the British-based Reuters group and more recently Agence France Presse (AFP). Such news agencies supply a continual stream of material to news offices all over the world, in effect dominating the world's supply of news information. Other similarly influential news organisations include the television agency Viznews, more recently Cable News Network (CNN) and even the major stand-alone news organisations such as *The New York Times, The Wall Street Journal, The Times*, CBS, NBC and the BBC, which also syndicate news material. While these news organisations do dominate the international flow of news, UNESCO's criticism was expanded by many individual states to also include more local or regional news organisations, such as *The Sydney Morning Herald* and the Australian Broadcasting Corporation (ABC) and its overseas service, Radio Australia (RA). The belief was, somewhat justifiably, that such news organisations dominated the international flow of news and information, reflected particular cultural, political and economic perspectives and wielded enormous influence in international affairs. This influence rarely favoured developing countries.

It was further thought by UNESCO and a number of developing countries that information could be harnessed as a development tool, to provide constructive input into the development process—the 'how to' and 'lead by example' type of stories. Although most governments of such countries realised they had little hope of influencing the international media to adopt this position, they were much more successful in bringing to heel their domestic media.

In many cases having the domestic media run more 'constructive' stories resulted in government disinformation and propaganda; stories that painted a more rosy picture of affairs than might have been warranted, that reported government statements without criticism or analysis or which even praised the admirable qualities of the government of the day, regardless of the sometimes negative facts. The corollary of so-called 'positive' stories was that 'negative' stories—those dealing with government or other failure—were usually reconfigured or censored.

It is worth noting here that the assistant director-general of UNESCO, in charge of Culture and Communications, at the time of the introduction of NWICO, was Makaminan Makagiansar, a 'very nationalist' Indonesian

(Righter 1978:232). Indonesia's history of control of its own media has been amongst the most stringent examples of media control in a developing country, with information outlets being banned or closed, journalists being black-banned and sometimes jailed and there being a constant stream of both informal and formal 'advice' about what stories should or should not be reported and how they should be presented.

Indonesia's Subrata said that Indonesia justified its control over the media by two means, one of which was the need to maintain national cohesion. The second justification he cited was the even more strict media controls of its neighbours, Malaysia and Singapore. Singapore has an extremely circumscribed media environment, with the government owning and, in relation to news, directly controlling all electronic media. Singapore's print media such as *The Straits Times* is officially limited in its independent reportage and bans exist on a range of imported media, including satellite television and more recently censorship of the internet. Beyond the government's direct control of the media, it has also freely used the judicial system to silence critics, particularly through the threat or practice of defamation suits. In Singapore, a politician can successfully bring defamation charges for the most ordinary of criticisms or perceived criticisms. In the final instance, the government of Singapore can use the Internal Security Act—detention without trial—to silence critics both in the media and in the more broad community.

Similarly, in Malaysia the media is officially constrained by legislative requirement, its defamation laws can be used at will (particularly given Malaysia's seriously compromised judiciary), there is a system of official and unofficial 'advice' to journalists and editors and Malaysia, too, holds the Internal Security Act in reserve for special cases. Like the Indonesian government, the Malaysian government, through its developing 'crony capitalism', has also captured a large segment of the news media through direct ownership by government party members or their friends.

The Singaporean approach to censorship has been called 'hands-off' because the media is well aware of the limits imposed on it (Economist Intelligence Unit 1992:8), although it attacked the *International Herald Tribune* for alleged contempt of court over a report on the lack of separation of powers between the executive and the judiciary in a non-specific Asian state, and has 'severely curtailed' distribution of the *Asian Wall Street Journal*, the *Far Eastern Economic Review* and *Time* (Economist Intelligence Unit 1991–92). Similarly, Malaysia banned the 22–23 November 1990 issue of the *Asian Wall Street Journal* for canvassing Malaysia's official objection to an Australian television series *Embassy*.

Apart from formal and informal methods, such as the 'telephone culture', the Indonesian government has also increasingly exercised control over the media through ownership by government members. For example, the Information Minister, Harmoko, owned 40% of ten publications in the Pos Kota publishing group, 20% of other publications, 50% of another two, and 5% of one in the Kompas-Gramedia Group and between 5 and 100% of 14 further media outlets (*Independen* 1995). Suharto family members also owned media outlets. All three of the commercial television stations, and a major publishing group, Media Indonesia, were controlled by family members (Vatikiotis 1993:108; Hill 1994:99). In any case, all television news must be rebroadcast from a government supplied bulletin. In 1985, ten Golkar leaders bought 60% of *Pelita*, which replaced the modernist Islamic publication *Abadi* (banned in 1974). In 1988, then vice-president Sudharmono became an official 'adviser' to *Pelita*'s editorial board (Hill 1994:45). Family members were also involved in other publications (Hill 1994:100; 102). From May 1998, the Indonesian media began to liberalise, reflecting the political space after the fall of Suharto. Banned publications reappeared and new publications sprung up, often in amore open style than before.

The political environments of Indonesia, Malaysia and Singapore have tended towards a lesser or greater degree of authoritarianism and by various means have exhibited a tendency to repress dissent. In each case, such political legitimacy that they do have invariably fails to take into account the persuasive effect of governments whose current tenures in office are longer than the average age of their citizens, where they have structured the political environment to suit their own needs and desires and where there is no longer a viable political opposition. Political pluralism, including that which may be expressed by the news media, is not only regarded as politically undesirable but is actively suppressed.

Censorship is, or in Indonesia's case, was a fact of life in these countries and these governments would, generally, like to see and often do impose restrictions on foreign as well as domestic journalists. Domestic journalists are not only censored, they exercise self-censorship. Self-censorship is a survival technique and it is easy to be critical of such compromise from an outsider's perspective. While in many cases such criticism is warranted, it often takes considerable courage and skill to continue to operate within the margins of what is permitted to be said. Many journalists in Indonesia, Malaysia and Singapore are fined or in other ways legally punished and very often find themselves unemployed and unemployable. The cost to the individual can be very high indeed.

To illustrate this climate of repression, a Singaporean journalists I knew could not get a job again in Singapore after having worked in Australia.

Another illustration was a Malaysian colleague who reported for Australian news media from Kuala Lumpur. He existed on the edge of arrest and eventually jumped before being pushed. He is now an Australian resident.

For Indonesian citizens, only registered members of the Indonesia Journalists' Union (PWI) were allowed to work as journalists between 1966 and 1998. Like other unions, the PWI 'has been tightly regulated and directed by the New Order Government' (Hill 1994:67). This situation was challenged by the establishment of an independent journalists union in 1994. It should be noted that a year later the present and a senior member of the new union, Achmad Taufik and Eko Maryadi, who also published the monthly magazine *Independen*, were sentenced to 32 months imprisonment each for 'spreading hatred' against the Indonesian government (*Time* 1995:27).

There is also the celebrated case where the editor of *Monitor* published the results of a public opinion poll that listed the most popular figures in Indonesia in order. The Islamic prophet, Muhammad, was rated eleventh in the poll, which upset a number of devout Muslim (*santri*) Indonesians as opposed to the majority nominal Muslim (*abangan*) Indonesian. As a consequence, the magazine was closed and the editor, Arswendo Atmowiloto, was charged with blasphemy and jailed for five years. The magazine in question was owned by the Kompas-Gramedia Group, the company that published *Kompas*, which is Indonesia's biggest selling daily newspaper, and a large range of other publications. Although they were operating within government guidelines, it was fairly widely suggested in Indonesia that, at least in part, the closure of *Monitor* was meant as a warning to Kompas-Gramedia. These are but a few examples, and this is not to mention the hundreds of journalists who continue to work between the cracks of government control.

One way in which cracks in government control are beginning to appear is in the field of technological change, in particular the electronic media. Satellite television services are rapidly replacing short-wave radio as the most influential source of foreign and often uncensored information, and for this reason satellite receiving dishes were banned in Singapore. In Malaysia, ownership of satellite dishes is restricted, although in Indonesia the relatively high cost of buying and setting up a receiving dish has been circumvented by the mass production of miniature receiving dishes, which pick up transmissions from larger nearby receiving dishes.

While the Indonesian-owned Palapa satellite is the source of much theoretically unrestricted information for Indonesian citizens, informal agreements such as that with Australian Television International limit the supply of critical information. The Palapa satellite is controlled by Satelindo, which is owned by Bambang Trihatmojo, son of former President Suharto.

Similar voluntary 'restrictions' on news apply to other satellite broadcasters, as a consequence of deals done with regional governments. News, such as it is broadcast by the networks that feed to Southeast Asia, is usually self-censored and there is a more broad move away from 'news' as such to more innocuous, political palatable programming.

The internet has also become a popular topic of discussion in the field of government control of the media, with anyone who has access to a suitable computer, the appropriate software and a telephone line being able to gain access to news and information from all over the world—including one's own country. However, after the first brief wave of euphoria over the introduction of the internet, a few home truths have diminished its immediate importance as a tool for breaking government control of information.

The first problem with the internet is that it requires a considerable up-front payment to acquire a computer capable of running the internet software and continuing payments for access to a service provider. For most citizens of Indonesia and to a large extent Malaysia, this is simply not economically feasible. Further, the government of Singapore can and does, track and locate people viewing material it regards as offensive. Although the technological and human organisation required to do this for all of Singapore's current or future internet users might be prohibitive, the possibility that an internet user logging onto a banned internet site might be detected and punished can act as a definite disincentive, particularly as there is no way of hiding one's activity. The risk for the person putting out banned information is significantly greater, as they are immediately exposed to all viewers. The Indonesian government has similarly warned against 'irresponsible people using the internet to spread misleading information' (Crawford 1996).

But the final problem of the internet, at least in its current form, is not that it is difficult to access or that such access could be tracked by a concerned government agency. Rather, the quality of the information on the internet is often extremely poor, and wading through the dross, particularly in the 'news groups', is time-consuming and often unrewarding. The 'news groups', where anyone can 'speak', could be likened to talk-back radio, where there is a preponderance of uninformed comment about often trivial issues. The difference is that with talk-back radio there is some sort of screening process and the subject matter is guided by a presenter who is usually at least moderately informed.

This then leaves short-wave radio, less popular than it once was as a method for conveying information to audiences without access to uncensored news and views, but still relatively affordable, often portable and not requiring literacy. As a relatively inexpensive medium to produce, it has long been possible for short-wave broadcasters to broadcast on a range of channels in a number of languages, ensuring relatively high rates of audience penetration. But it is particularly because of the success of short-wave radio in gaining access to audiences where information is often constrained or censored that governments of such countries have been most critical of it and opposed to assisting journalists who work for it.

Journalists who have worked for Radio Australia, for example, have often found themselves black-banned from entering any one of a number of regional countries at various times, in some cases for years. If foreign news reporting can be claimed to be an interference in another country's internal domestic affairs, then broadcasting critical material into that country in its own language is a great affront. Such was the case with Radio Australia and Indonesia, and some Indonesian officials have subsequently said that the prime focus of their concerns over the Australian news media was Radio Australia. As a former ABC Jakarta correspondent and RA editor of news and current affairs, Errol Hodge believed that RA directly contributed to poor relations between Australia and Indonesia after 1975 (Hodge 1995:182). In particular Hodge noted concern in Indonesia with RA using Fretilin information on East Timor sourced out of Darwin, although he added that the Indonesian government itself worsened this perception by refusing to comment on events in East Timor. RA's broadcasts to Indonesia were, he said, an 'intrusion that many of its leaders regarded, not without cause, as cultural imperialism' (Hodge 1995:182). Hodge did not, however, explain how such reports constituted 'cultural imperialism'.

The foreign editor of *The Sydney Morning Herald*, David Jenkins, also noted that:

> One perennial irritant in Australian–Indonesian relations is Radio Australia, the overseas broadcasting service of the ABC...Quite often, the news is about developments in Indonesia itself. For the Indonesian government, which seeks to control the information received by its own people, this is at best an annoyance and at worst an interference in Indonesia's internal affairs. (Jenkins 1986:160)

Jenkins himself was at the centre of what was probably Australia's most damaging regional dispute since the period of the Confrontation with Indonesia over the founding of the state of Malaysia (1963–66). On 10 April 1986 *The Sydney Morning Herald* published a front-page article by Jenkins entitled 'After Marcos, now for the Soeharto billions', which documented official corruption by Suharto, his family and his close associates. The Indonesian reaction was profound and Indonesia downgraded and came close to breaking off diplomatic relations with Australia.

There were a number of contributing factors to Indonesia's reaction towards Australia after the publication of the article. These included high-level anger with Australia over its official and unofficial responses to Indonesia's invasion of East Timor in 1975, during which six Australian journalists were killed. Indonesia was also unhappy about continued Australian reporting of East Timor, in particular reports of atrocities and widespread human rights abuses, which resulted in Australian journalists being expelled from Indonesia over the next five years. After three times opposing Indonesia in the UN, even when Australia gave *de jure* recognition of the incorporation of East Timor into Indonesia in 1978, Indonesia correctly regarded it as being a recognition of the fact of the matter but not an endorsement of that fact.

Indonesia operated on something of a political knife-edge throughout the 1990's, with the country's political elite divided into pro- and anti-Suharto's camps. It has been suggested in a number of quarters that the issue of Suharto's corruption was highlighted by an anti-Suharto group to embarrass him (which it did) and perhaps hasten his retirement (which it failed to do). The manner in which Suharto's corruption was highlighted was not by holding up the Jenkins article and using it to castigate Suharto, which is more the Australian style, but by drawing attention to the article by criticising it, which is peculiarly Javanese. Therefore, both pro- and anti-Suharto factions were highly critical of the article's publication, even though no-one in Indonesia ever disputed its contents, which were locally fairly well-known.

Perhaps Malaysia's most vociferous response to Australia did not focus on its news media, but was a more general critique, even though it came after a period of tensions over news media reports, as well as more general media portrayal. The dispute came to a head when, after being badgered by Australian journalists about his non-attendance at the 1993 Asia-Pacific Economic Co-operation (APEC) forum meeting, the then Australian Prime Minister, Paul Keating, described Malaysia's Prime Minister as a 'recalcitrant'.

Searle's analysis of the subsequent dispute located it on both a policy and ideological level and on an institution and operational level (Searle 1994). Searle noted that Australia's relations with Malaysia had been on the wane since the late 1970s, when Malaysia's then Deputy Prime Minister and Minister of Trade and Industry, Dr Mahatir, claimed that relations with Australia were deteriorating 'like a house on fire'. This was exacerbated in 1986 by Australia's then Prime Minister, Bob Hawke, referring to the hanging of two convicted Australian drug traffickers as 'barbaric' and in 1987 by some Australian parliamentarians protesting over the arrest of Malaysian activists protesting over rainforest logging, which was widely reported in the Australian news media.

Similarly and soon after, an SBS television documentary on Malaysia showed a photograph of Mahatir accompanied by the question 'Is this man running a police state on our doorstep?' and an ABC television documentary, 'Five Faces of God' showed Malaysia as backward and tending towards religious fundamentalism, referred to in the program as 'the Malaysian disease' (Searle 1994:2–3). The ABC television series *Embassy* in 1991, which depicted the fictitious state of Ragaan, created further tension with Malaysia, with the Malaysian government not unreasonably believing that Ragaan was modelled on Malaysia. The movie *Turtle Beach* in the following year, which depicted atrocities against Vietnamese boat-people by Malaysian villagers, further exacerbated tensions.

In a bid to normalise bilateral relations with Malaysia, then Australian Foreign Minister Senator Gareth Evans apologised to Mahatir, accepted responsibility for Australia's fault for the deterioration in the relationship and officially 'disassociated' Australia from critical views of Malaysia expressed in its media (Mellor 1991). 'Grovelling, toadying, cringing and abject were just some of the adjectives used by commentators to describe the apology' (Mellor 1991). Mahatir responded on the following day by renewing his criticism of Australia's media, saying that:

> In Australia, press freedom stretches beyond normal freedom…the press is free to come up with all sorts of lies', he said. Malaysia believed that press freedom did not mean the press was free to undermine others (Murdoch 1991).

However, the most troublesome aspect of the relationship followed the establishment of APEC, which was opposed by Mahatir who instead wanted to establish an East Asia Economic Caucus, which precluded Australia (as well as other non-Asian states). It was his disinclination to be further drawn into the Asia Pacific Economic Co-operation forum (APEC) that earned Mahatir the 'recalcitrant' reference from Keating and that precipitated a three-week diplomatic spat with Australia in late 1993. Malaysia only drew back from the brink of a full-scale anti-Australian policy when it realised that the costs to it would outweigh any potential benefit such a dispute could offer. Clearly the Australian news media played a marginal role in Australia's dispute with Malaysia, but it did play some role in keeping the issue alive and consequently remained a convenient target for the Malaysian government.

It is almost a political cliché, too, that political leaders can rally support behind them in a dispute with another country. Mahatir was under internal political pressure in 1993 and may have been looking to bolster his own stocks at home by rallying his country behind him against the 'enemy'. A similar scenario could be presented for some of Indonesia's various responses to Australia. Even criticisms of Australia emanating from Singapore could be said to be playing to a domestic audience—a kind of 'See how successful we've become compared to an off-shoot of our former colonial masters'. Ironically, this represents Said's 'politics of self-congratulation' in reverse

The politics of culture

Having made such observations, it is important to note that criticism of the Australian news media for their lack of cultural sensitivity does beg the question of cross-cultural interpretation: how well or otherwise an outsider such as myself is able to distinguish cultural authenticity from political manipulation. If one accepts the idea of fundamental cultural difference, then not only is cultural offence more likely to be caused, inadvertently though that may be, but analysis of and a method by which such difference might be overcome would itself be culturally located and, consequently, compromised.

Such cultural relativism would mean that no-one could offer any sort of critical analysis within any other cultural context without being at least insensitive and probably ignorant. I do not, however, subscribe to this view. While regarding cultures as different, I do not believe they are radically so (see Ricoeur 1981:49–50; Todorov 1986:374). The quality of being human underpins culture, and supersedes it. Hence, for example, that controversial subject of many news stories from the region, human rights, is by definition universal rather than culturally specific. If issues of human rights are, as claimed by many regional leaders, culturally specific, then what is being referred to is Indonesian 'rights', or Malaysian 'rights' or Singaporean 'rights', not rights that are founded on the quality of being human.

And for those who do argue for the cultural specificity of human rights, my experience in countries where such abuses take place has overwhelmingly confirmed that ordinary people don't like being jailed, tortured or killed no matter what their cultural or political affiliation, or the affiliation of their government.

Further, and perhaps more immediately, what is represented as one country's culture is often that which is constructed by its political elites, usually to their own advantage and that of their colleagues. Given the cultural diversity of the countries under consideration, claims to cultural uniformity are patently nonsensical.

Yet Australian journalists are generally not anthropologists, nor are they usually sufficiently immersed in the particular country they report on not to miss some subtleties, especially given that foreign postings are usually for no more than a few years at a time and are often just short-term assignments. Australian journalists sometimes *do* get facts wrong, but it is very rarely 'getting it wrong' that causes angst, or alleged angst, amongst the region's leaders. More often they express concern when Australian journalists 'get it right'. No-one ever disputed the facts of the 'Suharto billions' affair, or that

Malaysian timber companies were logging rainforests at the expense of the homes of indigenous peoples, that the governments of Indonesia, Malaysia and Singapore have little time for a meaningful political opposition or that constraints on free political activity, expression and peaceful dissent were often suppressed by means that constituted a breach of human rights as defined by the United Nations, of which these countries are members.

But that Australian journalists sometimes do slip up, as they do at home, and that they cannot often immerse themselves deeply into the culture or cultures on which they report does not necessarily preclude cultural sensitivity, nor does it imply that meaningful communication is unavailable. Those who argue that cross-cultural communication is inherently flawed and probably impossible generally base their case on the Whorf-Saphir hypothesis in linguistics (Whorf 1956), which proposes the basic untranslatability of language and hence conceptualisation. The idea is that conceptualisation is relative to language, and that cultural difference is therefore impenetrable.

This theory has again been made fashionable by some post-structural theorists intent on recognising difference rather than similarity, and comes in reaction to the universalist approaches of structuralist theories, fashionable from the 1950s through to the 1970s. The main critique of such universal positions was that it imposed a uniformity of type and precluded regional identity, which had negative implications for ethnic minorities, women and non-mainstream groups and individuals. By asserting difference, such groups were able to retake ground commandeered by the universalist position.

Yet this has led to a fragmentation and closure of debate, all arguments being concluded by a resorting to difference, which is shallow logic. And unfortunately for supporters of the Whorf-Saphir hypothesis, people can learn languages, translation does work in a meaningful and practical sense, and conceptualisation is available across and between people from different cultural backgrounds.

Australian journalists based in the region tend most to report politics, and the practice of the exercise of power varies very little in its basic premise from one culture to another. One need only reread Machiavelli (1963), Weber (1964) or Lukes (1974) and compare their theoretical approaches with the political practice of the region to see that the attainment, maintenance and exercise of power has been and remains the primary goal of the governments of Singapore, Malaysia and Indonesia.

On balance, then, I do not believe that issues of concern expressed by regional governments can be sustained on the basis of cultural insensitivity. Rather, what is at issue is political insensitivity, and in the broadly liberal society to which Australian journalists report, 'insensitively' to often questionable methods employed in the maintenance of power is not regarded as a legitimate complaint. Such sensitivities would be to engage in self-censorship, or the production of propaganda.

Having noted that, some Australian journalists working in the region have told me that they *do* practice self-censorship, in order to maintain their bureaux in difficult political environments. The issue of regional reporting is also complicated by the costs of maintaining overseas bureaux. When an expensive bureau can be closed because an Australian journalist has simply done his or her job, then the case for maintaining such bureaux becomes problematic, especially when there are cheaper, though less precise, options such as wire services, satellite feeds and so on.

The politics of the region are sufficiently potentially volatile to displace Australian journalists, regardless of their sensitivity or lack thereof, and may be exacerbated by the political shake-ups to come. Indonesia's political landscape after Suharto, Malaysia after Mahatir and Singapore after Lee Kuan Yew (who is still the power behind the government) will raise whole new sets of political sensitivities that could challenge and even threaten the positions and perspectives of journalists trying to report the region. But it is precisely because of the inevitability of such fundamental changes to the politics of the region—a region which identified as crucial to Australia's future—that Australia needs its own journalists there, viewing regional developments from an Australian perspective and communicating in a style that addresses the interests and concerns of Australian audiences.

References

Alatas, A 1994, (fax) 'Answers by H E Minister Ali Alatas to Written Questions by Mr Damien Kingsbury of the *Bulletin and Newsweek*', Department of Foreign Affairs, Republic of Indonesia, 12 January.

Burger, W and Bogert, C 1988, 'Mahatir's Heavy Hand', in *Newsweek*, 2 May.

Byrnes, M 1994, *Australia and the Asia Game*, Allen and Unwin, Sydney.

Crawford, M 1996, 'Information revolution', in *Inside Indonesia*, October–December.

Economist Intelligence Unit, *Country Profile: Singapore*, 1991–92, London.

—— *Country Report: Singapore*, No 3, 1992, London.

—— *Singapore Country Report*, 3rd quarter 1994, London.

Geertz, C 1993, *The Interpretation of Cultures*, Fontana Press, London.

Hill, D 1991, *The Press in New Order Indonesia: Entering the 1990s*, Asia Research Centre, Murdoch University, Perth.

Hodge, E 1995, *Radio wars: truth, propaganda and the struggle for Radio Australia*, Cambridge University Press, Cambridge.

Jenkins, D 1986, 'Indonesia: government attitudes towards the domestic and foreign media', in *Australian Outlook*, Vol 40, No 3, December.

Lukes, S 1974, *Power: A Radical View*, Macmillan, London.

Machiavelli, N 1963, *The Prince*, Pocket Books, New York.

'Malaysian High Commission Press Release Re: SBS TV Programme 'Dateline' on Malaysia on Saturday, March 26, 1988', Canberra, No 2, 1988.

Mellor, B 1991, 'Entirely to Blame', *Time*, 5 August.

Milne, J 1989, 'Australia–Indonesian media relations: how to bridge the gap', *Pelangi*, Vol 5, No 3.

Murdoch, L 1991, 'Media tells lies, says Mahatir', *The Age*, 29 July.

New Straits Times 1991, 5 August.

Ricoeur, P 1981, *Hermeneutics and the Human Sciences*, Cambridge University Press, Cambridge.

Righter, R 1978, *Whose News? Politics, The Press and the Third World*, Times Books, New York.

Said, E 1981, *Covering Islam: How the Media and the Experts Determine How We See the Rest of the World*, Routledge and Kegan Paul, London.

—— 1991, *Orientalism*, Penguin Books, London.

Searle, P 1994, 'Recalcitrant or Realpolitik?: The Politics of Culture in Australia's Relations with Malaysia', paper for *Looking North: Reassessing the Framework and Unravelling the Myths* workshop, Asia Research Centre, Murdoch University, 18–19 November.

Subrata 1993, interview with the author, Jakarta, 23 December.

Time 1995, 18 September.

Todorov, T 1986, '"Race", Writing and Culture', trans Mack, L in Gates, H L Jr (ed), *'Race', Writing and Difference*, University of Chicago Press, London.

United Nations Educational, Scientific and Cultural Organisation 1978, 'Declaration on Fundamental Principles concerning the Contribution of the Mass Media to Strengthening Peace and International Understanding, to the Promotion of Human Rights and to Countering Racialism, Apartheid and Incitement to War', Paris.

Vatikiotis, M 1993, *Indonesian Politics Under Suharto*, Routledge, London.

Webor, M 1964, *The Theory of Social and Economic Organisation*, Parsons. T (ed), The Free Press, New York.

Whorf, B 1956, *Language, Thought and Reality: Selected Writings of Benjamin Lee Whorf*, Carroll J (ed), The MIT Press, Cambridge, Massachusetts.

New Order regime style
and the Australian media:
the cultural contributions to political conflict

Rodney Tiffen

The news media have played a more pivotal role in Australia's relations with Indonesia than in any other of our bilateral relationships. In mid-1989, the Foreign Minister, Gareth Evans, urged the Australian media to be more constructive in their coverage of Indonesia. The remarkable aspect of this statement is that we took it as unremarkable. Yet an Australian Foreign Minister has rarely, if ever, made such pleas about media coverage of Japan, China, Vietnam or any other country. Nor is it easy to envisage an American Secretary of State or a British Foreign Secretary urging their national media to temper its treatment of another country.

Yet when Senator Evans spoke, the previous 15 years of recurring conflict had so conditioned our expectations that the statement passed almost unnoticed. Without canvassing this history in detail, it is sufficient to note that the first serious conflicts began with the reporting of Indonesia's annexation of East Timor in 1975 and, of course, that issue has remained a sore point. The conflict next reached a crescendo in the years from 1978 to 1980, with the expulsion of several Australian correspondents, including the closing of the ABC bureau in late June 1980. It was preceded and followed by years of complaints about Radio Australia. There was then a lull, and after the election of the Hawke Government, two Australians, Leigh Mackay of Australian Associated Press and Michael Byrnes of the *Australian Financial Review*, were admitted as resident correspondents.

Nothing that had gone before, however, prepared anyone for the remarkable events of April 1986, following David Jenkins' article in the *Sydney Morning Herald*, published under the headline 'After Marcos, now for the Soeharto billions' (Jenkins 1986). This produced a more intense diplomatic conflict than any media issue that has come before or since (e.g. Tiffen 1991).

Eventually the conflict receded. The first resident correspondent in Jakarta for an Australian news organisation was Ian McIntosh of the ABC, who returned in late 1991, not long before the Dili massacre. However, the tentative moves to normalisation continued, and by 1996 there were five resident Australian correspondents, more than at any earlier time.

My aim is to explore one limited aspect of the conflicts that have arisen—the culturally derived oppositions in approach between the Australian media and the Suharto Government. The stress on cultural differences is a commonplace in discussing the difficulties in the bilateral relationship, including news coverage, almost to the point of unreflecting cliché. It is rare, however, to go beyond the general formulation, to articulate precise points of clashing expectations, and also to both acknowledge the pervasiveness of cultural influences, while also stressing the limited explanatory role that culture plays in the political conflicts that have arisen.

The limits of a cultural explanation

Culture offers a seductively embracing means of explaining anything. In politics, it figures as the most prolific residual explanation: 'The fatal attractiveness of the political culture approach is that it may be made to explain too much' (Kavanagh 1972:55). So before proceeding further, the limits and difficulties surrounding a cultural explanation of the conflict between the New Order regime and the Australian media need to be established. Two qualifications are fundamental:

- there is not one embracing, consensual contemporary Indonesian culture;
- the roots of conflict were more political than cultural.

Before talking about Indonesian culture, at least three complications must be acknowledged. The first involves sub-cultural variations. All large nation states embrace a wide diversity of groups and sub-cultures, but perhaps none more so than Indonesia. All observers of Indonesian politics make two points here: the need to distinguish between Java and the variety of outer island cultures, and, second, the need, as all post-Geertz scholars have acknowledged, to distinguish the different *aliran* within Java, especially the distinction between devout and 'nominal' Muslims.

Equally important, however, is to acknowledge the sub-cultural variations based upon social structure. The huge differences between social classes, between military and civilian, and between metropolitan and rural are all increasingly pertinent aspects of Indonesian society. Thus when employing the term political culture, the first danger is falsely to universalise it, to make it more embracingly consensual than it is. The second danger is to picture the political culture as eternal, beyond the fickleness of changing fashions and regimes.

The last 60 years of Indonesia history exhibit an enormous variety of political behaviours and government types. Such variety and change require, firstly, that any formulation of political culture should be able to embrace all the periods of modern Indonesian history, to encompass both Sukarno and Suharto as culturally authentic leaders.

Secondly, they indicate that we are dealing with a post-colonial, post-modernisation version of surviving traditional cultures. There is no pure indigenous culture now untouched by its encounter with the external world or by the complexities of modernisation. Typically, traditional cultures have been both attracted and repulsed by the new and the foreign, and various elements have sought both to embrace and to repudiate the past (see, Geertz 1972:328 on restorationist sentiment).

A further point about change and political culture needs to be emphasised. Nothing in Indonesian tradition envisaged many of the phenomena associated with the modern nation state. In particular, none envisaged the contemporary importance of international relations, or of the contemporary institutions associated with mass communications. What would a traditional *abangan* Javanese news service look like? The question is impossible to answer because the very notion of news is a modern import.

The third danger in discussing political culture is the temptation to over-simplify, to under-emphasise the ambivalences and inconsistencies in any complex civilisation. In the case of Java, it is difficult to describe a culture that on the one hand can produce such tolerance and subtlety and on the other some of the modern world's most terrible massacres. It is difficult to capture a history that is rich in evidence of both compliance and rebellion, of both ready adaptation and stubborn persistence.

Cultural approaches, at least on the issue of conflict with the Western media, need to be rescued from the realm of regime apologia and restored to political analysis.[1] Behaviour explained as culturally derived too often becomes sacrosanct, not subjected to further questioning or challenge. In the case of Indonesian culture and the Australian media, this has had two adverse consequences. The first is a gross underplaying of not only the degree of internal variety but of internal contestation that some of the claims arouse. In particular, the conflicts between the Suharto regime and domestic media suggest that Australian diplomats and others defending the regime's attitude on cultural grounds see themselves as more worthy arbiters of Indonesian culture than the Indonesian editors and journalists being suppressed. The second has been that only a limited, and indeed rather anaemic, version of Indonesian political culture was employed, one that emphasised traits of civility-cum-docility almost to the exclusion of all else.

For the rest of this paper I will abandon the term political culture, because its connotations are too embracing and constant, and further because it

---

[1] The 'culturalist' critics of the Australian media, former diplomats and others, are all doubtless aware of the importance of cultural variations within the state of Indonesia, but tend to take regime outlooks as the measure of Indonesian culture.

connotes not only that culturally derived responses are legitimate, but that no other response is possible.

Rather I will substitute the term 'New Order regime style'. The phrase emphasises that the responses were those of one sub-culture. It also suggests that the orientations were derived from political experiences as well as more universally cultural ones—that these were the views of elderly males who had spent their careers in a military institution, that they had endured earlier periods of threat, uncertainty and instability before entering their era of prolonged dominance, that most had become enormously wealthy, and had experienced social mobility and politico-economic change undreamt of by their parents.

The phrase 'New Order regime style' also leaves open the question of how much the particular world-view and ethos of the upper echelon *abangan* Javanese military officers of the independence generation were diffused through other sectors of the population.[2] It emphasises that the orientations dominant in the regime were culturally derived and culturally consonant, but that other equally authentic Indonesian cultural voices could take different views. Such a phrase also allows the recognition that the definition of culture is itself political, and frequently contested.

Having outlined the need for precision in situating the particular sub-cultural basis of the New Order orientations to conflicts with the Western media, we can more briefly address its logical accompaniment—that the orientations present among Western journalists over the last 20 years bear a problematic relation to the broader Australian political culture. They are not necessarily representative of Australian public opinion or of earlier generations. They are also shaped decisively by their institutional ethos and occupational experience. This is seen at its most aggressive in the gladiatorial ambience of the Canberra press gallery—the zero-sum, winner-take-all electoral contest between the major parties, the intense competitive ethos between the journalists, and the adversarial edge in their mixings with politicians all contribute to an apparent revelling in the expression of conflict. Several indicators suggest that the Australian public often deplore the tone of political reporting, and what they see as media sensationalism. On the other hand, journalists are probably more cosmopolitan and outward looking than Australian public opinion, more tolerant as well as more cynical. Moreover,

---

[2] Even now we run the danger of over-generalising, perhaps extrapolating too much from the President to the rest of the military elite, which also includes non-Javanese and people from other religions, eg the Catholic Murdani. Moreover, the New Order has now been in power for three decades, and many aspects have changed over time. More generally, 'in Indonesia, it is widely believed today that the Islamic current has been expanding for the last half-century at the expense of the Javanist one' (Liddle 1996:11).

those Australian journalists who become foreign correspondents in places like Jakarta are usually far more attuned to the nuances of cultural difference and diplomatic pressures than their domestic counterparts.

In discussing the role of regime political style as an ingredient in conflict with the Australian media, it is timely to recall that its intensity has been far from constant. In accounting for the rhythms of the contention, one must go to political rather than cultural sources. Indeed from 1966 to 1974 there was little discernible conflict. The New Order regime, while not covered intensely or extensively, received a predominantly favourable press.

On at least one occasion escalation in the cycle of conflict with the international media broadly coincided with a peak in repression of the domestic press. The period 1978–1980 was one of regime consolidation after the political crisis of early 1978. In media terms that crisis peaked on 20 January 1978, when 'the Indonesian Government in one swift stroke closed down two-thirds of the metropolitan press in Jakarta' (Anderson 1978).[3] Similarly, no cultural factors can explain the different responses to US and Australian media, how critical articles in the *New York Times* and *Washington Post* in 1986 went unpunished while the Jenkins article created such a furore. The calculus determining differential regime response here is rooted in international political power, not cultural affront.

The difficulties in discerning the role cultural differences might play are compounded because culture is often cited as an acceptable rationale for actions whose real motives may lie elsewhere. An appeal to cultural incompatibility is more likely to gain sympathy than the naked profession of a wish to protect political or commercial interests. Before proceeding therefore, it is necessary to emphasise that culture alone is never a sufficient explanation for any governmental behaviour, but may be one necessary part of an explanation. Citing culturally derived differences is very far from citing the bases of actual conflicts. There are deep cultural differences between the Western media and every regime in Asia, whether they draw on Buddhist, Confucian, Islamic or other traditions. When looking for what transforms divergence into direct antagonism, we need to examine political events and interests.

The explanatory claims being made for the oppositions sketched below between regime style and journalistic orientations then are moderate indeed. They are not the roots of the conflict, but once antagonism exists, the

---

[3] The earlier domestic crisis for the Suharto regime in January 1974, followed by the collapse of Pertamina the following year, produced widespread criticism of the regime in international circles of diplomats, businessmen and academics, but didn't achieve a sufficiently sustained focus in the Western media to warrant a reaction.

differences are likely to exacerbate rather than mollify its intensity. Moreover, to the extent that there is latitude for calculating the definition and pursuit of political interests, the cultural oppositions are pertinent to the exercise of discretion. They are also helpful in seeking to capture the contrasting emotions and perceptions on each side, and for putting particular claims and statements into a larger interpretative framework.

Five points of opposition

What follows is writ in broad strokes, seeking to understand some politico-cultural oppositions rather than to state all the qualifications and variations on each side, or to document precisely the different generalisations. Its aim is to articulate opposing assumptions and orientations, which the Indonesian Government and the Australian media have brought to their peculiar relationship.

A strong, authoritative political centre vs an adversarial orientation

According to Anderson's influential and provocative essay (1972), in Javanese thinking, power is concrete and has a single source, and the total amount of power is constant. Concentration produces strength while diffusion produces weakness. Such notions are antithetical to Western liberalism, which emphasises the need for checks and balances, which values the pluralism of influences, and which believes that unaccountable power corrupts. Fundamental to the Western press's self-conception is its role as watchdog, the servant of the public interest in opposing vested interests, and promoting disclosure and discussion.

In Anderson's account, the leader is the embodiment of unity (1972:22). In this view, the presence of a strong, unchallenged leader is not culturally alien. The result is to set the leader somewhat above the political manoeuvring, and to ascribe to that person a national rather than sectional role. In consequence, normal political debate assumes that the head of government will remain so, and has ultimate control. Criticisms are raised in a generalised, indirect form, and especially when political discretion works in tandem with cultural indirectness, are intended to affect arrangements and policies, not to overthrow or replace the top hierarchy.

In contrast, the very notion of representative democracy emphasises the public's ability to replace one set of rulers with another as the most basic means of downward accountability. In consequence, especially perhaps in Australia, in the conduct of political debate and media reporting the focus is upon the leader. Not only is blame personalised, but personal denigration becomes the common currency of political rhetoric, reaching far beyond the debating of policy differences. Personal vitriol has long been the common discourse. We are not shocked that during the 1980 election Deputy Prime Minister Anthony called Opposition Leader Hayden a 'sissy', that in 1984 Opposition Leader Peacock called Prime Minister Hawke a 'cheap little crook', or that in 1987 Treasurer Keating called Opposition Leader Howard a 'wimp'. Indirectness is hardly in evidence.

With both the political opposition and the media there is a strong adversarial attitude, which some have claimed extends into a 'tall poppy' syndrome, which takes delight in cutting leaders down to size. The news media treat government statements as claims to be tested. The methodology is one of gathering reactions and balancing viewpoints, highlighting the extent of contention. Sometimes, especially when a leader is succeeding politically, there is deference and ready acceptance of official viewpoints, but more often the tone is of impartial detachment verging into judgemental moral superiority.

An ethic of restraint and caution vs an ethic of disclosure and assertiveness

In Southeast Asian journalism, there seems to be wide acceptance that news reporting should pay attention to its likely consequences, that if a story were likely to cause a race riot or religious violence, it should not be published. There is what we might broadly label a culture of caution, an ethic of restraint, based upon the experience or fear of widespread social conflict and disorder. 'There can be very few Indonesians now who do not know that, however clouded, the abyss is there, and they are scrambling along the edge of it' (Geertz 1972:331).

In extreme situations, such as total war or terrorists holding hostages, the Western media will adopt similar attitudes. However, in most normal circumstances, Western journalism displays a culture of confidence, an ethic of disclosure, in the belief that openness, whatever its short-term consequences, will be ultimately beneficial. This produces not only an impatience with secrecy, and a reluctance to acquiesce to others' desire to suppress information, but develops into an assertiveness of the prerogatives, and a directness-cum-sensationalism in presentation.

This divergence has an ironic consequence: just as the Western media insist on probing the motives behind official actions, so the Suharto government was always interpreting Western news reports in terms of hidden motives. Such a search is quite consonant with various Javanese cultural motifs—the search for *pamrih*, or a concealed personal motive. Especially when there is criticism of the leader, or a report is unexpected and causes consternation, there is a tendency to look for a plot.[4] For example, after the Jenkins article was published, theories abounded to explain not just the content, but the timing of the article.

In contrast, the Western media, with their belief that disclosure has value for its own sake, and their professed creed of 'telling the truth without fear or favour', are indignant over accusations of ulterior motives. They claim that intrinsic judgements of newsworthiness, able to be assessed by no-one but themselves, are their sole motivation. While refusing to take officialdom at face value, they insist on their own institutional purity.

Maintaining public facades vs penetrating private realities

Many commentators have argued the importance in Indonesia culture of maintaining public unity, that ceremonial expressions of solidarity and order play an important role in Indonesian political life. This emphasis on preserving facades, of maintaining the appearance of respect, and of expressing differences within an over-arching framework of unity is alien to the Australian media. In contrast they place great value on going 'behind the scenes', to get the 'real' story and expose the operations of power. They are impatient with any 'fake' public consensus or misleading 'cover stories' designed to conceal conflicting interests, and they regard conflict as more newsworthy.[5]

The idea of *halus* (smoothness) and Anderson's argument that 'the man of power should have to exert himself as little as possible in any action' (1972:42) easily lend themselves to a preference for discretionary secrecy (common to most military institutions) and a *modus operandi* which emphasises the importance of behind-the-scenes manipulation, which sometimes even suggests an appetite for conspiracy. The Suharto regime's preference for protecting its privacy, in contrast for example, to allowing due processes to occur, was illustrated many times. Most substantially, it was apparent after the collapse of Pertamina in the mid-1970s. Even though this was clearly due to mismanagement and corruption on a massive scale, there were no open inquiries or court proceedings.

This example raises again the question of whether the preferred regime style is also a widely shared cultural trait. Within Indonesia, how do we draw

[4] Some Indonesian friends said to me in the mid-70s, that when there is an internal critic, political gossip asks who outside is involved; and when there is criticism by foreigners, political gossip asks who domestically is behind it?
[5] Western journalists tend to be sceptical towards foreign slogans and symbols, and towards behaviour designed for expressing solidarity rather than achieving substantial results. In their frame, material substance matters more than symbols and proclamations. *Realpolitik* and the pursuit of interests count for more than agreement on an abstract consensus.

the line between cultural restraint and political control? For example, what were the implications of the emphasis on indirect criticism, public unity and deference for how Indonesian editors would have responded to the Jenkins material on the Suharto family's business connections? Would they have been offended by its very existence? Would they have relished it in private gossip but refrained from publication? Or if they could have published without fear of political retribution, would they have done so?

Tolerance for patrimonial prerogatives vs an emphasis on due process, checks and balances

The dominance of the leader easily lends itself to a patrimonial system, where the prerogatives of power include considerable scope to shape arrangements. Formal procedural norms are weak. Political norms embody aims, including ones of order and consensus, more than formal representation. Both Sukarno's populist rhetoric and Suharto's developmental rhetoric claimed a general mandate to act far beyond simple or passive representation.

Most obviously in contrast, the media tend to view the exercise of such patronage as corruption (as, of course, do many Indonesians). Less obviously, a central part of the Western media tradition has been the eschewal of open ideologising in favour of the description of action.[6] The result has been an emphasis on descriptions of events, in which the propriety of processes easily becomes a more pronounced point of reference than the substance of policy, except insofar as substance is reflected in the unfolding controversies surrounding official actions (cf Tiffen 1989:ch8).

Nationalist sensitivities vs assertion of universal ethics

Whether because of the sensitivities of a post-colonial state, or for other cultural reasons, a recurring theme in Indonesian criticisms of the Australian media is that it constitutes an intrusion into their national sovereignty and an interference in their domestic affairs.[7] Such protests are of course most pronounced in relation to Radio Australia, where the choice by millions of Indonesia to listen to RA's news broadcasts is resented by many prominent figures. Beyond Radio Australia, the same themes are raised over criticisms about Indonesian conduct in East Timor since its official incorporation, and to

---

[6] For an early, interesting account of this tendency in Western, as opposed to Eastern bloc, reporting (see Gerbner 1962).

[7] Such sensitivities were prominent in post-Second World War Australia, and earlier, for example, at the founding of the League of Nations, over international criticism of the White Australia policy and treatment of Aborigines. But there has been a change in Australian political proclivities since in our adherence to and debating of international covenants, not only in human rights, but as part of a redefining of Federal and State responsibilities on the environment, for example.

human rights criticisms. Certainly there are strong historical grounds for these sentiments, and contemporary examples are easily assimilated into the former resentments.

In contrast, the Western media are strong believers in open borders, and in the universalism of moral stances to do with human rights. In Australia, for example, there is often (although not always consistently) a strong emotional response to humanitarian issues beyond our national borders. The outrage and the sorrow that were widely expressed in so many ways following the Beijing massacres in 1989 were a dramatic illustration of a tendency that no doubt complicates the lives of our diplomats.

Under duress or in extreme form, the Indonesian nationalism can grow into isolationism, even autarchy. Similarly, the moral concerns of the Western media can easily escalate into a tone of superiority.

Having outlined these oppositions, we must conclude with further qualifications about their explanatory role. Firstly, it should be emphasised that there are other journalistic values consonant with favourable coverage of the Suharto regime. There are contradictions and ambivalences in Australian media attitudes just as there are in Indonesian culture. They appear to abhor centralised, strongly entrenched power, yet at least as basic is their admiration for effectiveness. They profess democracy more fervently than anything else, but also display an intolerance of disorder, weakness and other phenomena which often appear as the alternative to authoritarianism.

Secondly, there are other influences on news at least as important as journalists' orientations, including a responsiveness to newsworthy events and influential sources. The most important single determinant of how Indonesia is covered is what sorts of events are occurring there. Similarly, what foreign diplomats, businessmen, the Indonesian intelligentsia and parts of its bureaucracy and so on are saying about the government is filtered into news reports and judgements, and play a direct role in shaping journalists' attitudes.

Thirdly, the above arguments are for culturally rooted preferences. They should not be extrapolated, as is sometimes done in culturalist critiques of the Australian media, into any assertion about a cultural incapacity among Indonesians to understand the workings of a democratic press. At the least that argument falters because of the deliberate efforts the Indonesian government has sometimes made to affect such coverage.[8]

To conclude this discussion, the Suharto Government was dramatically successful at maintaining a low profile in international news coverage, at least

---

[8] See, for example, Manheim and Albritton 1984 on Indonesia's hiring of a PR firm in America.

until the collapse of the Indonesia economy and Suharto's fall from power. This began as a deliberate point of contrast to the flamboyant, erratic Sukarno. It continued primarily because Indonesia did not become a large focus of controversy in American politics. Nor has it had any of the major eruptions that catapult a Third World country into American headlines.

Indonesia is the fourth most populous country in the world, and is not unimportant economically or strategically. Yet there are much greater concentrations of foreign correspondents in Tokyo, Hong Kong, Delhi, Beijing, Bangkok, Singapore and Manila. It is unlikely that Indonesia will forever maintain the relative inattention it has received from the Western media (excepting Australia) for the last quarter of a century. This state of affairs existed prior to the events of May 1998, which led to the fall of Suharto. One of the many transitions Indonesia is having to make in the post-Suharto era is how to cope with more intense and sustained attention from the Western media.

References

Anderson, Benedict R O'G 1972, 'The Idea of Power in Javanese Culture', in Holt, Clair (ed), *Culture and Politics in Indonesia*, Cornell University Press, Ithaca.

—— 1978, 'Last Days of Indonesia's Suharto?', *Southeast Asia Chronical*, Issue No 63, July–August.

Geertz, C 1972, 'The Politics of meaning', in Holt, Clair (ed), *Culture and Politics in Indonesia*, Cornell University Press, Ithaca.

Gerbner, George 1962, 'Ideological Tendencies in News Reporting', *Journalism Quarterly*.

Jenkins, David 1986, 'After Marcos, now for the Soeharto billions' the *Sydney Morning Herald*, 10 April.

Kavanagh, Dennis 1972, *Political Culture*, Macmillan, London.

Liddle, R William 1996, *Leadership and Culture in Indonesian Politics*, Allen and Unwin, Sydney.

Manheim, Jarol and Albritton, Robert 1984, 'Changing National Images: International Public Relations and Media Agenda Setting', *American Political Science Review*, 78, 3.

Tiffen, Rodney 1989, *News and Power*, Allen and Unwin, Sydney.

—— 1991, 'The Australian Media and Australian–ASEAN Relations', in Broinowski, Alison (ed), *Australia and ASEAN into the Nineties*, Macmillan, London.

Foreign correspondents and knowledge broking in Indonesia

Angela Romano

The majority of foreign correspondents who operate in Indonesia base their offices in central Jakarta, near to what were once the sodden swamplands of old Batavia. The largest group of correspondents congregates in the building of the national *Antara* newsagency. From the towering *Wisma Antara*, they gaze down upon the Presidential Palace, the nation's political centre, its ritziest shopping malls, luxury hotels, and the headquarters of national and multinational banks and corporations, all joined by roads commonly congested by interminable traffic jams.

Two smaller groups have converged a kilometre to the south. The first is located in the complex of the international news agency *Agence-France Presse* (*AFP*) in the quiet, tree-lined Jalan Indramayu, while the second is nearby in the Deutsche Bank building in Jalan Imam Bonjol. Still within the city centre, these two groups are conveniently closer to most of the foreign embassies as well as a newer source of influence in Indonesia's politico-economic realm, the stock market.

A shifting population of stringers tend to establish itself in less central, less expensive locations. Most are fringe dwellers to the *Wisma Antara*, *AFP* and Deutsche Bank complexes, regularly visiting colleagues based there because the bigger news offices provide freelance and part-time work as well as various financial and news resources.

In short, foreign correspondents are nestled, at least geographically, in the national heartland of political power, business and economic consumption. The location of journalists around the hubs of politico-economic activity and authority is hardly unique to foreign correspondents in Indonesia. Studies of media in the West have long found that the news industry's insatiable appetite for fresh information is most commonly satisfied by concentrating journalistic resources around the pulse points of government and business. Fishman (1980:143) dubs this 'the principle of bureaucratic affinity: only other bureaucracies can satisfy the input needs of a news bureaucracy'.

Such proximity also arises from the journalist's perceived function as a conduit between the general public and sources of power. The news media play an important role in civil society—the social domain in which the citizen and community attempt to regulate, bargain with and control the government and other power sources. Through the gathering, filtering and dissemination of information, journalism has great potential to expose and redefine the ways in which social and power relationships are organised, exercised, negotiated and maintained. Because of their strategic importance, the media's role and the media's relationship with other sectors of society are the subjects of debate, contest and manipulation. Much of the foreign correspondent's work is consumed outside of Indonesia,[1] so Western journalists are not usually direct negotiators of power relations between their host society's populace and the elite. Despite this, foreign correspondents remain bound by Indonesian social rules and expectations regarding the conduct of the news media because they deal with local sources who have different assumptions regarding the functions of the news media.

This article results from in-depth interviews with 20 foreign journalists who work or have previously worked in Indonesia. The interviews were conducted between 1994 and 1996 with a sample of four correspondents from newspapers, four from weekly magazines, six from radio and television and six from wire services. All but one of the journalists interviewed were based in Indonesia for periods ranging from one to seven years. The majority of foreign correspondents in Indonesia are male, and consequently only four of the interviewees were women. The names of most of the reporters have been concealed, at their request, because of their expressed concerns about possible repercussions.

The foreign correspondents studied are located at a nexus point between Western and Indonesian journalistic practice. They work within Asian geographic, political and ideological domains but their socialisation, training, audiences and news organisations are predominantly Western. This study does not aim to critique those foreign correspondents' performance or *modus operandi*, their potential role as agents of neo-colonial domination, their potential to foster or reduce global information imbalances, or related issues. Instead this chapter presents a view of Indonesia's information culture as perceived by 'strangers' who arbitrate and work within an alien culture. Because of their cross-cultural experience, foreign correspondents may provide insights that local news gatherers may take for granted due to their very absorption into the system. This study is also limited for the same reason—that it centres on outsiders, rather than those who have developed from and dwell within the culture examined.

Foreign correspondents have been defined in a narrow sense as journalists of Western origin. Although there are significant numbers of foreign correspondents from non-Western nations working in Indonesia—the most

---

[1] Exceptions are those services that attract sizeable Asian audiences, including Radio Australia, Australian Television International, the BBC World Service, the Voice of America, the *Far Eastern Economic Review* and the *Asian Wall Street Journal*.

sizeable number from Japan—a study of non-Western correspondents is beyond this chapter's scope. Australian journalists have been classed as Western correspondents, despite Australia's geographic location and shifting ethnic identity, in acknowledgment of the dominant cultural frameworks within Australian society.

This research utilises Garnham's (1986; 1994) notion that the mass media's role as mediators and knowledge brokers within the public sphere is delimited according to their societies' definitions of the 'public good'. The survey examines how the journalists' relocation into a new political sphere in a new country—which is guided by different assumptions about the public good, political accountability and decision-making processes—affects their day-to-day working habits and news gathering practices. It outlines the challenges that Indonesia's culture of political opacity and personalised decision-making create for foreign correspondents, with a specific focus on how these journalists establish and maintain their source networks in a closed political and information environment.

In Indonesia, policies of depoliticisation and exclusion, and the centralisation of power, have clearly influenced the shape and activities of the public sphere. Among the factors that can be considered both causes and symptoms of this closed political system are the dominance of the president and his self-appointed cabinet in political decision-making; the weakness of the parliament and legislature against the executive; the lack of autonomy of political parties; the absorption of organisations representing labour, farmers, women, youth, and other social groupings into state-controlled functional groups; the restriction of political rights, such as the rights to assemble and to associate, which are essential components of the rights to free speech and to seek information; and the prevention of the majority of the population, the so-called 'floating masses', from participating in party political activities outside of designated election periods. Furthermore, political decisions are often conducted around client-patron groupings and political factions (which may tend to function in a personalised and arbitrary fashion) rather than through standardised bureaucratic channels (which usually follow procedure or organisational rules)[2].

---

[2] These characteristics of the socio-political environment have been discussed in length by many scholars of and participants in Indonesian politics. Some of the better-known contributions of recent years include Bourchier and Legge 1994; Bresnan 1993; Budiman 1990; Ramage 1996; Schwarz 1994 and Vatikiotis 1994.

Closed information culture

The political bureaucracy

The agenda and space permitted for public debate in Indonesia are strongly influenced by the state's promotion of the ideology that the national character has given birth to *negara integralistik* (an integralistic nation)—a system of institutions, practices and ways of living that encompasses, protects and yet also transcends the interests of all individuals and groups (Hariyati 1995:1). The philosophy of *negara integralistik* is derived from a selective revival of the ideas of Supomo (Bourchier 1993; Simanjuntak 1994), a scholar of traditional law and a key contributor to the 1945 Constitution, who drew inspiration from sources such as Georg Hegel, Baruch Spinoza, Adam Muller and pre-Second World War Japanese 'family-oriented' political philosophies. Supomo (1945:113) envisaged the model nation as an organic whole, with rulers and the ruled linked in harmony and all groups joined in unity by 'the spirit of mutual co-operation, [and] the spirit of familial solidarity'.

This conceptualisation specifically rejects individualism and the idea of 'social contract' as the basis of protecting individuals. Supomo went so far as to argue—admittedly with limited success (Mahfud 1993:41; Nasution 1993:67)—that the Constitution should not contain safeguards of human rights and civil liberties on the grounds that such provisions would violate the solidarity between state and society (Supomo 1945:114). The moral state is instead built upon Javanese notions of the king (or president) as God's vice-regent and 'Father of the Nation', *Pancasila*[3] as a unifying state philosophy, *gotong royong* (mutual assistance), *persatuan* (unity) and *kesatuan* (integrity), and decision-making through *musyawarah* (deliberation) and *mufakat* (consensus). In such discourses, the nation is idealised as 'the "traditional village" where social harmony reigns, neighbours pitch in for the common good and where decisions are reached by consensus under the guidance of a wise leader' (Bourchier 1993:2).

In the integralistic vision, sovereignty of the masses is the result of through their delegation of power to the nation and infrastructure of government. Office holders are obliged to remember their responsibility to the masses and to deliberate with the people, but ultimately the strength of the executors rests upon 'inner control' rather than external checks on their power (Hariyati

---

[3] The five principles of *Pancasila* are:
- belief in the One and Almighty God;
- a just and civilized humanity;
- national unity;
- democracy, led by the wisdom of consensus among representatives;
- social justice for all Indonesian people.

1995:12). Habermas (1989:19) notes that Hegel, and by implication other supporters of the integralistic state, 'took the teeth out of the idea of the public sphere in civil society' by lionising the state apparatus's dominance as an integrating and guiding force essential for the 'public good'.

The state further bolsters its dominance and legitimacy by continuously promoting itself as the 'bringer of "development"' (to borrow a phrase from Robison 1982:135). The New Order government's[4] self-proclaimed role as the director of development conferred key power holders with the authority to define the goals and processes development (and once again, the 'public good') in restricted terms. By blending theories about the need for political 'order' and 'modernisation', the state developed an extensive rationale for its patrimonial form of rule (Higgott and Robison 1985). Journalists were furthermore considered the government's 'partner in the process of nation building' (Soeharto 1989:134), a role that implies considerable co-operation with the power centres that direct development strategies. As a member of the development team, 'the press is not outside the political system...and is not expected to hold the other parts of that team to account' (Schwarz 1995).

On arriving in Indonesia, foreign correspondents immediately encounter a philosophy of public responsibility and information sharing that has been moulded from the these integralistic and developmentalist frameworks. In the 'New Order pyramid' (Liddle 1985), power and the exercise of authority flowed downwards from the dominating presidency, to the armed forces, to an enormous bureaucracy which forms the hub of decision-making, to Indonesian society. There are, accordingly, relatively few mechanisms to ensure an appearance of bureaucratic and institutional accountability, and little emphasis on informed participation of the polity in decision-making. Despite passing references in official rhetoric about the media's role 'as a channel for the people's aspirations' (Soeharto 1989:132), communications also tended to flow from the decision-makers down to the society below.

Since the political system does not maintain an ongoing open dialogue between state and citizens over the management of the nation, many Indonesian government departments have done little to develop administrative structures and personnel for disseminating information and dealing with the media (Romano 1996a:50). The foreign correspondents surveyed faced unfamiliar obstacles to obtaining information because state organisations usually lack extensive systems of records and documentation about their activities. Even basic figures and statistics are difficult to obtain.

---

[4] Indonesia's New Order government came to an end on 21 May 1998 with the resignation of Suharto during his 32nd year in the presidency.

The Deputy Head of the Central Bureau of Statistics, Sutjipto Wirosarjono, admits that data in government socio-economic surveys are weak and unrealiable because of incomplete and inappropriate procedures for information gathering (Wirosardjono 1993; *Wakil Kepala BPS* 1991). The head of *Kompas* newspaper's research department, Daniel Dhakidae (1993:6–13), further reveals that surveys and polls on politically or socially sensitive topics are limited because of the pressures on researchers. Correspondents attempting to gather such data found that little had changed since the late 1970s, when former Australian Broadcasting Commission (ABC)[5] reporter Warwick Beutler (1982:28) found that: 'Statistics are notoriously wrong, often exaggerated or invented for the sole purpose of pleasing a superior'.

Foreign correspondents quickly discovered, furthermore, that it is frequently impossible to ring an organisation's press spokesperson for instant comments and analysis on the topic issue of the day, as they would expect to in their home countries (Kakiailatu 1994:71). Press secretaries often feel insecure about making frank on-the-spot statements to journalists, tending 'to be ignorant of decisions and issues, or deliberately evasive' (Beutler 1982:28). Australian Associated Press's Tom Hyland (1995) gives the example of an armed forces (ABRI) press officer, who would often claim to be 'unavailable' when journalists called, or who would make statements that were 'plainly not believable'. Foreign correspondents find that they gain information from such departments on 'an ad hoc basis' (Schwarz 1995), with the success of their interactions largely dependent on their personal relations with individuals in the institutions.

A bureaucratic culture, in which public servants must more commonly demonstrate accountability to their superiors on the institutional ladder rather than the masses they serve, also influences information flow. Foreign correspondents found that, as a general rule, public officials were less forthright and confident in dealing with the media. Adam Schwarz (1995) of the *Far Eastern Economic Review* (*FEER*) found that middle level officials would often be unwilling to talk about topics within their area of expertise, 'for fear of showing up their minister or the next person higher up on the bureaucratic chain'. Another correspondent said that bureaucrats were more reluctant to talk to their superiors or reporters about 'bad news' because of fears the information might reflect poorly on their administrative abilities. Tom Hyland (1995), by contrast, believed that the reason bureaucrats are inclined 'to only tell reporters good news' is because 'they think that's what reporters want to hear'.

---

[5] Later to become the Australian Broadcasting Corporation.

From his experience in the 1970s, Warwick Beutler (1982:28) described ministers and first-level government servants as 'the only reliable sources' of information within the state apparatus. The foreign correspondents surveyed, however, found that even though there is never any shortage of formal occasions in which ministers and other public officials will deliver what one described as 'sterile pronouncements', direct media access to senior government figures is limited. Michael Byrnes (1995) explained that at press conferences and similar occasions, information and viewpoints tended to be 'presented as set pieces. You don't really expect to learn very much from that'. Western journalists generally prefer individualised interviews with sources that allow them to be more probing, to engage in debate, and to take greater initiative in directing the range and depth of topics discussed (Tiffen 1989:37).

Correspondents found substantial practical obstacles to obtaining personalised audiences with the top echelons of Indonesian bureaucracy. Former AAP correspondent Terry Friel (1995) explained that:

> To organise an interview it took a good hour or so just to get through to the secretary and put in your request. Then often a day, or two days, or three weeks later you'd suddenly get a phone call saying there would be an interview in the minister's office in half an hour. It was generally an hour and a half trip in the traffic to the minister's office.

Even when access to senior bureaucrats and ministers was arranged, reporters found that such figures were frequently unaware of important policies or activities within their portfolio or area of responsibility. Foreign correspondents attending a media briefing on the 1998 presidential elections, for example, were bemused to find senior politicians studying from piles of textbooks and holding emergency consultations in huddles because, even as participants in the political process, they did not have enough information to answer basic questions about political procedures. One politician was greeted by 'a roomful of laughter' when, following a question about special powers that were about to be granted to the President, she replied: 'It's a special power, but nobody knows what kind of power this is' (Golkar defends its policies 1998:2).

Indonesia's largest political organisation, the armed forces (ABRI) is organised around *dwi fungsi* (the dual function)—the philosophy that it is the military's 'duty to run the state as well as to guard it' (Vatikiotis 1993:3). Members of the armed forces do not vote, but are allocated a block of seats, 100 under Suharto but reduced to 75 in recent years, for non-elected ABRI representatives in the parliament. The dual military and political function of ABRI is consonant with integralistic principles, such as 'paternalism, the legitimacy of non-elected rulers and the idea that it is possible for an elite to represent the whole society's interests rather than simply its own' (Bourchier 1993:13). Indonesian editor Mochtar Lubis argues that ABRI's dominance of political activity has been accompanied by an unwillingness to share power with other sources, ultimately creating 'a very closed society' in which the local press is 'completely intimidated' (Hill 1987:33).

Foreign correspondents all agreed with the analysis of one of their colleagues that the military typically resists 'any attempt to expose the way in which power is wielded'. A radio reporter commented that it is 'useless' to ask army representatives for on-the-record statements, especially on controversial subjects like East Timor, because 'they're invariably going to lie' and an intrinsic part of ABRI's function is 'to cover up'. ABRI operates an information centre but, as mentioned above, some correspondents expressed scepticism about the veracity of material provided by its spokesperson.

Certain elements of ABRI—often discontented with and disenfranchised by the circle of power around the President—began promoting greater social and press freedom (known as *keterbukaan* or openness) in the 1990s. As ABRI–press relations shifted in the early 1990s, journalists noted that the army became more accommodating about providing information. Groups within the armed forces were apparently motivated by a desire to facilitate criticism of the Suharto government (HRW-A 1994:5). In this context, the increased accessibility and openness appears the result of a political desire to use the public sphere as a zone for elite power contestations rather than any commitment towards the renegotiation of power between the elite and masses or the mass media (Romano 1996b).

The very pinnacle of the political ladder, the Presidential Palace, was the most remote source of information during the Suharto era. The political structure shielded President Suharto from direct systems of accountability, as he was not directly answerable to the electorate through popular mandate[6] and the Parliament never questioned or attempted to significantly alter the decisions of Suharto and his cabinet. President Suharto's engagements with the media were also managed in a fashion that prevented interrogation or frank questioning of his actions or policies. He was frequently quoted in the news, but those statements tended to come from second-hand or staged contacts with the media—speeches; comments at formal, pre-organised events; or reports from ministers and friends who relayed announcements to journalists as they left his office. AAP's Tom Hyland (1995) compares Suharto to a king 'who issues pronouncements—but never directly, never

---

[6] The president is elected by the members of the Congress, only 40% of whom are elected by the public through general elections.

himself—to somebody else who then comes out and says, "The President told me this." Further, journalists required special security passes to work in the Presidential Palace, and Suharto's staff carefully vetted and groomed applicants to ensure that those covering the President's activities were confined to merely reporting verbatim transcripts of comments from his official visitors.

President Suharto rarely agreed to press conferences or direct interviews. The Index on Censorship group (1975:83) reports that Suharto held the first press conference of his presidency in 1974, seven years after he was formally appointed to the nation's number-one position. Even then, the conference was held only to deny claims in a popular magazine that he had an aristocratic background in contrast to the official family tree, which shows that he hails from peasant stock. Hyland (1995) recalls that during his two years in Indonesia, from 1989 to 1991, Suharto held only two press conferences, both with senior journalists on the Presidential plane while returning from overseas trips. Suharto's press conferences were so infrequent that when they were held, journalists were inclined to lead their stories with the fact that he had agreed to hold a conference, rather than what he had actually said (eg Goh 1998:4). The few journalists granted audiences with Suharto interviewed him in a respectful fashion, with only the mildest of probing (Tiffen 1978:195; Berry et al 1995:18).

After conducting an in-house training course for Indonesian reporters at the *Jakarta Post*, Melbourne journalism lecturer John Wallace concurred with the findings of this research—that Indonesian political and bureaucratic sources were not as 'compliant or responsive' to journalists as their Western counterparts (Wallace 1996). This culture arises from the bureaucracy's conceptualisation of 'public information' within a system that largely frees them from the demands of continuously competing for legitimacy and mass support, and that limits the mechanisms by which the public scrutinise, participate in and negotiate over public issues. The environment is one in which information is not perceived as an openly accessible communal possession, but something dispensed at the discretion of state guardians.

This outlook affects the media's performance of their two main functions in the public sphere: to collect and distribute information, and to furnish a forum for debate (Garnham 1986:49). The state depicts the media's role in terms of the first function, with one Indonesian minister describing the media's duties as education, motivation and persuasion (Asean Regional Workshop 1972:5). With an 'almost complete ban on political activities beyond the framework established for them by government' (Van Dijk 1989:2), the state often suppresses the second role of journalists as mediators of discourse in the public sphere on the grounds that it is socially disruptive and destabilising. In the terminology of James Carey (1983), the 'information' role subsumes that of 'conversation'.

Sociologist Gaye Tuchman (1978:3) notes that 'news imparts to events their public character as it transforms mere happenings into publicly discussable events'. In integralistic ideology, many of the events and issues that foreign correspondents consider worth bringing into the public domain—such as issues related to the system of authority, the processes of decision-making, and the merits of policies and activities—are 'not up for discussion' (Byrnes 1995). This is not to imply that all actors in the Indonesian state apparatus are characterised by withdrawal and secrecy regarding their functions and activities, nor that they do not perceive the media as a site of hegemonic struggle. Rather, it indicates that the state ideology tends to naturally submerge those social realities that the foreign media assume should be displayed for the 'public good'.

Private enterprise

Private companies have also been reluctant to build relationships with the media, even in cases that may generate favourable publicity. Companies often decline to release even rudimentary information about apparently inoffensive topics such as new business opportunities, business expansions and mergers. Correspondents noted that this started to change during the 1990s with the increasing power of Stock Exchange supervisory bodies and the trend for listing companies overseas. The requirements of company listing forced the appearance of increased transparency in the economic arena, encouraging many businesses to publicly disclose more about their activities.

Symptomatic of the unwillingness to deal with the media is the apathy demonstrated by public relations companies, which work mainly for private businesses. Although there are some good PR operators, foreign correspondents found that most were ill informed and provided little useful information. Responding to my comment that Indonesia's public relations industry was underdeveloped, the *Australian Financial Review*'s Greg Earl (1995) laughed and replied that I had chosen a 'very polite way of describing it'. A television and radio correspondent said:

> It's basically a bunch of good looking women walking around and trying to promote their clients, usually through lunches, or if a press conference is held, by pressing little envelopes of money into the hands of journalists in order to ensure their client gets some column inches.[7]

_____

[7] Indonesian journalists are often offered money by individuals or organisations seeking press coverage, in a practice known as *wartawan amplop* or the 'journalist's envelope'. The envelope culture has been discussed by a variety of sources including Awanohara 1984:30 and Cornish

FEER's John McBeth (1995) went further, describing the activities of PR companies as 'running interference'. Others complained that some companies know so little about their clients that they were unable to provide information as simple as correct spelling of names. There was, furthermore, little evidence of PR operators attempting to direct media output through manipulation of information to suit deadlines and news routines, displacing real news by 'created news', and other sophisticated techniques of information management.

The apparent indifference of business and public relations professionals to the news media may arise from the close integration of the Indonesian economy with the state. The private sector is relatively small, since much of the economy is still controlled by state and/or military institutions. Many private enterprises are also controlled by political and/or military leaders, their families or their close associates. The survival of a large portion of private businesses has furthermore been heavily reliant on state support and market control in the form of government patronage, access to state facilities, state-imposed monopoly conditions in certain areas of trade, special licences, subsidies and so on. Since financial success has often revolved around obtaining benefits and concessions from the state, many business enterprises are predisposed to rely 'on personalized political connections rather than on the kinds of organized lobbying activities and institutions found in many other countries' (Mackie 1990:89).

In Western political systems, where government officials and business people are subject to greater pressure to maintain an image of public accountability, more emphasis is placed on structures that provide communication links between government or business bureaucracies and citizens and journalists. The public relations sector is one of these structures. This is not to suggest that the public relations industry inherently opens political or business organisations to greater public accountability. Often its function is exactly the opposite, promoting images of transparency and responsibility through complex techniques of concealment and diversion. The industry's existence and status, however, indicates a consciousness of the weight of public pressure, the importance of securing public support, and the need to generate productive relations with other political and economic power sources. In a climate in which commercial interests are mainly advanced through 'informal and personal contacts' (Mackie 1990:91), Indonesian organisations have apparently not perceived sufficient benefits to warrant substantial investment in the public relations sector.

1992:76. The envelope is usually only given to journalists working for the local press. Foreign correspondents are rarely offered financial inducements to cover stories.

Openings in the closed culture

It must be acknowledged that the communications culture cannot be considered as uniform. While many state institutions are difficult to access, correspondents find there are some that are very co-operative with the media. The Ministry of Finance hires public relations staff, for example, who are described as very skilled, experienced and sophisticated. ABRI is generally considered a closed institution. However the ABC's former Jakarta correspondent, Ian Macintosh (1995), acknowledges that while some army staff hindered his activities, others 'went out of their way' to provide assistance. Certain public figures furthermore have developed reputations for their readiness to meet with journalists and to discuss issues candidly. While some foreign correspondents experienced recurring difficulty in obtaining access to the institutions of state and leading figures, Friel (1995) states that he found Indonesian ministers were more accessible than their Australian counterparts.

The outlook of bureaucrats and their departments towards the media is often shaped by contingent factors that can alter the perceived desirability of navigating the social spaces between and within the community and the elite. The openness of the Finance Ministry to the media, for example, may be because many of its senior staff have studied in universities in the US and other Western countries and may have absorbed liberal ideologies through their education. On a more pragmatic level, the Ministry's staff have been acutely aware of the need to attract attention and support from foreign business investors, lenders and aid donors, and have worked hard to cultivate the confidence of international businesses and aid organisations. They have also perceived a need to generate local support for the Ministry's strategies, such as those relating to economic liberalisation, which have sometimes been contrary to the interests of other government ministries, sections of the army and even the Suharto family.

Groups and individuals outside government and business bureaucracies, who have less access to bureaucratic decision-making processes or who oppose the bureaucratic hegemony, are usually notably accessible. Correspondents found it far easier to approach and obtain information from Indonesia's intellectual community—non-government organisations (NGOs), academics and even certain retired generals—than from politicians, public servants or business-people.

The open relationship of these organisations and individuals with the media is the result of their wider involvement in social and political struggle (see Eldridge 1995; Uhlin 1995). Many of the more vocal retired generals, such as Sumitro and Ali Sadikin, were formerly key players in elite political circles. Subsequently excluded from such realms, they have been active in conceiving and promoting alternative political and social visions. Islamic organisations, such as Nahdlatul Ulama and the mosques, have been venues for discussion of political and cultural issues, and as such have been relatively free of state manipulation. Many leading scholars, authors and journalists—such as academic Arief Budiman, the poet Emha, and journalist Gunawan Mohamad—have become popular public figures. Individually, or working in groups with other intellectuals and activists, they have attempted to stretch the bounds of debate and to reformulate the ideologies that underpin existing the socio-political relations. The NGOs also attempt to promote counter-hegemonic viewpoints and to address economic, socio-cultural, political, civil and environmental problems and inequities. These advocacy groups frequently centre around the activism of students who, due to restrictions on political activities in university grounds, have shifted their interests off campus.

Since opposition political parties and most adversarial groups have been absorbed into the state apparatus, the NGOs and the intellectuals play important quasi-oppositional roles to government and big business. Indonesia intellectual Ariel Heryanto (1996) says that the masses rely on these figures 'to legitimate their cause. Intellectuals say nothing new, but by saying it they give authority to the common wisdom'. The intellectuals not only express the views of the largely silent polity, they also seek to expand the limits imposed on mass-engagement political processes. The willingness of NGOs and intellectuals to co-operate with the media thus corresponds with their own endeavours to legitimise a wider range of interactions between the state and civil society.

Negotiating the information culture

Due to the challenges that arise in information gathering, foreign correspondents can be tempted to focus on sources of easily obtainable, easily digestible information. Western embassies and multi-national businesses are usually avenues of readily accessible data, with the information often already evaluated for its international significance. One freelance magazine correspondent disparagingly noted that there is

> an over-reliance by many reporters on diplomatic sources where you go into the embassy, you sit down with the political attaché, and you get your tablespoon full of political analysis. And it's all right there for you, clear as day.

Not surprisingly, Rodney Tiffen's study in the 1970s of Western correspondents in Southeast Asia found that the most notable aspect of their source structure was 'the symbiotic relationship between journalists and diplomats' (1978:61). Alan Knight similarly found in the 1990s an intense reliance on Western sources. 'Diplomats, particularly Australian foreign affairs officials remained Australian journalists' most favoured sources in East and Southeast Asia' (Knight 1995:11).

The tendency to rely on Westernised sources decreases as foreign correspondents personalise their relations with a range of contacts. It is a truism in any country that the journalists who cultivate close relations with their sources are those who produce the best copy. Journalists who confine their activities to press conferences and brief liaisons with official institutional representatives are less likely to produce stories of great depth, reveal new insights, or uncover new issues. It is, however, still possible for journalists in Western nations to perform creditably through relatively impersonal contacts with sources who, in the age of tele- and computer communications, they may never meet. Local Indonesian newsworkers, by contrast, are known for developing far closer relations with the ruling elite and other potential sources. Former editor Nono Makarim notes that the relationship between news workers and ministers can become so intense that the editor has a virtual 'hot-line' to the minister's desk, or that younger journalists are considered as a 'favourite son of the minister' (1978:271). Foreign correspondents rarely attempt to forge such strong links, but they still find that the need to establish personal networks is more critical in Indonesia than in their home societies.

Because of the limits of formal access to news sources, correspondents make greater efforts to establish extended informal networks through the social circuit. Cocktail parties, celebrations, seminars, business launches, diplomatic functions and other social occasions are important venues for establishing, renewing and widening connections. Foreign correspondents can expect to receive dozens of invitations to such events each week. One journalist described such gatherings as a key means by which 'the Indonesian elite keeps its channels of discourse flowing...It's the substitute for the telephone'.

Correspondents unable to contact ministers or other public figures through regular channels often make an effort to calculate which social functions such sources were likely to attend, and then attempt to meet those sources on a social basis. From such events the journalist might gain a commitment for an interview from a previously inaccessible source, obtain leads for stories, or occasionally gather on-the-record quotes. Friel (1995) estimates that a journalist might meet four to six significant sources at a social event; this becomes a very time-efficient way of working when compared to the process (described above) of arranging contacts through formal channels.

The 'social circuit' is also important because it increases the potential to cultivate a relaxed sense of intimacy between journalists and potential information providers. Correspondents found that sources who had been difficult to contact often become far more approachable after a meeting, even a brief one. The ABC's Michael Maher (1995) observed that: 'Even if you speak to them for five minutes and thrust a name card in their hand, it's worthwhile.'

The process of building and preserving personal relationships, however, is usually a long-term process of winning trust and confidence. *FEER*'s former Jakarta correspondent Adam Schwarz said:

> After you develop a reputation of not damaging your sources, or of protecting your sources, and of doing your homework on stories, and of making a commitment to the story and to the country by the very fact of staying for a couple of years and learning the language, gradually people open up to you.

Until that stage, however, sources will 'speak in platitudes which say nothing' (Schwarz 1995).

Correspondents found that as the bonds of confidence build, even senior military figures will become, in the words of one reporter, 'extremely helpful and revealing'. Foreign reporters who have established particularly strong contacts with important army figures include the doyen of Indonesian foreign correspondence, David Jenkins, and the ABC's Ian Macintosh. Jenkins (1994) says the military sources were the most difficult in Indonesia to obtain information from, 'but once they felt that confidence had been established they were remarkably free and frank'. He and several other correspondents note, however, that such briefings from military sources are generally off-the-record. Jenkins (1986:156) further warns that those few foreign correspondents admitted to 'the inner circle' of military factions must be aware of the possibility of jeopardising relations with the circle through critical reportage, and of risking alliances with other groups by identifying too closely with any one faction.

Time becomes a significant factor that can prevent correspondents from establishing trusting, open communications with such power holders. Jenkins (1986:156) notes that the military will only open up 'once they feel that a particular journalist can be trusted...and they are slow to make that assessment'. He estimates that it took him four years to win the confidence of ABRI's major factional groups (Jenkins 1994). As many correspondents are stationed in Indonesia for periods of only one or two years, they usually lack sufficient time to overcome the hesitancy that some sources hold in relation to the media.

Women correspondents enjoy some advantages in such an environment. Patriarchal stereotypes of women being neat, decorative, passive and non-aggressive can benefit female reporters. Wolf's (1992) study of factories found that female workers were often preferred because factory owners viewed men as lazy and aggressive, while women were thought to be more diligent, less likely to complain or engage in labour protests and easier to control. While the work of factory hands differs considerably from that of journalists, the women journalists found—and journalists worldwide might agree—that paternalistic sources are often more accommodating with reporters whom they believe to be naïve, submissive and non-threatening. A radio reporter says that men in senior positions often adopted the approach of: 'Let me sit you on my knee and explain things to you.' She acknowledges that although it can be limiting and irritating to be treated less seriously than men, 'it does give you an access which you might otherwise not have simply because you are seen as less of a threat'. In a culture where personal contact is important, women are also at an advantage because sources tend to remember the names and faces of female reporters faster than those of males; this occurs because there are relatively few women journalists in Indonesia, so women tended to stand out more.[8]

Tensions between conflicting political ideologies

The activities of foreign correspondents in Indonesia have often led to international political tensions. The uneasy relations between Australia and Indonesia that followed the publication of Jenkins' 1986 'Soeharto billions' story on the front page of the *Sydney Morning Herald* is one of the best-known cases. The strains that arise around the activities of foreign correspondents in Indonesia are often due to divergences in expectations about the obligations and openness of the state. Many of the foreign correspondents surveyed have found their activities hampered by what they perceived to be the unresponsiveness of bureaucracy. Western correspondents, in turn, have been accused by Indonesia (and by many other Third World nations) of imposing inappropriate Western, liberal frameworks in their writings (see Rodgers 1982:21). The frustrations of both sides have been aired in debates about the new world information and communication order, development journalism, 'Asian values', and so on.[9]

Most foreign correspondents have been socialised into Western cultures that espouse the openness of bureaucracy to scrutiny and the sensitivity of social leaders and organisations to public opinion, even though the social

---

[8] Figures from the Indonesian Department of Information (Departemen Penerangan, 1996–1997) show that in 1996 only 12.8% of Indonesian journalists were women.
[9] See for example Berry et al 1995; Horton 1978; MacBride et al 1980; and Schiller 1976. Innumerable articles on these debates have been published in many 'journals of record', with *Media Asia*, *Journal of Communication* and *Gazette* among the more prolific international contributors.

reality may often fail to match such ideals. The correspondents' professional routines have been constructed around premises that the news media have both a right and responsibility to access and audit the internal workings of the structures of power on behalf of the polity. When operating in Indonesia, the correspondents encounter a system in which the mechanisms and culture required to facilitate public and media scrutiny is often circumscribed—sometimes because economic underdevelopment has hindered the growth of appropriate facilities that aid media–elite communications; sometimes because the elite do not perceive any benefit in direct interaction with the polity or media; and sometimes because of a conscious rejection of 'adversarial', 'liberal' ideology in favour of an organic political system.

It should be noted that such tensions are not merely the result of East–West cultural and political differences. Similar divergences in outlook have existed within Indonesia and other developing nations for decades. On the one hand are those Third World theorists who argue that in order to foster cultural and economic development:

- journalists must build confidence in the nation's 'fragile political structures', which they argue cannot withstand the 'endless scrutiny' of Western-style journalism (Ng'weno 1978:128);
- journalists should work with the government in nation building and development (Soeharto,1989:134); and
- the state may sometimes be obliged to restrict the news media according to the economic and development priorities identified by policy-makers (Mahatir 1985:215; Soeharto 1989:132).

In the extremes of this approach, '[i]nformation (or truth) thus becomes the property of the state; the flow of power (and truth) between the governors and the governed works from the top-down' (Hachten 1987:31).

On the other hand, those Indonesians who contest such concepts of guided freedom and a press–government partnership usually wish the press to expand its role in the public sphere by monitoring development processes, probing human rights violations, and reminding the government to respect the rule of law. Todong Mulya Lubis points out that although those in this group 'do not feel comfortable with the term *liberal press*, it must in all fairness be admitted that their attitude resembles the attitude of this type' (Lubis 1993:260). The discord that sometimes occurs around the activities of foreign reporters is comparable to similar conflicts that arise around the Indonesian citizen's relationship with sources of power and the local news media's role in mediating such relationships.

Foreign correspondents find that stresses also arise around their need to obtain information within time frames that suit Western news corporations. Time delays in obtaining interviews and information increase the difficulties of operating within the deadlines. Inability to meet deadlines was, for example, a daily complaint of the hundreds of journalists who converged on Jakarta and Bogor for the 1994 APEC forum meetings but found they were unable to arrange their schedules to accommodate the vagaries of their Indonesian bureaucratic sources (Kakiailatu 1994:71). In the West, the journalists' routine is generally organised around presumptions that the bureaucracy will respond instantly to their requests for information; in Indonesia, work practices had to be readjusted to suit the reality that the less information-centred bureaucracy tended to reply eventually, rather than immediately. Friel (1995) said: 'The Western need for haste left a few people bemused. They just couldn't understand the idea'. This creates considerable pressures for Western news reporters, especially those working for wire services that may consider important stories 'late' if they arrive seconds after those of their competitors.

Reporting from post-Suharto Indonesia

The collapse of Indonesia's economy in late 1997 led to protests and riots throughout much of 1998 over the issues of rising prices, increasing unemployment and the prevalence of KKN (*korupsi*—corruption, *kolusi*—collusion and *nepotisme*—nepotism) in the bureaucracy. The economic crisis forced President Suharto's resignation and major changes to the political structure, at least for the short term. Previously unquestionable mainstays of the New Order are being reviewed, including the dual function of the ABRI, the status of *Pancasila* as the sole ideology for all social institutions, and the status of the 1945 Constitution as the basis for all legal and political culture. The new government of B J Habibie enacted legal reforms or announced plans to amend laws regulating many areas of social, economic and political life, including those laws relating to licensing of the mass media, the organisation of labour unions and professional groups, the activities of political parties and the right to gather and demonstrate, among others. The weakness of the new President forced him to attempt to portray an appearance of championing human rights, of responding to public opinion and of accommodating the demands of a wide range of political interest groups.

The change in the political structure has impacted noticably on the activities of the mass media. Topics once considered taboo, such as Suharto's wealth, are now under public discussion (eg Greenlees 1998:7). Sources who were once hesitant to speak to journalists now regularly court the news media.

The change is most conspicuous in the upper echelons of political power. Habibie's adviser, Dewi Fortuna Anwar (1998) said that Suharto had advised his protégé not to talk with the media, but she later counselled him that journalists would write about him, regardless of whether he spoke to them, so he had best take the opportunity to present his point of view. Habibie surprised journalists in the first days of his presidency by seizing the microphone to make impromptu speeches at public gatherings. He has subsequently held weekly meetings with foreign journalists and conducted regular question and answer sessions with local journalists (Habibie 1998; Kelly 1998:23; Price 1998:9).

Habibie, admitting that many people regard him as 'the puppet of his former master', told journalists that he intended to separate himself from the culture of the Suharto era. 'You have transparency. You could never talk to President Suharto the way you can talk to me...I am not the king,' he said (Mydans 1998). While Suharto almost never talked to journalists, the *Australian*'s Paul Kelly (1998:23) notes that Habibie 'talks, and talks, and talks. Above all he's an extravagant storyteller and myth-maker'.

It is difficult to predict whether the spirit of reform will be maintained. It is interesting to consider observations from *New York Times* journalist Seth King about Indonesian newspapers breaking out of their previously 'subservient' behaviour, demonstrating 'new freedom and daring' in their reporting. In an article for the *Times*, he quotes the Information Minister promising that he will not attempt to dictate to the press. King furthermore cites editorials in the nation's leading newspapers warning that they will be ready 'to hit' politicians and bureaucrats 'whenever they deviate'. King's article, however, was not written in 1999 but in 1966, during the dying months of the Sukarno presidency, when then Minister of Defence, Lieutenant General Suharto, was seen as part of 'the fresh wind blowing' economic and political reform into the nation (King 1966:12). Veteran Indonesian journalist Rosihan Anwar (1973:4) notes that the 'honeymoon' was over within a few years, with Suharto and ABRI 'tightening up' controls on the media and the civil society once they had 'the self-confidence that they could well go alone without too much reliance on civilian co-operation'. It is too early to determine whether the current wave of reform will lead to long-term changes in the political and information culture or whether, as in 1966, the present climate of reform is merely the result of the political elite's desire to establish short-term legitimacy.

Conclusions

This chapter has traced the practical ways in which the foreign correspondent's ability to access sources and gather information is inhibited by an environment in which the lines of accountability between the elite and the masses are not direct and transparent. In his analysis of correspondents in Southeast Asia, Rodney Tiffen (1978:139) wrote that:

> The lack of press freedom and the absence of a liberal tradition, where talking to newsmen is a common and recognized way of airing grievances, means officials and politicians are much less likely to talk to either the local or foreign press about regime problems. Lack of access at the highest levels in most Southeast Asian countries means more can remain secret and makes many questions of truth much harder to establish.

Until 1998, the broad thrust of Tiffen's findings remained valid in Indonesia. It was not until the collapse of the political regime of President Suharto and his New Order that the culture shifted significantly, and sources have begun seeking rather than shunning the attentions of journalists.

During the Suharto era, the emphasis on an 'information culture' was reduced because the political structure limited the public's capacity to demand responsibility from political and economic bureaucracies. The community had relatively few options for legitimate involvement in the public sphere, and a climate of opacity developed and perpetuated. Many of the journalists correspondingly noted that the politico-economic elite did not usually perceive openness to the media, especially to the foreign media, as being important or beneficial. One bureau chief said that he found it 'a permanent struggle' during the late years of the Suharto presidency to convince government and business bodies that they had an interest in presenting 'their side of the story'.

With formal channels of communication relatively closed, foreign correspondents were compelled to redirect their activity towards opening informal channels. The personal bonds of familiarity and trust became significantly more important with sources who did not accept the taken-for-granted assumptions of Western political thought that both the public and the media have rights of access to state information.

The public sphere is not merely characterised by vertical communication or, in other words, communication between the government down to the people. It is further constituted by horizontal and diagonal lines of communication among and between groups at different levels of the political heirarchy (Curran 1991:31). In Indonesia, such horizontal and diagonal lines have often expressed themselves as contestation and challenges across and between factions and allegiances, and have typically led to greater activity in the public space. Foreign correspondents are best able to fulfil their role by attempting to drill for information in the cracks that emerge in the closed communications culture when elite alliances shift, contract or break, often creating new needs to win media attention and public support. The correspondents also increase productivity by shifting their focus away from institutional sources of information to intellectuals and activists outside the politico-economic power structure, because such sources desire to expand the immature public sphere. The correspondents must thus position themselves to take advantage of the continuously shifting nature of the information environment, which opens and closes depending on the benefits that different individuals and factions perceive in submitting to media attention. It is currently in the interests of the new Habibie government to solicit the media spotlight, but Indonesian history suggests the environment could easily close again, requiring journalists once more to play against the different lines of communication that constitute the public sphere.

References

Anwar, D F 1998, 'The Habibie Presidency', *Indonesia Update conference proceedings*, Australian National University, Canberra.

Anwar, R 1973, 'Newsmen Can Take Heart when They Look Across the Border', *IPI Report*, November–December.

ASEAN Regional Workshop 1972, *Communication Problems in Development*, Yayasan Tenaga Kerja Indonesia and Friedrich-Ebert-Stiftung, Jakarta.

Awanohara, S 1984, 'An Industry in Better Shape Than Ever Before', *Far Eastern Economic Review*, 1 March.

Berry, C, Birch, D, Dermody, S, Grant, J, Hamilton, A, Quilty, M and Sen, K 1995, *Perceiving 'the Media'*, Canberra: Australian–Asian Perception Project Working Paper No 8, Academy of Social Sciences and the Asia–Australia Institute, Sydney.

Beutler, W 1982, 'Comment', in Broinowski, A (ed) *Australia, Asia and the Media*, Nathan, Griffith University, Brisbane.

Bourchier, D 1993, 'Totalitarianism and the "National Personality": Recent Controversy about the Philosophical Basis of the Indonesian State', revised version of a paper written for the *Indonesian Culture: Asking the Right Questions* conference, 28 Sept–4 Oct 1991, Adelaide.

Bourchier, D and Legge, J (eds) 1994, *Democracy in Indonesia: 1950s and 1990s*, Monash Asia Institute, Clayton.

Bresnan, J 1993, *Managing Indonesia: The Modern Political Economy*, Columbia University Press, New York.

Budiman, A (ed) 1990, *State and Civil Society in Indonesia*, Monash Asia Institute, Clayton.

Byrnes, M 1995, Former Jakarta Correspondent for the *Australian Financial Review*, Personal interview conducted August 1995.

Carey, J 1983, 'The Press and Public Discourse', *Center Magazine*, no 20.

Cornish, P 1992, 'Journalistic Jawa: a Personal Look at Journalism Training in Indonesia', *Australian Journalism Review*, vol 14, no 2.

Curran, J 1991, 'Rethinking the Media as a Public Sphere' in Dahlgren, P and Sparks, C (eds) *Culture and Citizenship: Journalism and the Public Sphere in the New Media Age*, Routledge, London.

Departemen Penerangan 1996–1997, *Data Kewartawan Berdasarkan IPPPN Tahun 1996* (Journalistic Data Based on IPPPN 1996), Jakarta: Direktorat Jenderal Pembinaan Pers & Grafika, Proyek Pembinaan Pers, Departemen Penerangan RI.

Earl, G 1995, Jakarta Correspondent for the *Australian Financial Review*, Personal interview conducted in September.

Eldridge, P J 1995, Non-Government Organisations and Democratic Participation in Indonesia, Oxford University Press, New York.

Fishman, M 1980, *Manufacturing the News*, University of Texas Press, Austin.

Friel, T 1995, Former Jakarta correspondent for Australian Associated Press, personal interview conducted in September.

Garnham, N 1994, 'The Media and the Public Sphere', in Calhoun, C (ed) *Habermas and the Public Sphere*, MIT Press, Cambridge.

—— 1986, 'The Media and the Public Sphere', in Golding, P, Murdock, G and Schlesinger, P (eds) *Communicating Politics*, Holmes and Meier, New York.

Goh, A 1998, 'Suharto on How Press Could Have Helped the People Cope with Crunch', *Straits Times*, 18 January.

'Golkar Defends its Policies to Foreign Press' 1998, *The Jakarta Post*, 7 March.

Greenlees, D 1998 'Habibie Feels Lash of Unshackled Press', *Australian*, 8 June.

'Habibie: I Don't Need to Talk Much' 1998, *Kompas*, 7 June.

Hachten, W A 1987, *The Third World News Prism: Changing Media, Clashing Ideologies*, 2nd edition, Iowa State University Press, Ames.

Hariyati M T 1995, '*Pandangan Faham Integralistik Indonesia*' (An Observation on the Integralistic Concept of Indonesia), paper delivered at a meeting of Coordinators of *Pancasila* lecturers, Semarang, 4 December.

Heryanto, A 1996, private interview conducted in April.

Higgott, R and Robison, R (eds) 1985, 'Theories of Development and Underdevelopment: Implications for the Study of Southeast Asia', in *Southeast Asia: Essays in the Political Economy of Structural Change*, Routledge and Kegan Paul, London.

Hill, D T 1987, 'Press Challenges, Government Responses', in Tickell, P (ed) *The Indonesian Press: Its Past, Its People, Its Problems*, Annual Indonesia Lecture Series, No 12, Monash Asia Institute, Clayton.

Horton, P C (ed) 1978 'All Freedom is at Stake', in *The Third World and Press Freedom*, Praeger Publishers, New York.

Human Rights Watch—Asia (HRW-A) 1994 The Limits of Openness: Human Rights Violations in Indonesia and East Timor, HRW-A, New York.

Hyland, T 1995, former Jakarta correspondent for Australian Associated Press, personal interview conducted in September.

Index on Censorship 1975, 'Indonesia', *Index on Censorship*, vol 3, no 3.

Jenkins, D 1994, Asia editor for the *Sydney Morning Herald* and former Jakarta correspondent, personal interview conducted in October.

—— 1986, 'Indonesia: Government Attitudes Towards the Domestic and Foreign Media', *Australian Outlook*, vol 40, no 3.

Kakiailatu, T 1994, 'Berubah Pandang Setelah APEC' (A Change of Opinion After APEC), *Gatra*, 26 November.

Kelly, P 1998, 'B.J. in a Bind', *The Weekend Australian*, 8–9 August.

King, S S 1966, 'Indonesian Press Becomes More Daring as Curbs Are Eased', *New York Times*, 12 April.

Knight, A 1995, 'Re-inventing the Wheel: Australian Foreign Correspondents in Southeast Asia', *Media Asia*, vol 22, no 1.

Liddle, R W 1985, 'Soeharto's Indonesia: Personal Rule and Political Institutions', *Pacific Affairs*, no 58.

Lubis, T M 1993, *In Search of Human Rights: Legal-Political Dilemmas of Indonesia's New Order*, Gramedia, Jakarta.

Macintosh, I 1995, Former Jakarta correspondent for the Australian Broadcasting Corporation, personal interview conducted in September.

Mackie, J 1990, 'Indonesia: Economic Growth and Depoliticization', in Morely, J W (ed) *Driven by Growth: Political Change in the Asia–Pacific Region*, M E Sharpe, New York.

Mahatir M 1985, 'A prescription for a socially responsible press', *Media Asia*, vol 12, no 4.

Maher, M 1995, Jakarta correspondent for the Australian Broadcasting Corporation, Personal interview conducted in September.

Mahfud, M 1993, *Demokrasi dan Konstitusi di Indonesia* (Democracy and Constitution in Indonesia), Liberty, Yogyakarta.

Makarim, N A 1978, 'The Indonesian Press: an Editor's Perspective', in Jackson, K D and Pye, L W (eds), *Political Power and Communications in Indonesia*, University of California Press, Berkeley.

McBeth, J 1995, Jakarta bureau chief for the *Far Eastern Economic Review*, Personal interview conducted in August.

MacBride, S et al 1980, *Many Voices, One World*, UNESCO, Paris, Kogan Page, London, and Unipub, New York.

Mydans, S 1998, 'Indonesia's New Leader, Self-Styled Reformer, Hopes to Stay a While', *New York Times*, 3 June.

Nasution, A B 1993, 'Adakah Hak Asasi Manusia di Dalam UUD 1945?' (Is There Human Rights in the 1945 Constitution?), *Forum Keadilan*, no. 2.

Ng'weno, H 1978 'All Freedom is at Stake', in Horton, P C (ed) *The Third World and Press Freedom*, Praeger Publishers, New York.

Price, M 1998, 'Talks the Talk, Walks the Walk But...', *The Australian*, 27 May.

Rodgers, P 1982, 'Australian Reporting from Asia: Interpretation or Intrusion', in Broinowski, A (ed) *Australia, Asia and the Media*, Griffith University, Nathan.

Richard R 1982, 'Culture, Politics, and Economy in the Political History of the New Order,' in Anderson, B and Kahin, A (eds) *Interpreting Indonesian Politics: Thirteen Contributions to the Debate*, Cornell Modern University Project, Ithaca.

Ramage, D 1995, *Politics in Indonesia: Democracy, Islam and the Ideology of Tolerance*, Routledge, London.

Romano, A 1996a, 'Piecing Together the Jigsaw: The Professional Culture of Foreign Correspondents in Indonesia', *Media International Australia*, no 79, February.

—— 1996b, 'The Open Wound: *Keterbukaan* and Press Freedom in Indonesia', *Australian Journal of International Affairs*, vol 50, no 2.

Schwarz, A 1995, Former Jakarta correspondent for the *Far Eastern Economic Review*, Personal interview conducted in September.

—— 1994, *A Nation in Waiting: Indonesia in the 1990s*, Allen and Unwin, St Leonards.

Schiller, H 1976, *Communication and Cultural Development*, International Arts and Sciences Press, White Plains.

Simanjuntak, M 1994, *Pandangan Negara Integralistik* (The Philosophy of the Intergralistik Nation), Pustaka Utama Grafiti, Jakarta.

Soeharto 1989, 'Role of the Press in National Development', in Mehra, A (ed) *Press Systems in Asean States*, Asian Mass Communication Research and Information Centre, Singapore.

Supomo 1945, 'Pidato Pada Tanggal 31-5-1945 Dalam Rapat Badan Penjelidikan Untuk Persiapan Indonesia Merdeka, Digedung Chuuoo Sangi-In Di Jakarta' (The Speech of 31 May 1945 in the Inquiry Body for Preparations for Indonesian Independence, in the Chuuoo Sangi-In Building in Jakarta), in Yamin, M (ed) 1959, *Naskah Persiapan Undang-Undang Dasar 1945* (Minutes of the Preparations for the 1945 Constitution), Jajasan Prapantja, Jakarta.

Tiffen, R 1989, *News and Power*, Allen and Unwin, St Leonards.

—— 1978, *The News From Southeast Asia: The Sociology of Newsmaking*, Institute of Southeast Asian Studies, Singapore.

Uhlin, A 1995, *Democracy and Diffusion: Transnational Lesson-Drawing Among Indonesian Pro-Democracy Actors*, Department of Political Science, Lund University, Lund.

Van Dijk, C 1989, *Political Development, Stability and Democracy: Indonesia in the 1980s*, Centre for South-East Asian Studies, Hull.

Vatikiotis, M R J 1994, *Indonesian Politics Under Suhart—Order, Development and Pressure for Change*, revised edition, Routledge, London.

'Wakil Kepala BPS: Distribusi Pendapatan Belum Bisa Dideteksi' 1991, *Kompas,* 2 May.

Wallace, J 1996 RMIT journalism lecturer, Personal interview conducted in September.

Wirosardjono, S 1993, 'Peta Kemiskinan' (Poverty Map), *Tempo*, 15 May.

Wolf, D L 1992, *Factory daughters: gender, household dynamics, and rural industrialization in Java*, University of California Press, Berkeley.

The Flor Contemplacion case as a media event

Philip Kitley and Warwick Mules

[An event] is not a decision, a treaty, a reign, or a battle, but the reversal of a relationship of forces, the usurpation of power, the appropriation of a vocabulary turned against those who had once used it... (Foucault 1981:154)

Introduction

Media relations between Australia and its regional neighbours have been the site of diplomatic and cultural tension over the last 20 years, and have been the subject of academic, political and at times lively popular analysis and comment (Frost 1982:81–84; Hurst 1987:345–356; Kessler 1991:57–73; Perera 1993:15–29; Byrnes 1994; Searle 1996:56–84).

In scholarly discussions, the focus has generally been on the media as vehicle for the bilateral representation of different, domestic, regimes of value. It has not focussed on the way the media, under conditions of globalised communications, interact and create a transnational public sphere where, beyond the control of any single media interest, a wide and shifting array of voices, interests, audiences, sources and actions effects the representation of relationships and events. Our argument is that the Flor Contemplacion affair indicates the need to rethink a number of theoretical and conceptual positions concerning international relations and public affairs in a world where the barriers between official culture and public culture are dissolved by the flows of information and imagery within global contexts of telecommunications and media.

We suggest further that while cultural differences inflect the language and style of a specific event, they may not necessarily be constitutive of the event. 'Culture' is a device that may be strategically played for political purposes in international relations. Journalist David Jenkins makes the point bluntly:

> I become deeply suspicious when Indonesians wheel out the words 'values' and 'culture' to explain and justify their treatment of the local and foreign press. More often than not, 'Indonesian culture' is invoked as a smokescreen by people whose deeper motivations have little to do with culture and everything to do with power maintenance. (Jenkins 1996:151)

The cultural meanings protagonists invest in their speeches, releases and other forms of publicity are re-signified in the transnational public sphere, which shifts representation and interpretations of the event. An example of the strategic use of culture was Dr Mahathir's opportunistic representation of the Asian currency crisis as just the latest instance of a historic clash between

Asia and the West. And while ASEAN foreign ministers jointly declared (*Economist* 1997a) that foreigners were to blame for the crisis, Mahathir's intemperate comments in July and August 1997 were not endorsed by other regional leaders. When stock markets around the region fell sharply after Mahathir's comment that 'speculators deserve to be shot', he was left exposed for his simplistic and prejudiced cultural perspective and re-cast domestically and internationally as out of touch (*Economist* 1997b).

This essay is part of a larger collaborative project and leads on from an earlier discussion (Mules and Kitley 1998) of the Flor Contemplacion affair, where we theorised the idea of the transnational public sphere and characterised 'people power' in Philippines political processes as an example of a mediated counterpublic. In this essay, we will not traverse those issues further. Our interest here is primarily on the way the transnational public sphere affects international relations and diplomacy. In this discussion our focus is on a media event that involved the Philippines and Singapore as primary protagonists, but that also drew in other ASEAN neighbours, Australia and the United States. Our analysis of the cultural politics of the Flor Contemplacion media event shows that media relations problems between Australia and its Asian neighbours ought not necessarily be understood as an expression of essentialised cultural differences (Hurst 1987; Kessler 1991), but are inherent to the mediasation[1] of international relations, and can occur between nations that claim a high degree of shared 'Asian values' and cultural heritage. We argue further that while culture may be employed strategically in international relations, the specificities of local history and meaning frame the different voices in the transnational public sphere, which becomes the site of re-framing of cultural meanings and relationships in ways that are unexpected, unintended and beyond the control of the official voices trying to contain the dispute. The implications of these findings for Australia's media relations with regional countries are commented on in our concluding remarks.

The Flor Contemplacion affair

In 1995 a dispute broke out between Singapore and the Philippines over the execution of Flor Contemplacion, a Filipina overseas contract worker (OCW) employed in Singapore. Flor Contemplacion was tried and convicted of the murder of a Filipina maid in Singapore in 1991. The dispute drew in

---

[1] The concept of mediasation is adopted from Thompson (1990:3ff). Mediasation accounts for the general condition of social mediation by electronic media. Unlike the term mediation, which suggests an interim process between media and society, the term mediasation, as used in this essay, is proposed to signify the thoroughgoing spread and intercalation of media within and across social contexts.

other ASEAN nations as it became clear that the extensive media coverage of the events surrounding the execution and its aftermath put the representation of the events beyond the restricted channels of official action and administrative control that normally frame relations between the ASEAN nations. In this paper we will follow some of the trajectories of this dispute as it appeared within the Singapore and Philippines public spheres.

A useful way in which such a transnational perspective might be gained is through rethinking the concept of the public sphere as articulated by Jurgen Habermas (1989). Based on the 18th century ideal of rationally determined communicative exchange/debate, the bourgeois public sphere assumes face-to-face communicative relations between disputants in personalised, unmediated space. Habermas' development of the concept acknowledges the crucial role of the media in the late 20th century, but fails to take note of the great diversity in modes of action in the public sphere. The Habermasian ideal presupposes forms of speech (discussion, debate) and print as the predominant modes of communication in the public sphere.

In our discussion, the public sphere is thought of as a discursive space where, in a wide variety of ways, such as debate and discussion in meetings, on radio, satellite television and the internet, through telecommunications and in printed publications, and also through performance, exhibitions, representation and lobbying, and public action such as street marches and demonstrations, diverse social groups constitute themselves as identities with their own public face and profile. Understood in this way, the location of the public sphere is dispersed, and has simultaneously a real and a virtual character. It may no longer be understood as 'that space between civil society and the nation-state' as Martin Hirst puts it (1995:14), for state authorities, elite representatives and other social groups are present, and interact in a variety of ways across the same communicative space(s). Indeed, in events such as the Flor Contemplacion affair, the public sphere is occupied not only by local actors, but also by official and non-official voices from beyond the national territory, creating a transnational public sphere (TPS). As Miriam Hansen put it, 'the accelerated process of transnationalization makes it difficult to ground a concept of the public in any territorial entity, be it local, regional, or national' (Hansen 1993:183). Understood in this way, the public sphere is strategic and evanescent, and will expand and contract according to the needs actors have to maintain their public contestation. In the Flor Contemplacion affair, the presence of ASEAN voices apart from those of the two national disputants was transitory, but reminded those directly involved that a dispute in one part of the system was recognised necessarily as a problem in other parts of the system, emphasising again the transnational character of contemporary media events.

Although governments make extensive use of electronic communications in the conduct of international relations, contemporary conventions of diplomatic relations and representation are still often premised on pre-electronic communications. The formal, stylised symmetry of exchange of 'Third Person Notes' and recall of resident ambassadors enacted during the Flor Contemplacion affair derive historically from a period of pre-electronic communications, and sea and land travel. In that period governments spoke to each other privately, and at a distance, through accredited representatives in high level, personalised exchanges. Even today, as Adam Watson argues, 'oral communication, face to face, mainly through expert intermediaries but where necessary by personal meetings of heads of government, remains the fundamental method of diplomacy' (Watson 1982:84). Indeed, Searle has pointed out that this is the way the *Embassy* affair was resolved. In July 1991, the Australian Foreign Minister, Gareth Evans, hand-delivered a private letter from Mr Hawke to Dr Mahathir acknowledging Australia was at fault. In October, Prime Ministers Hawke and Mahathir met privately and agreed that their two governments would 'dissociate themselves from "inaccurate" news reports about each others affairs' (Searle 1996:60).

Before the advent of globalised electronic communications, and the widespread penetration and linkage between newspapers and television, states were able to quarantine news of diplomatic manoeuvring and communications within a privileged political and cultural elite. Diplomatic missions were able to pursue their governments' objectives largely without public scrutiny or criticism precisely because signification did take time and space, despite the myth of the presence of the ambassador and personalised communications. For an ambassador was always a sign of a deferral. His (they were mostly men) presence and person masked an absence of power, for he was far from home and only ever representative.

In the present context of almost instantaneous transnational communications, however, the symbolic break in relations traditionally signalled by the recall of ambassadors is radically subverted. The temporal and spatial modalities of diplomatic conventions associated with personalised representation are radically altered by electronic communications as the clamour of voices in the public sphere takes the rhetoric of stately relations as simply another topic for debate. Where once the recall of ambassadors symbolically and literally signalled a period of official silence and a break in relations, in the present era news of such high cultural official action is propelled into the media spaces of the transnational public sphere and becomes itself the catalyst for a further round of comment and action. Despite Australian Foreign Minister Evans' express preference for working 'quietly and patiently' through the 'recalcitrant' affair, for example, the dynamics of the transnational public sphere rendered such an approach anachronistic (Searle 1996:65). The anger in the Philippines that greeted the diplomatic note (*note verbale*) that expressed Singapore's 'shock and outrage' (*Philippines Star* 1995) at the burning of the Singapore flag illustrates very well how circulation of news of official communications in the public sphere dissolves its formerly privileged, private status and thrusts the action of governments into a wider public debate. In the Australian context, Searle has pointed to the way the *Embassy* and 'recalcitrant' affairs were mobilised by the Opposition and domestic political groups to question the government's approach and handling of the affairs (Searle 1996:72–75). Indeed, public debate over its competence may prompt a government to publicly justify and even announce its actions, turning inside-out the formerly largely privileged and confidential processes of government-to-government relations. Throughout the Flor Contemplacion affair, this became obvious in the way President Ramos and the Prime Minister of Singapore used the press, public speeches and television interviews (CNN) to reveal the content of diplomatic correspondence between them over the affair (*Straits Times* 1995a; 1995b; 1995c; 1995d; 1995e).

Thus the role of electronic communications in the public sphere has contributed to a radical shift in the tenor of international diplomacy. The media are far more than media of representation. The media actively interact with and transform the practices of diplomacy that they seem to represent in a simpler sense. Electronic communications facilitate the scrutiny of public action and erode distinctions between high and popular culture and politics. This occurs not so much by penetration of traditional barriers of secrecy by intelligence leaks or investigative journalism, but more simply through the sheer speed and radical deterritorialisation of national action. In the electronic mediascapes of the contemporary world, an action taken in one political/cultural space can be simultaneously signalled in another and becomes itself the site of popular comment, leaving government with little time to erect defences or institute damage control, drawing it into the clamour of the public sphere as one voice among many. The satellite relay to Baghdad on 18 February 1998 of television images showing Ohio State University students shouting down and disempowering the United States' premier diplomat, the Secretary of State, Madeline Albright, as she defended her government's proposed strike against Iraq, is an illustration of the way globalised communications disrupt governments' desire to manage the representation of foreign policy issues. On relays from Baghdad, Americans saw that in Iraq, the images were interpreted as an indication of a popular lack of support for Clinton's policies. President Clinton was forced to address publicly the issue of opposition. He asserted that 'most people support our policy', and that the rowdy meeting represented all that was good about American democracy (*Washington Post* 1998).

The TPS leaves government with little choice but to use the media as an alternative form of diplomacy. Not to do so is to risk leaving the field open to critics and opponents (Hamilton and Langhorne 1995). Australian journalist Michael Byrnes has argued that Indonesia has played a strategic press 'game' with the Australian press to exert its psychological control and 'keep Australia in retreat' (Byrnes 1994:130). President Ramos used the press as a diplomatic tool when he sent the Prime Minister of Singapore media clippings that expressed the 'emotion, passion, excitement, even the outrage of Filipinos from all walks of life'. President Ramos explained he had sent the clippings because he believed the Singaporean Ambassador, Tan Seng Chye, may not have properly informed his Prime Minister about how Filipinos regarded Flor's execution (*Straits Times* 1995f).

To make these abstractions more concrete, we will draw attention to the interplay of official and public discourses between the Philippines and Singapore early in the Flor Contemplacion affair. Indeed, were it not for the interplay to be described, the Flor Contemplacion affair, would, like so much of international relations, have remained part of routine consular business. The Philippines government's initial appeasement (*PDI* 1995a) of the Singaporean stance with respect to the execution of Flor became the focus of considerable antagonism in the media. Many columnists and other contributors expressed opposition to the government's stance, arguing that Flor was being sacrificed because of the Philippines government's desire to protect its favoured nation status with Singaporean investors. When President Ramos shifted ground, established a fact-finding commission and declared that he would end diplomatic relations with Singapore if forensic evidence suggested Flor had been a victim of injustice, the general view was that it was popular action that had motivated the President's policy change:

> President Ramos is angry at last. The widespread indignation over the execution of Flor Contemplacion has exploded in his face and torn into his Philippines 2000 program. The heavy fallout might have shaken him to realise that, in a crunch, his constituency is the Filipino people, not the applauding businessmen, diplomats and officials who attend official functions whenever he travels abroad. (*PDI* 1995a)

Flor was imagined as a martyr in the struggle of the Philippines people to overcome their impoverished circumstances, which have forced millions of Filipino women and men to work overseas in generally menial occupations in countries such as Hong Kong, Saudi Arabia, Malaysia and Singapore.

> '[Flor] died for us, so the plight of our countrymen abroad could be brought to our attention' (PDI 23 Mar, 1995).

'Flor is a symbol of how oppressed our workers are in foreign countries' (*Philippines Star* 23 Mar 1995).

'The loneliness, the degradation, the fears, and yes, the hopes, but always the sacrifices are met in one OCW named Flor Contemplacion...She's only one of them, but all at once she's all of them' (Editorial, PDI 26 Mar 1995).

'...a policy of labour export that has made of the Philippines a fount of modern-day slaves' (Editorial PDI 27 Mar 1995).

In this discourse we find the appearance of an imagined Flor Contemplacion, the embodiment of a populist version of Philippines national identity quite at odds with the perceptions of the Philippines foreign policy elite, which has shown little interest in linking the economic, humanitarian and moral welfare of its citizens abroad to bilateral relations with countries where the migrant labourers work (Romana 1995:78–82). This counter-imaginary, drawing on the language of the Catholic tradition, became the focal point for rallies and oppositional practices within the domestic space of Philippines public affairs.[2] What these extracts signify is that the popular construction of the Philippines community reaches beyond the national borders of the Philippines and gathers up the millions of Filipinos abroad into an imagined community that is simultaneously global and local.

After Flor's execution, outspoken criticism in the press of government handling of the affair, and of the government's economic (mis)management, was maintained and accompanied by protest action such as flag burning, rallies and memorial ceremonies, which culminated in a public funeral in San Pablo City attended by an estimated 40,000 mourners. All of these actions took place in the (local) public sphere of the Philippines. But the domestic space of the Philippines is not sealed off from the 'outside' world. It is traversed by flows of official and commercial communication, and hence is already incorporated into the TPS. Thus the local image of Flor as martyr, as the embodiment of a Philippines popular national identity inscribed in editorials, in midnight vigils and spectacular events such as rallies and the ceremonialism of her funeral, also appeared on the television screens and in the daily newspapers of the Singaporean public sphere.

When discussing the contribution of electronic communications to the creation of a TPS, it is easy to think mainly in terms of the technology of transnationalisation, and focus on the aspect of images arcing over and dissolving spatial boundaries. Indeed, many observers writing about communications and their contribution to globalisation focus more or less exclusively on uni-directional electronic flows across borders and on the

---

[2] Historian Rey Ileto has shown how opposition movements in the Philippines in their parades, street art and hymns traditionally draw on secularised versions of Catholic tradition (Ileto 1979).

impact of the flow(s) at the point of reception (Schiller 1985:11–20; Straubhaar 1991:39–59). The idea that flows create relationships that do not reflect a world already created, but are constitutive of (virtual) social and cultural relationships literally constituted in flows of imagery has received little attention. In the case of media events, transnational communications draw the parties into a relationship in which the two (or more) nations no longer see themselves as separated but as inextricably related (at least for the while). The TPS simulates the transnational relationship and becomes a space for mutual, reflexive examination of the dynamics and meaning of that relationship. In the Flor Contemplacion media event, the TPS foregrounded the economic interrelatedness of Singapore and the Philippines, as well as notions of community and shared histories of colonialism, articulated through perceptions of shared Asian values and ASEAN fraternity.

The reason that Flor, just one among many oppressed and mistreated OCWs, generated such passion, may be attributed to a clash between competing ideological representations of Singapore and the Philippines. Filipinos were disillusioned when their own government and Singapore, which has vigorously promoted the representation of itself as an Asian nation, founded on 'Asian values' of collective welfare, social harmony and family, set aside these supposedly shared values in favour of more narrowly defined economic relations. It seemed a double betrayal—of carefully managed representations of ASEAN community, and of a sense of shared history. After all, in both Singapore and the Philippines, the pain of separation (from family members working overseas in the Philippines, and from Indian, Malaysian and Chinese homelands and the Malaysian federation in Singapore), is recent and deeply felt. If, in Singapore, as Chua Beng Huat argues (1996:87–107), ideas of the national interest, social welfare and community have been reductively culturalised into economic development, in the Philippines popular imagination they have not, and this disjunction in representations of the idea of community generated a sense of hurt and outrage that similar incidents in the Middle East had failed to.

In the mediaised, virtual relationship, there is a tendency for familiar (local or national) lived practices (*habitus*) (Bourdieu 1977:83) to be the deictic anchor point for each party in maintaining the relationship. This means that unlike a relationship (even if it is a confrontational one) where there is a shared habitus, in a transnational, transcultural relationship there is likely to be a disjunction of values, of ways of talking and ways of acting. This is very obvious in the different styles of reporting in the Philippines and Singapore. In the Philippines, reporting on the Flor Contemplacion affair was presented in editorials, essays, columns, letters to the editor, features and news reports, and circulated in the views of a diverse range of columnists and journalists. In a journal such as the *Philippines Daily Inquirer* (the newspaper with largest circulation and a reputation for investigative journalism), on any one day during March and April 1995, as many as four writers could be found commenting on different aspects of the affair. The affair in Singapore received more limited in coverage, attracted far less correspondence and was generally presented in the form of news reports. The language of the Singapore press was more formal and impartial than that of the Philippines press, which at times was bitter and provocative. The representation of Flor as a martyr, for example, as if she died for a noble cause and not as a result of due process, is a perfect example of the way the familiar language and imagery of one habitus may be deeply resented in another. The Prime Minister of Singapore's comments in his National Day Address, in August 1995, provide ample evidence of the point:

> President Ramos sent me several video cassettes and thick files of newspaper cuttings, to let me appreciate the mood, and his predicament. At first I was outraged by their media's lies, distortions, and total irresponsibility. But as they went on I decided it was a waste of time and energy to get angry. The Filipinos and the Singaporeans are totally different people. We have different cultures and political systems. Some of their journalists are a special breed from the wild west of cowboy movies. The media stories would have been hilarious, except that the Filipinos believed them and consequently damaged bilateral relations.

Thus, although the TPS is constitutive of a relation between (national) players, the pragmatic meaning of the relationship has to be negotiated and is likely to be strained cross-culturally. The strain is related to the lack of a shared habitus, but is also related to the virtual quality of the simulated relationship. As Ochs argues, 'the greatest part of sociocultural information is keyed implicitly' (Ochs 1990:291), and successful communication depends not so much on propositional meaning as on inferences drawn from subtleties in communication such as manner, gesture and choice of register. These are largely erased by the speed of electronic communications, which bring widely differing communicative styles into juxtaposition and leave little time for reflection.

The possibility of a transnational relation, or 'we-feeling', between Singapore and the Philippines is crucially linked to ideas of relative economic development and ideas of community that provide each society with a way of ordering their relations. We suggest further that these concepts function indexically and allow 'social identity to be defined and affirmed in difference' (Bourdieu 1994:103). In both Singapore and the Philippines, the ideal national community is imagined as an economically developed, well-managed society living securely at home within the national territory. In the Philippines, however, the 3.5–4.5 million contract workers (OCWs) spread throughout the world are accepted as an index of underdevelopment and incompetent national management. At the same time, the estimated annual US$2.6 billion contribution that OCWs make to the domestic economy is recognised and valued by families throughout the Philippines who depend on remittances from overseas for their everyday survival (*FEER* 1995:43).

Thus, on one level, the OCWs index poor management and the relative underdevelopment of the Philippines, and their absence overseas indexes the breakdown in the idealised construct of the national community. On another level, the OCWs' absence is recognised as constitutive of the very survival of the home community. OCWs are thus present while absent, and the economic circumstances of the Philippines have shifted the pragmatic meaning of community to include a social network of 'shadow households' (Caces et al 1985:5–28). The community-in-place remains an ideal, but absent workers, present to all in their sacrifice and in their remittances, have redefined the Philippines community as a spatially dispersed global/local or 'glocal' community, to use Featherstone's term (Featherstone 1995:9, 118). The language that constitutes the global Philippines community is grounded in the Christian habitus. OCWs are typically praised for their sacrifice, their suffering and, in the case of Flor, their martyrdom. The resonances with Christian doctrine and ethical exemplaries are powerful. More than just income, remittances from abroad enter the economy as windfall gains, being well in excess of the income workers could earn at home. In this sense the remittances take on the character of gifts to the community. But while freely given, the gifts are not freely bought. They entail considerable costs—of separation, of loneliness, the pain of family breakdown, and vulnerability to personal harm and exploitation. These costs, understood as selfless sacrifices, are the root of the feelings of solidarity and compassion that are central to the popular Filipino construct of the OCWs.

Relative underdevelopment is thus the ground for the deterritorialisation of the idea of community in the Philippines. In Singapore, the presence of Filipino OCWs amongst Singaporean citizens was not understood as constitutive of a transnational Philippines–Singapore community in which OCWs might enjoy the same status as in the Philippines. In Singapore the OCWs index the economic power and relative development of the small island nation. Their presence indexes a break up in the Philippines community and highlights the ethnically diverse, but imaginatively intact national community of Singapore, secure 'at home'. The lack of any recent history of out-migration, a tightly defined national community and a largely non-Christian religious culture as habitus meant that in Singapore the presence of OCWs was understood largely within an economic heuristic. In the Singapore model of the economy, OCWs are part of the supply or production side. As such, they are accepted as highly substitutable commodified labour units rather than as individuals contributing to the Singapore community. Put another way, we might say that in Singaporean constructs, the OCWs were denied the symbolic capital they enjoy within the Philippines habitus. As the President of the Foreign Maids Employment Agencies Association put it, the 'row' over the hanging of Flor did not affect the maid business because:

> we were more or less prepared and have managed to get an average of about 1,500 maids from countries like Sri Lanka, Indonesia and India. We will still recruit [Filipinas]. However, in the past we had depended a lot on Filipino maids but we would not put all our eggs in one basket now. I think we have learned a lesson—not to be totally dependent on one source. (*Straits Times* 1995g)

It is the disjunction in the habitus of Singapore and the Philippines and the resultant asymmetry in the understanding of the constitution and possibility of community that lie at the heart of the dispute between Singapore and the Philippines. When the TPS brings nations into relation, the pragmatic meaning of the relationship for each side comes under pressure from the habitus of the other. As we have noted, both parties to the relationship share a common valuation of economic development, and idealise a secure, territorially-centred community. The Philippines acknowledges its relatively inferior economic position and the significance of Singaporean investment in the Philippines, so there is no disagreement over relative economic power and status in the relationship. It is the different status accorded to migrant workers by each party that denied the Philippines the we-feeling they expected from Singapore as an Asian nation and ASEAN partner. Simply put, from the Philippines perspective, OCWs are part of the community, even though absent, because of their vital economic contribution. The emotional costs of the contribution have invested the OCWs with considerable symbolic as well as economic capital in Philippines eyes. From the Singapore perspective, the OCWs are not part of the community, even though present and even though they contribute to the economy. They are not part of the community because they are 'foreigners', and because their relative poverty defines them as different from the relatively affluent Singaporean community. From the Singapore perspective, OCWs possess (limited) economic capital, but no cultural or symbolic capital exchangeable for membership in the Singapore community.

From the Philippines perspective, the Singapore focus on the poor, outsider status of OCWs fails to acknowledge that its relatively superior economic position owes something to Filipino workers, and fails to accept that the OCWs constitute a reciprocally beneficial bond of transnational community between the two nations. Rejecting the reductionism of the economic model, the Philippines media argued that Singapore failed to acknowledge the social and emotional significance of the OCWs' work in building the Singapore community. Separated from their own families, OCWs ironically find themselves at the heart of domestic life in Singapore, where for many families they perform the intimate, nurturing roles Singaporeans have chosen to put aside in their drive for economic development.

In Singapore, the transnational, dispersed community of the Philippines is both a real and simulated presence in the public sphere. The presence of Filipina maids is understood by Singaporeans as an endorsement of the success of the economic development of the island state. At the same time, the contract workers disquietingly display dependency relations historically associated with Western colonialism but denied in the Singaporean construction of itself, which selectively foregrounds the Asian cultural heritage of its pluralist population rather than its Western colonial origin (Ang and Stratton 1995:179–192). In the Singaporean public sphere the appearance of Flor as martyr became a sign of the 'Other'. All the positive values associated with Flor in Philippines (martyr, hero, victim, good woman, family saviour and selfless worker) were reversed, and Flor became the sign of Filipino emotionalism and irrationalism, even envy (*Straits Times* 1995g). This process of re-signification and re-territorialisation of the image of Flor in Singapore can only happen because the public sphere is no longer contained within the territorial domain of the nation state. As we have argued, the public sphere is already transnational. Therefore any counter-imaginary, even if addressing local issues, is always already transnational. Thus in a state such as Singapore, where an authoritarian government restricts public expression of political opposition (Rodan 1993:5–108), images and narratives that threaten the master narrative of Singaporean national identity may still appear and have an effect within the Singapore community. The counter imaginary, circulating in the Singapore public sphere is not 'Singaporean' as such, but still serves to set the parameters of debate and discussion about what constitutes Singapore, its identity, its values and its policies.

This re-reading of Flor needs to be understood in terms of Singapore's nation-building project, which has been underway for the last 30 years. The Singapore government has constituted a unified Singapore national identity through an ideology of multicultural pluralism. Singapore's three main ethnic groups (Chinese, Malay and Indian) are encouraged to imagine themselves as separate ethnic and cultural identities and, at the same time, as members of a unified nation. This policy of syncretic identification reduces 'difference' to a symptom of the 'same', so that all manifestations of difference are interpreted as so many problems to be solved in terms of the coherence and unity of Singaporean national identity (sometimes writ large as a general Asian character). The appearance of the Flor Contemplacion affair, challenging Singapore's procedural rigidity, lack of compassion and departure from an essentialised 'Asian way' of doing things, constituted a clear sign of difference for Singaporeans, who responded by Othering.

At the same time that Singapore read the Philippines' construction of Flor-as-martyr as a sign of the Other, the counter-imaginary of Flor in Philippines popular discourse also involved a process of Othering of Singapore, and its vehemence was a measure of the recognition that what was despised in Singapore was a reflection of historical processes that had shaped both nations, but which appeared to reinstate the very dependency that both nations had found intolerable.

If the Singaporean Othering of the Philippines involves an Orientalist discourse that represents the Philippines as irrational, overly emotional, weak, chaotic and vulnerable, the Filipino counter-attack is Occidentalist, knifing in on Singapore's 'arrogant' pride in its orderly society, an (excessive) attachment to the rule of law and a readiness to exploit the weakness of a neighbouring country (*Manila Chronicle* 1995; *PDI* 1995c; *Philippines Free Press* 1995). This last point prompted charges that Singapore is not what it represents itself to be. Lacking indigenous authenticity, it is not an Asian nation but, by implication, a colonial artefact and power that has not escaped its historical legacy of Westernisation (*Today* 1995). What the Philippines accuses Singapore of, then, is a dangerous lack of cultural memory. Singapore stands accused of denying its own history, of denying the memory of a time when its citizens were vulnerable and far from home:

'Singapore can't seem to understand why Filipinos are equating Flor's case with society's need for compassion' (*PDI* 1995c).

'Singapore finds it difficult to understand our sympathy for a mere housemaid and, in their eyes, a convicted criminal. Our reactions are seen as those of a poor, victimised people, not of a people aspiring to greatness in this era of globalisation' (*PDI* 1995b).

The East–West binarism inherent in Singapore's nation-building project is used against it and Singapore stands accused of mimicry, of being almost Asian but not quite, of being unable to remake itself as a fraternal member of the ASEAN family (*PDI* 1995c). Singapore's willingness to rely on the Western model of the rule of law and individual responsibility and agency as the basis of its claim for its scrupulously fair treatment of Flor sits uneasily beside its vehement criticism of the individualism of Western values and its championing of 'Asian' collectivism (Chua cited in Ang and Stratton 1995:187).

At the same time, the desperation in the Philippines' Othering masks the recognition that what Singapore is accused of may also be turned against its accuser, which shares a colonial past with Singapore, but unlike Singapore, is still dependent. Representing itself as Asian involves the Philippines in re-territorialising its own Spanish Catholic and later American post-colonial legacy as 'Oriental'.

But Singapore's apparent readiness not to recognise the Philippines' situation as part of a long-term historical process in which they were also involved, its willingness to use the Orientalist discourse of colonialism against the Philippines, and its acknowledged smugness over its economic development (*Straits Times* 1995g), left the Philippines with little choice but, in a kind of reciprocal blindness, to deny any shared history and position Singapore not as a victim but as an oppressor.

Conclusion

By mid-May 1995 the press in Singapore and the Philippines were beginning to use phrases such as 'in the wake of the Flor Contemplacion tragedy', and to discuss the possibility of movies of the affair, foreshadowing the ultimate simulation of the event and a sure sign that the intensity of the event had played itself out. The Philippines and Singapore governments had regained control of the narrativisation of the affair in late April, when both governments agreed to a joint autopsy and agreed further that, if necessary, the findings of an independent panel of foreign forensic scientists would be mutually binding. Throughout the affair both governments attempted to regain control of the event and their relations, which had been so unexpectedly and dangerously upset by the execution of Flor for a crime committed four years previously. State authorities and national leaders attempted to reassert their control first of all by acknowledging and working with the diverse publicity that constituted the affair. They also made significant concessions (different in the two states), of which the agreement that a neutral forensic team would decide the matter was just the last and most decisive. The concessions and the recruitment of an independent team in early June re-positioned both sides as flexible and co-operative, and in this way asserted a mode of communal relations. Ironically, the nations reasserted their essentialised 'Asian' qualities and character and ASEAN fraternity through the institution of Western science. Both countries had relied upon positivist notions of forensic science during the affair, but each believed that its practice might have been 'contaminated' by the intrusion of national and political interests. Nevertheless, a master narrative of forensic science performed by independent experts became the site of remaking the relationship through images and processes that the two sides agreed to decode in a similar way.

The Flor Contemplacion media event seriously tested the conventional framing of the relationship between Singapore and the Philippines. The event moved beyond the immediate control of official voices and led to a break in diplomatic relations and a mutually damaging process of Othering that opened up sensitive issues for each country, such as their imagined Asian/ASEAN identity, their status as nations and the nature of the relationship between Singapore and the Philippines. At the theoretical level, our analysis has shown that in conditions of electronic communications, local public affairs are traversed by media flows that deterritorialise represented events into transnational space. This means that the appearance of oppositional voices, or a counter imaginary within a national domestic context, is also already an appearance within a transnational public sphere, present in other local contexts and having diverse effects. Thus globalisation or postmodern theory is necessary for the understanding of the emergence and nature of media events, but our analysis has also shown that, at least in the case of Southeast Asia, postmodern theory needs to be informed by post-colonial analysis, as we have shown that the modern nations of Singapore and the Philippines were always transnations, if not globalised, through their complex relations with metropolitan powers and institutions. The articulation of post-colonial analysis with postmodern theory is powerful in the way it furnishes insights into the history of the trajectories that inflected the constitution of the media event and provided its rich, situated meaning.

Finally, and very briefly, a comment on the implications of our analysis of transnational media events for Australia's relations with regional neighbours. We have presented a theoretical analysis of the impact of the TPS on diplomacy elsewhere and will not reiterate that here (Mules and Kitley 1998). The key point is that electronic communications technologies make it impossible to quarantine international disputes and restrict their management to the private processes of privileged elites. In both democratic and authoritarian states, electronic communications thrust diplomatic relations into the full glare of publicity and action. The behind-the-scene becomes front-of-scene. The autonomy of the state is restricted to what it is capable of internalising. When, as we have seen, communications technology makes the inside outside, makes the splits and fissures of national politics and events transparent to a transnational audience, then states must exert themselves to preserve areas of sovereignty they hold dear. States must become 'masters of appearances', in Cynthia Weber's words (1995:38). Because Australia seeks to become, and is more and more, integrated into the region and its politics, it is crucial that Australia re-think the national in terms of the transnational, and reflect critically on the 'in-betweenness' of language, imagery and cultural policies.

This does not mean that diplomatic relations will be turned over to the pages of newspapers, television and computer screens. But it does mean that what is called 'public diplomacy' (Logan 1994:55–59) will become the norm rather than an irritating distraction. It should also mean that all those who have the day-to-day carriage of international relations are highly skilled in communications, and highly attuned to the strategic use of various forms of publicity. Indeed the delivery of Australian official public affairs programs is a topic of discussion within the Department of Foreign Affairs and Trade. But it is regrettable that at a time when media skills seem critically important, the Department pulled Australia-based public affairs officers out of all overseas posts except for Washington, Tokyo and Jakarta, and closed down the Overseas Information Branch of the Department in 1996. On the face of it, removing skilled personnel from overseas posts where they have daily access to the nuances of local politics is likely to damage Australia's capacity to master its appearances.

References

Ang, Ien and Stratton, Jon 1995, 'Straddling East and West: Singapore's Paradoxical Search for a National Identity' in Perera, Suvendrini (ed), *Asian and Pacific Inscriptions: Identities Ethnicities Nationalities*, Meridian, Bundoora.

Bourdieu, Pierre 1977, *Outline of a Theory of Practice*, Cambridge University Press, Cambridge.

—— 1994, [*La Distinction* 1979, Minuit, Paris] cited in Friedman, Jonathan, *Cultural Identity and Global Process*, Sage, London.

Byrnes, Michael 1994, *Australia and the Asia Game*, Allen and Unwin, St Leonards.

Caces, Arnold, Fawcett, James T, Gardner, Robert W and Adelman, Irma 1985, 'Shadow Households and Competing Auspices: Migration Behaviour in the Philippines, *Journal of Development Economics*, Vol 17 No 1/2.

Chua Beng Huat 1996, 'Culturalisation of Economy and Politics in Singapore' in Robison, Richard (ed), *Pathways to Asia: The Politics of Engagement*, Allen and Unwin, St Leonards.

Economist 1997a, 2 August.

—— 1997b, 6 September.

Far Eastern Economic Review 1995, 30 March.

Featherstone, Mike 1995, *Undoing Culture: Globalisation, Postmodernism and Identity*, Sage, London.

Foucault, Michel 1981, *Language, Counter-Memory, Practice*, Cornell University Press, Ithaca.

Frost, Frank 1982, 'Asia and the Australian Media', *Media Information Australia*, No 23.

Habermas, Jurgen 1989 [1962], *The Structural Transformation of the Public Sphere: An Enquiry into a Category of Bourgeois Society*, Polity Press, Cambridge.

Hamilton, Keith and Langhorne, Richard 1995, *The Practice of Diplomacy: Its Evolution, Theory and Administration*, Routledge, London and New York.

Hansen, Miriam 1993, 'Unstable Mixtures, Dilated Spheres: Negt and Kluge's The Public Sphere and Experience, Twenty Years Later', *Public Culture* 5.

Hirst, Martin 1995, 'The Coming Republic: Citizenship and the Public Sphere in Post-Colonial Australia.' *Australian Journal of Communication*, Vol 22 No 3.

Hurst, John 1987, 'A Clash of Cultures: Indonesia and the Australian Media.' *Australian Quarterly* Vol 59 No 3

Ileto, Reynaldo Clemena 1979, *Pasyon and Revolution: Popular Movements in the Philippines, 1840–1910*, Ateneo de Manila Press, Quezon City.

Jenkins, David 1996, 'Culture and Convenience: the Press in Indonesia' in Brown, Colin (ed), *Indonesia: Dealing With a Neighbour*, Allen and Unwin, St Leonards.

Kessler, Clive S 1991, 'Negotiating Cultural Difference: On Seeking, Not always Successfully, to Share the World with Others—or, in Defence of *Embassy*', *Asian Studies Review*, November.

Logan, Sandi 1994, 'Public Diplomacy and Global Media: A DFAT Information Paper', *Media Information Australia*, No 71.

Manila Chronicle 1995, 7 March.

Mules, Warwick and Kitley, Philip 1998, 'People Power, and the Transnational Public Sphere: the Flor Contemplacion Affair as Media Event in the Asia Pacific', *International Journal of Cultural Studies*.

Ochs, Elinor 1990, 'Indexality and Socialization' in Herdt, G, Shweder, R and Stigler, J (eds), *Cultural Psychology: Essays on Comparative Human Development*, Cambridge University Press, Cambridge.

Perera, Suvendrini 1993, 'Representation Wars: Malaysia, *Embassy*, and Australia's *Corps Diplomatique*' in Frow, John and Morris, Meaghan (eds), *Australian Cultural Studies: A Reader*, Allen and Unwin, St Leonards.

Philippines Daily Inquirer (*PDI*) 1995a, 24 March.

—— 1995b, 26 March.

—— 1995c, 27 March.

Philippines Free Press 1995, 1 April.

Philippines Star 1995, 23 March.

Rodan, Garry 1993, 'Preserving the One-party State in Contemporary Singapore' in Hewison, Kevin, Robison, Richard and Rodan, Garry (eds), *Southeast Asia in the 1990s: Authoritarianism, Democracy and Capitalism*, Allen and Unwin, St Leonards.

Romana, Elpidio 1995, 'The Evolution of Philippines Foreign Policy and the Perceptions of Filipino Foreign Policy-Makers During the Aquino Regime', *Asian Studies Review*, Vol 19 No 1.

Schiller, Herbert I 1985, 'Electronic Information Flows: New Basis for Global Domination?' in Drummond, Phillip and Patterson, Richard (eds), *Television in Transition: Papers from the First International Television Studies Conference*, BFI Books, London

Searle, Peter 1996, 'Recalcitrant or *Realpolitik*? The Politics of Culture in Australia's Relations With Malaysia' in Robison, Richard (ed), *Pathways to Asia: The Politics of Engagement*, Byrnes, Michael 1994, *Australia and the Asia Game*, Allen and Unwin, St Leonards.

Straits Times 1995a, 13 March.

—— 1995b, 16 March.

—— 1995c, 22 March.

—— 1995d, 26 March.

—— 1995e, 27 March.

—— 1995f, 13 April.

—— 1995g, 15 April.

Straubhaar, Joseph D 1991, 'Beyond Media Imperialism: Assymetrical Interdependence and Cultural Proximity', *Critical Studies in Mass Communication*, No 8.

Thompson, John 1990, *Ideology and Modern Culture: Critical Social Theory in the Era of Mass Communication*, Polity Press, Cambridge.

Today 1995, 27 March.

Washington Post 1998, Online, 19 February.

Watson, Adam 1982, *Diplomacy: The Dialogue Between States*, Eyre Methuen, London.

Weber, Cynthia 1995, *Simulating Sovereignty: Intervention, the State, and Symbolic Exchange*, Cambridge University Press, Cambridge.

Foreign news for Australians: the case of the Philippines 1986–88

John Tebbutt

For Australian foreign correspondents, domestic concerns have a priority in determining the coverage of foreign events. This doesn't necessarily mean that big events are not covered; it means that covering any Australian angle is an imperative. The cultural practice of reporting, for a foreign correspondent, is conditioned by knowing what will interest the audiences. This knowledge determines the kinds of stories that can be told; it is a product of implicit and explicit directions from editors as much as the journalists' conception of their role as national correspondents and the political context of the host country. Rather than 'values', it is in this play of dependencies between journalists and these audiences—editors, nation, hosts—that power is exercised through the organised and organising practices of reporting and its administration. (Barrett 1991:134–7; Foucault 1980:115–6)

In this chapter I want to explore some of this 'play of dependencies' in the way Australian foreign correspondents reported the Philippines in the years immediately following the 'people's power' uprising in February 1986. In particular, I consider the home audience: how an interested nation, as the popular form of 'national interests', influenced the reporting of events in the Philippines. Following that, I have collected descriptions of work in three different institutional arrangements for gathering international news: the staff correspondent, the freelancer and the journalist 'on assignment', each of which provide, examples of different forms of reporting practice. Furthermore, I will look at the way in which the Philippines, as a contested political space, impacted on the stories and practices of journalists.[1]

Background: the February Revolution in the Philippines

During February 1986, major cities in the Philippines, and in particular the capital Manila, were caught up in political turmoil. In a pattern that was repeated in Eastern Europe and other parts of Asia (most recently Indonesia),

---

[1] I interviewed journalists who represented the major Australian media outlets in the Philippines between 1987 and 1988—the *Australian*, the *Sydney Morning Herald* (*SMH*) and the Australian Broadcasting Corporation (radio and television)—as well as staff and freelance journalists who went to the Philippines 'on assignment' during this time. These interviews were originally conducted for a series I produced for *Media Magazine*, 'The Philippines and the media', which was broadcast on 2SER FM. An earlier version of this chapter was presented as a paper to the Asian Studies Association of Australia, Biennial Conference, Griffith University, 1994.

thousands of civilians took to the streets in protest at political manipulation, repression and censorship. The 'people's power' uprising during that month was a major international news story. Apart from the implications of the mass involvement of a citizenry in extraparliamentary political change, there were other, more romantic, aspects that made the story attractive as international news. Opposition leader Corazon Aquino had taken on the mantle of heroine when she returned from America to contest the presidential elections after her husband, exiled opposition leader Benigno Aquino, was shot while leaving the plane on his return to Manila in August 1983. The campaign of Ferdinand Marcos, who had ruled through intimidation and violence since instituting martial law in 1972, was plagued by allegations of corruption, including a dramatic walkout of scrutineers who were ostensibly employed to guard against vote-rigging. Following the election on 7 February 1986, a standoff occurred where both candidates claimed victory, prompting former allies of Marcos, Defence Minister Juan Enrile and military commander Fidel Ramos to attempt their own coup. They took over Camp Aguinaldo, the military barracks in the centre of Manila, but were never in control of enough of the military to ensure their own victory. Here the role of the citizenry was crucial. They surrounded Camp Aguinaldo, preventing attacks from the loyalist Marcos military. In a standoff over four days, eventually other sections of society and the majority of the military openly declared their support for Aquino and the defectors, Enrile and Ramos.[2]

Media, crisis and hierarchy

David Brisbin, an American journalist who was working for a Manila television station at the time of the uprising, observed the international reporting of these events:

> Viewers in developing countries witnessed the whole crisis blow by blow…The foreign networks had multiple crews, the best equipment and fleets of drivers…Operating out of hotel suites, transformed into space age video centers, they beamed on-the-spot coverage around the world by means of temporary satellite dishes. (Brisbin 1988:49–64)

Brisbin drew a sharp distinction between these activities and the operation of the local media. 'Hard news was infrequent and there was little of that action footage with gunfire and burning choppers seen on First World television' (Brisbin 1988:63). The Philippines media had been wrested from

[2] There are many accounts of the dynamics of the military and political standoff between 22 and 25 February (see Chapman 1987:234–248; Johnson 1987; Mamot 1986). Chapman gives a detailed explanation of the role of the CPP in Philippine politics; Johnson was a journalist for the Toronto *Globe and Mail*; Mamot provides an extensive catalogue of events with an emphasis on the role of Catholicism and the Church.

their typical position as disseminators of authoritative reports, and thrust directly into the contest over who could be claim to be the President of the Philippines. Media institutions and broadcasts became strategic sites around which the revolution was fought. Brisbin notes that 'roughly half of the casualties and most of the major battles occurred at broadcast facilities' (Brisbin 1988:49).

Through a series of accidents and coordinated actions, Marcos was prevented from televising his inauguration live on the morning of 22 February, while Aquino's own ceremony on the same day was recorded and broadcast later on a secure television channel. By that evening word was spreading through Manila that Marcos and his family had fled. People broke through the gates at the presidential residence, Malacanang Palace, and ransacked it, a final sign of their victory over despotic rule. Brisbin notes that at this moment of victory, the new form of media that had emerged during the course of events was censored by the military, who insisted that the departure of Marcos and his family be kept off air: '...it was in this transaction that media began reverting to normal pyramidal structures of control...' (Brisbin 1988:61).

The formats of foreign news meanwhile had remained unaffected by the shift in power to a politicised citizenry, apart from the focus they provided to discuss the possibility of a transfer of power to Aquino. As a general point, Western journalists reported a change of regime rather than an uprising. Consequently, the events over those three weeks in the Philippines were presented as a clear case of good and evil, with Aquino as an appropriate heroine to the desperate tyrants—Ferdinand and Imelda Marcos. Following this simplified version of the conflict, which reflected a concern for stable hierarchies among mainstream international media, the story that the 'people power revolution' was a military coup that, despite civilian support for the new President, only reluctantly accepted Corazon Aquino as a political leader was a much more difficult story to tell. Yet such a view was crucial to an understanding of the continuing pattern of military coups in the Philippines that occurred in the five years following Aquino's ascendancy. Rather than portray this complex web of interaction, Australian news media settled instead for simpler scenarios.

Media institutions and audience

Of course it is a spurious contrast to place foreign media up against Philippines media; the institutions of foreign media were not overturned and in fact may well have been strengthened during the crisis. Certainly ABC journalist Peter Couchman, in reporting the departure of Marcos, claimed that Filipinos were personally thanking him for the role that international media played in supporting the uprising. Couchman's report naïvely demonstrates the way in which foreign media could be drawn into the domestic agenda of political forces while remaining 'on the sidelines'; it had ominous portents for foreign correspondents who would eventually be seen as enemies of President Aquino's military program to combat the communist insurgency.

However, when the events of February 1986 had been played out, Couchman left the Philippines. During the next two years ABC TV and radio was served by a staff correspondent based in Manila. At the same time the *Sydney Morning Herald* (*SMH*) replaced the stringer who had been for some time their regular reporter with a staff correspondent, while the *Australian* maintained their long-standing correspondent. However, even full time correspondents are transient, and by 1988 many Australian news organisations had begun to consider the Philippines a 'slow story'; at the end of that year all the Australian correspondents had left Manila for other posts. News organisations had decided to cover the 'running stories' in Southeast Asia at the time, particularly the developments around the United Nations intervention in Cambodia. They also wanted to be closer to some of the fast-growth economies in the region, such as Thailand. Consequently the ABC correspondent went to Singapore, the *SMH* journalist was sent to Bangkok to set up the paper's Southeast Asian Bureau and the *Australian*'s writer came back to work as an editor in the Sydney office. Between end of 1986 and the beginning of 1989 though, these journalists had to find ways to relate the on-going changes in the Philippines to an audience 'at home' in Australia.

Once again, this obscures a more complex set of circumstances. The journalists were embedded in a matrix of relations that at once facilitated and constrained the practice of reporting to home. In the first instance, the destination of their reports, the newsrooms of their respective employer organisations, was a more mundane 'home' than the abstract national audience the reports eventually reached. Particularly in regard to newspaper stories, journalists' reports were read, reread and edited, and maybe 'blended' with other reports before they were received by a media consumer. Sometimes they would not be published at all. One journalist reflected on this process, recalling:

> When I first came [to the Philippines] in 1986, I had a very, very rough time with my foreign editor of that time. I was producing a lot of copy on issues such as land reform, I was producing a lot of copy on the communist movement. I was producing a lot of copy on what I guess he considered 'bleeding heart' issues. Those stories were getting spiked.
>
> So you get to the point where you start to select what you write for what's going to get in. It's not a case of the foreign editor ringing you up and saying I want this or that. It becomes a case of you responding to what is favourably received. And that doesn't mean that you can supply something that you think

they won't like and they won't use it. That's not true at all. You can actually get a number of stories in that you never expect to see but, generally it's a matter of assessing what's going to get in.

Apart from editors' interests, and their explicit or implicit directions, there were other institutional forces that the journalists had to consider, including: reports from competing media outlets, in particular the major news agencies; specific publishing practices such as writing to deadlines; and the appropriateness of stories to different structures of writing, including 'straight' news or features and current affairs. A number of journalists also had to consider different publishing technologies; the ABC journalist reported for radio and TV news and current affairs, while the *SMH* journalist filed for Macquarie News, which broadcasts a network radio news service around Australia.

As well, the journalists would have been aware that many Australians already had particular knowledge about the Philippines under Marcos. There had been extensive coverage in Australia of the communist insurgency that had grown considerably after martial law was declared. At one stage, Australian government aid workers were held by insurgents for almost a week before being released with a request that the Australian government cease providing assistance to the Marcos regime. Many people were also aware of the Australian-owned bars in Ermita, the red-light district of Manila, and the traffic in women who were known as 'mail-order brides'. The arrest of an Australian Colomban priest, Father Brian Gore, the assassination of the Benigno Aquino and the widespread human rights abuses in the Philippines had also received wide media attention. These events sparked a range of reactions in Australia, from street protests and the formation of a solidarity movement to shifts in public policy and popular perceptions of the Philippines demonstrated—and at the same time generated—the range of interest in Australia about events in the Philippines.

Given this multiplicity of knowledge and interest on behalf of the general population of Australia, how can a foreign correspondent address a 'home' audience? The idea of audience itself requires some definition. The point needs to be made that a media audience is a totality that cannot be separated from media institutions: a nation-as-audience is produced by economic and political processes of production, dissemination and reception. In this way, Australia as an audience can be understood as an 'effect of power', the material effect of government regulation, economic imperatives and the apparatuses of publishing and broadcasting; it is in this sense—as the material effect of particular forces—that the nation-as-audience has cultural specificity rather than an inherent identity derived from national (typical) characteristics. It is also in this way that an audience attains a political position. As an effect of power—a site where specific forces that govern media institutions come together—Australia-as-audience operates as a condition for the production of truth.[3]

True Australian narratives

The shared nature Australian institutions that produce the nation-as-audience have with European traditions, global capital flows and information flows allows a national audience to be both unique and 'Western'. This in turn allows that audience to be set off as different from any other culturally specific audience, such as that in the Philippines (or even the United States or Britain), while at the same time providing a universality around liberal norms (for example, freedom, democracy, progress). The narration of the on-going story of the Philippines during 1987 and 1988 could only be 'true' if it could be invoked in terms and statements appreciated by such an audience. Consequently journalists often relied on Western understandings of conflict, crisis and liberalism. Here are some examples:

Example 1

As far as the story goes, Westerners see things in terms of crisis, in terms of a collision of values and a possible solution at the end of that, whereas that's not necessarily the case for Asians. For example, Westerners would see the insurgency in the Philippines as a crisis for the government which either has to be solved or will be successful. But in fact Filipinos don't see it that way...revolt and protest is very much a part of the Philippines psyche and the Philippines tradition. But we can't explain that. A Western reporter has to interpret that in terms of crisis and solutions.

Example 2

When you're covering the third world in any way you're applying Western democratic models to that country—whether you resist it or not that is your point of reference. You can work back from there but lets face it, we work from our models. So yes, you have to admit that you are writing for a Western audience from a Western perspective and you can't pretend to understand and to appreciate the situation from the perspective of Filipino...The cultural aspect is rather important and it's something we tend to ignore when we're writing up big stories, writing that sterile news wire copy about the tanks rolling and the country teetering on the brink of collapse...

---

[3] This definition draws from Foucault's concept of truth, where: '"Truth" is to be understood as a system of ordered procedures for the production, regulation, distribution, circulation and operation of statements. "Truth" is linked in a circular relation with systems of power which produce and sustain it, and to effects of power which it induces and which extend it' (Foucault 1980:133. See also Foucault 1981:48–78).

Example 3

...we're journalists, we're about telling stories. Particularly in the broadcast medium, to tell a story in simple terms, it doesn't matter about the names or the place. Struggles for power, struggles to effect change, struggles to change policies within an established power structure are the same in most places. I was talking earlier about Mrs Aquino and the struggle that was going to pull her to the left or pull her to the right. That's something that is understandable to any audience and it doesn't matter if it's the Philippines or the New South Wales Labor Party.

A survey of newspaper reporting of the Philippines in 1988 noted that: '...the Australian press coverage of the Philippines over the last two years [1986–88] reveals a sympathetic identification with the Aquino government and the problems they are facing. This is a reflection of the admiration of what is viewed as her liberal democratic style of government' (Fisher and Leigh 1988:10). The authors of the survey also pointed to an 'element of romanticism' when the Philippines government was being judged.

This was evident in the response of one media institution to the expulsion of their reporter from the Philippines in late 1987. The *Australian Financial Review* writer Michael Byrnes had reported on the negative aspects of President Aquino's policies. Despite the regime change he identified government corruption and an inadequate land reform program as ongoing issues. Three weeks after an article on corruption appeared in the *Review* he was presented with an expulsion order effective within 48 hours (Byrnes 1994:187). Despite this a *Review* editorial gave the new government the benefit of the doubt declaring:

It is difficult to believe that the Aquino government with all its commitment to free speech and the fight against corruption, would have taken this action on its own initiative without some foreign pressure. More logically perhaps it may have been influenced by the subtle pressures surrounding the ASEAN Conference (Heads of Government Summit) to be held in Manila... (*Australian Financial Review* 1987a).

The editorial went on to virtually accuse Indonesia of being behind the expulsion without presenting any substantiation of the allegation (although it was well known that Byrnes' critical reports were not liked by the Indonesian government either when he was based there). While the Secretary for Foreign Affairs, Raul Manglapus, quickly overturned the explosion order, Byrnes still left Manila for Hong Kong.

In the popular press there appeared to be an editorial requirement for 'happy stories' that continued for at least four years after Aquino came to power. Stories that challenged the 'good versus evil' scenario that brought Corazon Aquino to the attention of a mass audience in Australia were considered inappropriate by editors with an eye on the market. On the 9

February 1990, the *Herald* in Melbourne (before it was amalgamated with the *Sun* to form the *Herald-Sun* but while its audience was in serious decline) published an article on the dramatic increase in human rights abuses under the Aquino Government (Kizilos 1990a:9). The reporter, who had participated in a study tour of the Philippines organised by Community Aid Abroad, a non-government aid organisation, outlined the response of her employers to the article:

> [Prior to publication] a note was left on my desk telling me that my boss would prefer a 'happy story' on the Philippines...I was told by my features editor that a separate story on a massacre of Muslims in Mindanao would probably be unsuitable for the features pages because most *Herald* readers were 'right-wing and not interested'. The editor of 'WeekEnd', the section that ran my story, was told to run bright articles on sport and entertainment after my story had appeared. (Kizilos 1990b)

Work practices and foreign correspondents

As well as the concepts of audience, specific work practices and competing production demands play a determining role in the selection and shaping of stories. Often journalists fall back on familiar sources to cover the fast moving events. In this section I want contrast the work practices as described by three different kinds of foreign correspondent: a staff reporter, a freelancer and an Australian-based journalist 'on assignment'. Each has particular constraints that determine the kind of story they cover and the kind of reporting they can conduct.

The following is a description of work from the ABC correspondent who reported the August 1987 coup attempt—a major incident in the early life of the Aquino government. In this description he indicates the importance of other sources in the context of the competing demands of maintaining coverage of a fast moving story.

> When there is a big story it is often difficult to get out to see for yourself what is happening and to talk to people. If you like we could talk about the coup attempt by Gregorio Honasan on August 28th [1987].
>
> I had a phone call at three o'clock in the morning Manila time. That's 5 o'clock Sydney time. I was told there was a coup attempt going on I said 'Don't give me that' because we've had these calls a dozen of times before. 'No, this one is real, they're shooting at Malacanang.' So I think right, OK, start calling other people, find out what the early rumours are...I tried to call Camp Aguinaldo (a military base in the centre of Manila), I tried to call a diplomat, and I called my BBC colleague who lived near the Palace. No one knew clearly what was happening.
>
> I lived closish to Camp Aguinaldo, so I got in my car and drove straight there. But before I did, *AM* [morning radio current affairs program] is on the

phone saying 'What are you doing at the coup?' I tell them there are just fears, rumours, shots in the dark, I'll do something for you, I have to go and find out what's happening. Now that's five o'clock in the morning in Australia, the early *AM* program goes to air an hour and a half later.

I went down to the gates of Camp Aguinaldo. There were three or four hundred soldiers, clearly in a rebel mode, waiting outside the gate. There was a telephone in an all-night cafe outside the gates of Camp Aguinaldo. I establish that I own that phone for the foreseeable time. I explained to the fellow who owned the cafe the calls wouldn't cost him anything and I slipped him several hundred pesos. I was the only reporter there for hours.

So I file for the early *AM* and I do something for the news. Meanwhile I'm trying to call other journalists. They tell me what they've seen at Malacanang, I tell them what I've seen at Aguinaldo. Between the two of us we have an idea [of what's going on]. And then along walks Colonel Gregorio Honasan. I knew him very well, I knew he spent all his spare time plotting coups, I'd met him a dozen times or so. I see him, everything falls into place. We chat. I go back to the phone and try to file more reports. I badger him for an interview, he gives an interview—after I've already done a live Q&A [question and answer] for the [later] *AM* program.

And all this quite dramatic stuff! It's early morning now coming up over Aguinaldo—I've been told to keep out of the way in case shooting starts. I get the interview with Honasan—*AM* is ticking away. I go to another phone. I'd had some equipment brought out so I could send [recorded sound] over the phone lines and get that on in the last five minutes of *AM*—it was the only interview Honasan gave.

So there we are. It's 8.30 in Australia, 6.30 in Manila and I feel as if I've done a fair day's work. I get back to the office. Television is of course, wanting a story. Ten o'clock I do a Q&A for the *World Today* [ABC Radio]. I do another Q&A towards the end of the program. I have a breather but then news is on the phone saying 'Where the hell is our story, you're working for us as well!'. Fine, so I do something in the five minutes that remain and then I have two hours in which to try and get out of the office and try to find out what is happening and in the meantime try to put together a TV story. The real problem is on the competing demands of current affairs programs and the constant demand of news, is trying to fit television in as well. Television of course has a certain priority and a huge amount of money spent on satellite links from a place like Manila to Sydney.

Journalists other than staff correspondents have different pressures that effect the way they can work. The freelancer I interviewed talked about her work in relation to the resident correspondent's:

In comparison to the staff you don't have to stay in one place, you can travel around. You can decide what story you're going to do, who you're going to interview and how you are going to do the story and that gives you a great deal of freedom and satisfaction.

On the other hand, clearly you have many disadvantages: you can't afford to hire a car, you can't afford to buy a plane ticket whenever you feel like it. You haven't got free telephone calls and you haven't got any status or protection if anything goes wrong. It's harder to get interviews. It's much more difficult to operate on a financial level alone, being a freelancer.

Ideally the freelancer should be able to count on the staff correspondent, if you like. There should be a relationship between the staff correspondent and the freelancer and a staff correspondent should be happy that a responsible freelancer is there to go out and do the things that they aren't able to do. But they don't necessarily see you like that, they see you as a rival unfortunately. Quite a few of them are not just a little bit threatened by you because you're unpredictable, you might embarrass them. But ideally it could be a very good relationship.

An ABC journalist who visited the Philippines twice 'on assignment', spoke about his work:

The pressures aren't that different to the range of pressures that exist for journalists who are there all the time. The one thing about going 'on assignment' as it were, is that you can't come back without 'the story'. Your organisation is frequently paying a large amount of money to get you there and sometimes a large amount of money to keep you there. You have a very specific time and you can't really get on the plane without having all the material for the story you were sent to do. So that's a pressure in itself.

Even so he admits that 'the story' can actually change once you arrive in the country:

…it would be foolish to assume that you could go to some country, even having done all the best research, or as much as you could possible achieve, and then think that the story wasn't going to be very different by the time you got there.

That's happened to me in a very specific case. I went to the Philippines to do a story about the right-wing vigilantes. We had a particular reference of our own research here to look at the way some aspects of the religious right in Australia had played a part in the increasing polarisation in Philippines society. When we got there we found it was a much, much bigger story—that the Australian element was just one component of a very big international input into the polarisation in the Philippines.

So it's not as if you go with a whole range of preconceived notions and get there and follow those notions. You have to, to a certain extent, go where the story takes you because it's often evolving while you are there.

Making it true: news agencies, narration and disinformation

Foreign desks for Australian newsrooms are very small compared to some overseas operations. The larger US, Japanese and European newsrooms will have regionalised foreign editors and desks. These editors can liaise directly with their correspondents and build up expertise and a working relationship. Typically, Australian newsrooms will have a foreign editor and a deputy editor who will divide the work between themselves; any expertise is usually incidental. Much of the work of the foreign desks is to sift through the masses of information that come from international news agencies and the syndicated wire services of the larger American newspapers such as the *New York Times* and the *Los Angeles Times*.

These international agencies also have an effect on the work of staff correspondents. Usually newsrooms subscribe to one or two agencies, and foreign editors and news chiefs in Australia would use the 'wire copy' as tipping service. They will pick up a story from the wire that the correspondents had not reported and contact them to check whether it is a worthwhile story or not. Sometimes a correspondent will be asked to file a 'matching story', or provide a 'colour' piece to complement an agency story.

The news agencies are also 'used as a threat...to keep journalists up to speed'. The fact that major agencies work 24 hours a day creates what one foreign editor called 'a psychological imperative' for correspondents to stay on their toes. Often newspaper stories are made up of 'blended wire copy', which will consist of information from a number of agencies as well as the staff correspondent. While the correspondent's byline should be then followed by 'and agencies' or the news service name, sometimes agency copy is not even credited. Occasionally this can put the correspondent in the invidious situation of being associated with unreliable information.

At other times a foreign desk will find an agency story that completely conflicts with their correspondents information. In a clear case such as this, the editor could contact the agency bureau, telling them to check their facts. The agency may then send out an advisory message on the wire service warning subscribers that the story is being checked. One correspondent I spoke to criticised the larger news agencies for 'enhancing stories'—the journalistic jargon is 'needled'—claiming that they had to 'dramatise stories in order to justify their existence'. Another foreign editor said that the agencies tend to be 'hysterical'. The thrust of these criticisms seems to be that the massive volumes of information that the international agencies churn out leads to a lack of thorough checking of sources.

Given the conditions outlined in the previous section by foreign correspondents, it is not unusual for them to have their daily news agenda prioritised according to the stream of information that is being distributed by the large agencies. As well given the imperative to produce news at this rate, the agencies are particularly susceptible to vested interests who attempt to have their point of view written up as being 'in the true'. While the Aquino victory was also presented as a victory for Western liberalism, the Philippines remained the only Western ally in Asia facing an active communist insurgency. The political struggle intensified as the communists claimed a role in the removal of the Marcos regime. In February 1987, following the collapse of the post-Marcos cease-fire with the underground National Democratic Front (the broad political front of the communist-led insurgency), the Aquino government launched a 'total war' aimed at crushing the insurgents. An important aspect of this strategy was cutting the funds directed to the coffers of the illegal Communist Party of the Philippines from what was believed to be a 'diverse network of fronts' in Western countries.

This was most forcefully enunciated by the conservative American organisation the Heritage Foundation. To defeat communism and consolidate democracy in the former American colony the Foundation outlined a number of actions the United States government could take, including 'countering foreign support to the CPP [Communist Party of the Philippines] by working with the Aquino government to identify CPP fronts abroad, particularly in friendly countries' (Fisher 1987). This quickly became the most important 'hometown angle' or domestic imperative on the media's agenda. One television researcher on a commercial current affairs program told me at the time that it was the only Philippine story he was interested in: '...if we could just get footage of an Australian with the rebels, that'd be a big story'. The *SMH* staff correspondent in Manila duly produced an article that described naïve Australians and their romantic motives for wanting to hobnob with communists in the jungles, while providing no evidence of collusion between Australians and the Filipino rebels.

In November 1987, six months after the Heritage Foundation recommendations were published, an Australian Associated Press (AAP) journalist filed a story that ran in the *Sydney Morning Herald* accusing Australian organisations of funding the New People's Army, the military wing of the CPP. Similar stories from the news agency ran in the *Advertiser* in Adelaide and the *Age* in Melbourne. All the reports quoted 'military intelligence sources' who alleged financial support for the Filipino communists had been provided from Australia and named six organisations, including Community Aid Abroad and the Tasmanian Council of Churches (who at the time were involved in a battle against conservative Christians in the local churches). The reports were greeted with outrage and indignation. Letters were sent to newspaper editors and government officials. Two weeks later a four line brief appeared in the *Australian Financial Review* entitled 'Filipino Funding Claims', saying 'the Philippines military had backed down' on the allegations (*Australian Financial Review* 1987b). In my research I didn't find this retraction published in any other newspaper.

The links between the Heritage Foundation and 'military intelligence sources' in the Philippines were strong. They were based on a network of organisations and individuals known as the World Anti-Communist League (WACL). At the time of the AAP story the head of the Philippines National Intelligence Co-ordinating Agency (NICA) was also an official with WACL. As to how these sorts of accusations can originate, a rare insight was provided by the Australian-based Christian Anti-Communist Crusade (since renamed the Pacific Anti-Communist Crusade).

In 1986, CACC president John Whitehall sponsored a tour to Australia for Jun Alcover, head of a similar anti-communist organisation in the Philippines. Funding for the tour was provided by the Philippines Defence Ministry's Peace and Order Councils. Alcover was a regular broadcaster on a radio station in Cebu, the Philippines' second largest city. While in Australia he contacted the station and broadcast by telephone accusations that Jose Maria Sison, a leader of the CPP who had been arrested by Marcos but released under an Aquino government amnesty, was raising funds in Australia for 'the communists'. Sison was visiting Australia for a conference and public meetings. Following the broadcast of this allegation in Cebu it was picked up by the state-run Philippines News Agency and given national coverage. On the strength of these reports, the Philippines military initiated an inquiry into Sison's activities (*Sydney Morning Herald* 1986).

While in November 1987, 'Philippines military intelligence sources' had targeted non-government aid agencies, churches and solidarity groups, by May 1988 the focus had shifted to the journalists themselves.

It was reported that the military had secret dossiers on 112 journalists, including 77 foreigners. This coincided with military authorities charging a British Broadcasting Corporation crew with murder, and a warning that foreign journalists could be 'caught in the cross-fire' if they continued to report the war from the guerillas' side (Williams 1988a). Journalists were already aware that the military used them at times as 'trackers' for discovering the whereabouts of government dissidents when they went to interview them or contacted them by phone. However, the charges against the BBC seemed to raise the stakes in what had previously been considered an occupational hazard.[4]

The relationship between the Aquino government and the BBC had already been strained over the screening of a documentary, *The Flawed Madonna*, in 1987. The murder charges arose from allegations of a

---

[4] It was well known by foreign journalists that, for instance, taxi cab drivers at the Manila Hotel, the base for most foreign correspondents in the Philippines, would provide information to the military and were sometimes military intelligence operatives.

'communist surrenderee' who claimed that a group of 'foreign looking journalists participated in the planning and filming' of a guerilla ambush in which 12 soldiers were killed. The case went no further when the passport stamps of the crew concerned, who had returned to Britain by the time the charges were laid, showed that they had not been in the Philippines at the time of the ambush.

Many foreign correspondents were surprised at the military's warnings and allegations, and attributed the moves to a 'dirtier' phase of the war. The *SMH* journalist who had been the only staff correspondent in the Philippines at the time told me, 'it puts journalists in the ridiculous position of having to prove they are not leftists'. These incidents prompted the Foreign Correspondents Association of the Philippines to send a statement to then Defence Secretary, Fidel Ramos, saying journalists were 'deeply concerned about the series of damaging allegations, particularly the unsubstantiated charges against the BBC'. The Association went on to say that 'covering both sides of a guerilla conflict is essential to responsible journalism' (Williams 1988b).

Conclusion

In this chapter I have attempted to demonstrate the range of elements that operate to produce the kinds of stories written by foreign correspondents. In the Philippines between 1986 and 1988 there was a heightened contest for what could and could not be written within a discourse of Western liberalism in relation to an Asian country. While Australian foreign correspondents were engaged as crucial actors in this process, their reports were determined by relations of power that produced a knowledge of what could, and what should not, be reported.

References

Australian Financial Review 1987a, 'Philippines joins dismal parade of oppression', editorial, 3 December.

—— 1987b, 'Filipino funding claims', 9 December.

Barrett, Michèle 1991, *The politics of truth*, Stanford University Press, California.

Brisbin, David 1988, 'The electronic revolution', *Journal of Popular Culture*, vol 127 no 3, Winter.

Byrnes, Michael 1994, *Australia and the Asia game*, Allen and Unwin, Sydney.

Chapman, William 1987, *Inside the Philippines Revolution*, W W Norton and Co, New York.

Fisher, Richard D 1987, *The international anti-Aquino network; the threat to Filipino democracy*, Asian Studies Center Backgrounder, Heritage Foundation, New York.

Fisher, Lyn and Leigh, Michael 1988, *Australia–Asia media relations*, paper No 359, ANZASS Centenary Congress.

Foucault, Michel 1980, *Power/Knowledge*, edited by Colin Gordon, Pantheon Books New York.

—— 1981, 'The order of discourse', in Young, Robert (ed), *Untying the Text*, Routledge, London.

Johnson, Bryan 1987, *Four days of courage*, The Free Press, New York.

Kizilos, Kathy 1990a, 'Aquino's total war', *The Herald* (Melbourne), 16 February.

—— 1990b, *Media Watch*, Philippines Issues, March–April, Philippines Resource Centre, Melbourne.

Mamot, Patricio R 1986, *People power*, New Day Publishers, Quezon City, Manila.

Sydney Morning Herald 1986, 'Manila queries communist's Australian tour', 7 October.

Williams, Louise 1988a, 'BBC crew charged with murder', *Sydney Morning Herald*.

—— 1988b, 'Manila lists 77 journalists under surveillance', *Sydney Morning Herald*.

Australian news media constructing Asia: a case study of Malaysia, Indonesia and the Philippines

Barry Lowe

The Australian news media's relationship with Australia's Southeast Asian neighbours is often depicted as problematic. Politicians like to blame our news outlets for hiccoughs in bilateral relations with countries to the north; and academics often accuse the news media of displaying ignorance and insensitivity in their portrayal of those countries. This critique of the news media tends to focus on the effects of Australian reporting in the countries reported on, and not on the domestic Australian audiences who, must rely on the news media for much of their knowledge about the region. Allegedly hostile reporting on countries like Malaysia and Indonesia may be an irritant in the development of closer ties between those countries and Australia, but it can also impede the growth of closer bilateral ties by fueling and maintaining hostile attitudes of the Australian public towards those countries and their citizens. Consistently negative reporting on Southeast Asia by mainstream news media outlets might even draw the accusation that the news organisations are sabotaging Australia's chances of enmeshing closer with Southeast Asia.

This study provides an outline description of a sample of Australian news media reporting on Southeast Asia and relates that description to possible effects on the audience. It tracks the dominant themes, in terms of subject matter, and some of the reporting conventions used in the news media's Southeast Asia file, to construct a portrait of how Southeast Asia is packaged by the media for the Australian news consumer. It seeks to identify what is salient in this corpus of news reporting and speculates on how those salient notions might be internalised by the Australian public.

We learn about the societies of other nations from a range of sources: from visits to those nations, contacts with their expatriates, images of those societies incorporated in our cultural products and from images of those societies constructed and delivered to us by our news media. This last source is far more important for the societies we have little direct contact with. It also attains a high level of influence because of its sustained nature. Many Australians make occasional visits to Southeast Asian countries—for some just once in a lifetime—but they are more likely to have frequent and sustained 'contact' with those countries through their reading and viewing of the news media. Their visits no doubt have a much greater impact on their awareness of those countries and the adoption of attitudes towards those countries and their people. But their exposure to the news media's construction of those societies will also influence their attitudes through the accumulative effect of their continual narrative. The news media play a significant role in determining what we think about concepts that are largely beyond our direct experience. The less direct experience we have of those concepts the more we are likely to be influenced by the mediated experience of them provided by the mass media. The Australian news media therefore contribute—although the extent of that contribution is impossible to quantify—to the formation and maintenance of attitudes among the Australian public towards the nations and people to our north. It thus follows that a consistently negative or hostile corpus of reportage on a particular country—an emphasis on 'problems' such as political instability, natural disasters, poverty, crimes and social deviations for instance—can support negative or hostile opinions by Australians in relation to that country.

The news media determine how they report on various themes and issues by applying concepts of newsworthiness to different fields of reporting. These concepts of newsworthiness are shaped by the traditions and conventions governing news production and by the culturally-acquired attitudes of news producers. Statements made by the prime minister, for example, are usually considered newsworthy in Australia because our recent traditions and conventions of domestic political reporting determine prime ministerial statements are an important source of news, and because Australia's political culture links prime ministerial statements with important changes in the laws and policies that govern us. News outlets also apply pre-determined concepts of newsworthiness to foreign news in general and to different arenas of foreign news. The newsworthiness criteria applied to reporting on Southeast Asia are significant in shaping the profiles of Southeast Asian countries that are provided by Australian news organisations for their audiences.

What makes news

News selection conventions and concepts of newsworthiness have long been major foci of academic research into mass communication. Researchers have identified and developed theories for a number of key areas of news production practice. White (1950) described the news selection process in terms of the role of news gate keepers: those individuals who make decisions that determine which events were selected or rejected for inclusion as news in their news outlets. News media gate keepers—news editors, TV news producers, editorial executives, etc—are recognised as important elements in the news selection process. Their concepts of what makes news, influenced by their professional acculturation and their personal biases and prejudices, are key determinants of what events become salient in the news media and how those events are constructed by the media. Tuchman (1972) described aspects of the professional culture of news producers from a sociological perspective, and how this culture influenced their approaches and attitudes towards the selection and processing of news material.

McCombs and Shaw (1972) studied news selection practices in terms of their reflection of a predetermined agenda that the news media apply to the prioritising of news. This agenda-setting function of the news media explains for why some issues are consistently highlighted in media discourse and why others are deemed not newsworthy and therefore ignored. Molotch and Lester (1974) described the nature of events that attract media attention and how those events indicate a preoccupation by the news media with occurrences that are routine and predictable for some types of news reporting, and random and unpredictable for other types. Molotch and Lester also described the 'bad news' syndrome by which the news media prioritise reports about disasters and accidents. The first attempt to define newsworthiness was by Galtung and Ruge (1965; 1974) who devised a list of 17 separate attributes of newsworthiness. For an event to cross the threshold of news media interest it needed to display at least one of these attributes. Galtung and Ruge's model—although lately under challenge—has retained the position of the dominant paradigm in the field and is still used in media content studies to describe categories of news salience.

Investigations into the Western media's portrayal of Third World countries—Tiffen (1976, 1978) and Smith (1981)—have demonstrated a tendency by media outlets to describe developing societies in terms of the problems of development, constructing those societies as 'problem zones' by de-emphasising or ignoring those issues that are regarded as newsworthy in developed countries. Brooks (1986) examined the American news media coverage of the Philippines after the collapse of the Marcos regime and suggested the international media then needed to 'un-demonise' the Philippines by adopting a more balanced coverage of the country. Robinson (1995) applied a similar analysis to the coverage of African countries by the British press, while Ismail (1996) looked at the coverage of Asia by four US newspapers.

Constructing Asia

This investigation is based on a content analysis study of one year's reportage on three Southeast Asian countries—Malaysia, Indonesia and the Philippines—by two Australian news media outlets: the *Sydney Morning Herald (SMH)* daily newspaper and the 7.45am daily news bulletin broadcast on the metropolitan network of the Australian Broadcasting Corporation (ABC). The *SMH* was chosen because it is recognised as one of Australia's two quality, daily newspapers of record the other being the Melbourne *Age*. The two newspapers are owned by the same media group, have similar markets (in Australia's two biggest cities), achieve similar circulation figures in relation to those markets and are similar in their style and content (as with many international newspaper chains, they also share some overseas and domestic correspondents). So, the *SMH*'s coverage of Malaysia would not be expected to vary significantly from that of the Melbourne *Age*, although individual journalists might express perspectives that differ from one newspaper to the other. The ABC's 7.45am bulletin is Australia's most popular individual radio bulletin and has a high reputation for credibility and accuracy.

Both news outlets were monitored for the duration of one calendar year—1 January, 1993 to 31 December 1993—and all stories that prominently described a news event from or concerning Malaysia, Indonesia and the Philippines were transcribed onto a computer file. This amounted to a total of 350 stories reported by the *SMH* and 70 stories broadcast by the ABC. These stories were then classified into different categories and a concordance was constructed from the composite text of all the stories combined. The newspaper stories were measured according to the amount of space they occupied on the news pages. According to common newspaper production practice, this measurement was expressed in column centimetres, which measure the length of a story in regular four centimetre-wide columns (broadsheet news pages are normally seven columns across, although sub-editors sometimes vary this by using so-called 'bastard measure').

Table 1: Coverage of Philippines, Indonesia and Malaysia in 1993	
Philippines—*Sydney Morning Herald*	52
Philippines—Australian Broadcasting Corporation	13
Malaysia—*Sydney Morning Herald*	98
Malaysia—Australian Broadcasting Corporation	24
Indonesia—*Sydney Morning Herald*	200
Indonesia—Australian Broadcasting Corporation	33
Total—*SMH*	350
Total—ABC	70

Table 2: Highest rating stories from Philippines, Malaysia and Indonesia in 1993	
Sydney Morning Herald	
East Timor (Indonesia)	59
'Recalcitrant' affair (Malaysia)	29
Military (Indonesia)	22
Human Rights (Indonesia)	18
Australian bilateral relations (Indonesia)	18
Gillespie kidnapping (Malaysia)	16
Politics (Indonesia)	14
APEC summit (Malaysia)	11
Economics (Indonesia)	7
Marcos (Philippines)	7
Mount Mayon eruption (Philippines)	6
Australian Broadcasting Corporation	
'recalcitrant' affair (Malaysia)	11
East Timor (Indonesia)	10
Gillespie kidnapping (Malaysia)	7
Cebu AIDS clinic (Philippines)	5

This database was then compared with reportage by the same outlets of other foreign news over the same period of time. This comparison was considered a necessary validity check to determine if there was any significant difference in the coverage of the three subject countries compared to other countries. In other words: were consistent concepts of newsworthiness applied equally to all foreign news or did different news category and salience thresholds apply to different countries and different regions? If this test showed that a strong emphasis on 'bad news' was applied across the board by Australian foreign news editors, it would influence any conclusions drawn from evidence that Southeast Asian countries were consistently portrayed in terms of negative events and themes.

The data were also compared with news of the three countries 25 years ago, but only in the *SMH*. There are no records in existence—either in sound archives or transcripts—of ABC news bulletins from this period. The purpose of this comparison was to identify any changes in the prioritising of regional news by the *SMH* foreign editors over that 25 year period. Twenty-five years ago Australians did not consider themselves part of Asia, and there was no official campaign underway to challenge that concept of identity, so we might expect a change in the way the region is covered by Australian newspapers today to reflect the change in attitude as to Australia's place in the region. That does not necessarily mean a greater volume of news about the region. In 1968 there were strategic and national security reasons for Australians to be concerned about events in the region, particularly the escalation of the Vietnam War, Britain's decision to end its military presence in the 'Far East', and political instability in Indonesia. These issues all implied threats to Australia and as such were salient in the Australian news media at the time. But Australia's fear of Asia had greatly subsided by the 1990's, so we would expect a different focus and range of stories about the region in the contemporary Australian news media. With this shift in emphasis, one would expect that media coverage of the region would change to reflect this new engagement, which the government of the day defined in terms of mutual interests and friendship rather than fear and hostility.

This type of comparative analysis, however, has limitations. The main problem with comparing one year's output of news with another is that it is difficult to find a typical year to serve as a benchmark for the comparison. For the comparative analysis to produce conclusive evidence it ideally needs data that describe a normal or typical year in the Australian news media's relationship with the three subject countries. 1968, which was chosen only because it is a quarter of a century earlier than the 1993 study period, might not be regarded as a typical year. Malaysia was in the limelight because of a decision made halfway round the globe—London's announcement to pull its armed forces out of its Asian garrisons. Malaysia and the Philippines jointly shared a spotlight for much of the year as they squared off over their rival claims of ownership of the province of Sabah. And the political tensions in Indonesia, although down a few notches from their 1966 high point, made that country of more compelling interest to Australian foreign news editors than it was during the next few years. For that matter 1993 may not have been too typical, especially in relation to Malaysia's news profile in Australia, which was considerably inflated by two bilateral issues—the Gillespie case and the 'recalcitrant' affair. (On the other hand it may be impossible to find a 'typical' or average year in any historical context. News is essentially about change and thus tends to preclude the establishment of benchmarks of normality and typicality).

Another distorting factor in comparisons across a time span as great as 25 years is that newspaper design changes considerably in such a period. In 1968 the *SMH* used a much more cluttered layout for its foreign pages, with a tendency to run more stories, many of them reduced to just a few sentences each ('briefs', in modern news parlance). So while the number of individual stories may have been higher in 1968, a large proportion of those stories was dealt with superficially. There may have been a greater coverage of different countries in terms of frequency but a lesser coverage in terms of depth.

A more fundamental shortcoming of this study is its failure to include television news, arguably a more important source of public opinion and attitudes than the press and radio. This medium was not included because of the sheer complexity of doing so and because this would involve a heavily subjective analysis of the TV content that would compromise the press and radio analyses. TV content analysis is a field of research in its infancy, and a credible methodology for describing and annotating TV content is yet to be devised. The primary component of a TV 'text' is the broadcast frame, which is 1/25th of a second of real time viewing. Describing the textual content of just one frame—its image content, the prominence of some visual factors compared to others and the message implications of the juxtapositions of the different visual factors—is so complex and 'data dense' that it might take weeks to code just one TV news story. To run a comparative content analysis of a year's reporting on three countries by just one Australian TV network would require a huge input of research time and energy. TV content analysis studies to date (eg Glasgow Media Group 1982) have been anecdotal rather than scientific. While they offer some useful insights into the message content of TV news, they cannot provide a rigorous analysis of textual content in the same way that a text analysis of print or radio news can.

The Philippines

Of the 52 stories about the Philippines printed by the *SMH* in 1993, all but four could be grouped into 11 different categories (natural disasters, accidents, insurgency and terrorism, crime, the Marcoses, domestic politics, external relations, defence, economic issues, vice and sexual crimes, and overseas contract workers). Of the four ungrouped stories, two were about a calamitous blunder by the Pepsi corporation during a promotion that produced too many winners in a cash-prize competition, one was about a bogus AIDS cure, and the fourth was about Filipina mail order brides. The category that proved most newsworthy was natural disasters. This included the eruption of Mount Mayon and the impact of seasonal typhoons. Insurgency and terrorism was the second highest category, with reports on attacks by both the communist New Peoples Army and Muslim separatist guerrillas. The next highest category was the Marcoses. The Marcos stories occupied the most space of any category, accounting for a total of 378 column centimetres, compared to 193 centimetres for the natural disaster stories. There were six stories about the return of ex-president Marcos for burial in the Philippines and one story about his wife Imelda and her legal battle against corruption charges. The next highest scoring category was vice and sexual crimes, which included stories about prostitution, the Philippine activities of foreign paedophiles and sexual war crimes by the Japanese.

This narrative on Philippines by the *SMH* showed a low priority for issues relating to domestic politics and regional relations and a high priority for disasters of various kinds: natural disasters, economic disasters (the Marcos's kleptomania), political disasters (insurgency activity), social disasters (accidents and violent crime) and even corporate disasters (the Pepsi debacle). Taken together these stories represent an overwhelming majority of the individual events reported to its readers by the *SMH*. This portrayal of the Philippines shows a country characterised by dangerous natural and acquired conditions.

Table 3: Major story categories, Philippines 1993	
Sydney Morning Herald	
Natural disasters	10
Insurgency and terrorism	9
Marcoses	7
Vice and sexual crimes	6
Accidents	4
Crime	4
Domestic politics	2
Economic matters	2
Overseas Contract Workers	2
Australian Broadcasting Corporation	
Bogus AIDS clinic	5
Mount Mayon	3
Typhoons	1
Boating accident	1
Paedophiles	1
Marcos' burial	1
Amerasian kids	1

The ABC's 7.45am news bulletin only found the Philippines newsworthy on 24 occasions during 1993. The biggest story for the year concerned an Australian TV personality who became embroiled in a row over a clinic in Cebu offering an 'alternative' AIDS cure to foreigners. This story ran in five installments from 26 March to 24 April. The only other sustained subject was the Mount Mayon volcano, which generated three stories. Other stories were about typhoons, a boating tragedy, the burial of Ferdinand Marcos, Australian paedophiles and the abandoned children of US navy personnel at Subic.

Significantly absent were stories about domestic politics and relations with Australia and other countries. The one story that linked Australia with the Philippines—the bogus AIDS clinic—was essentially a story about vulnerable Australians being ruthlessly exploited by evil Filipinos.

Malaysia

The *SMH*'s coverage of Malaysia during 1993 was dominated by two major stories that achieved sustained front page status: the wrangling over the Gillespie children, taken from Australia by their Malaysian father, Prince Kamarul Bahrin Shah, and the diplomatic tiff sparked by the Prime Minister, Paul Keating, calling his Malaysian counterpart 'recalcitrant'. The Gillespie affair generated 16 separate stories in the *SMH* during that year, while the 'recalcitrant' affair accounted for 29 separate stories. Apart from those two issues there were five stories about the Malaysian royals (all these stories reported criticisms of their royal privileges), four stories about the tragic collapse of a Kuala Lumpur apartment block, two stories about the execution of a convicted Australian drug trafficker, six stories about military purchases by Malaysia's armed forces, six stories about domestic Malaysian politics, two stories about human rights in Malaysia, two stories about protests against rainforest logging in Malaysia and a number of other unrelated stories that all received single mentions only.

The Gillespie and 'recalcitrant' stories set the tone for the year's coverage of Malaysia, the former carrying hostile overtones—expressing outrage over the two 'Australian' children being kidnapped by their Muslim/Malaysian father and over Malaysia's implied complicity in allowing the crime to go unpunished—and the latter being initially critical of Paul Keating for his intemperate language at an international forum and later critical of the Malaysian Prime Minister for being over-sensitive and over-reacting to a mild and perhaps deserved rebuke. Many of these stories included exhaustive analyses of the situation. The longest occupied 246 centimetres of column space. Together they totalled 1,796 centimetres.

The two stories achieved a status that elevated them from the foreign pages to the news and feature pages because they involved Australian personalities and were therefore as much about domestic issues as they were about Malaysia. Beyond the loud events they described was a range of less prominent Malaysian domestic issues and events, from the introduction of harsh Islamic laws to Malaysia's relations with its neighbours and Prime Minister's Mahatir's occasional diatribes against the West. But the salient issues embraced by the *SMH*'s coverage were 'problems' in the relationship between Australian and Malaysia, and thus portrayed a nation that was not co-operating with Australia in a friendly and positive way.

The ABC's 7.45am metropolitan radio bulletin ran a total of 25 stories about Malaysia during 1993. Echoing the *SMH* coverage, the 'recalcitrant' and Gillespie affairs dominated this file, with 13 separate stories on the 'recalcitrant' imbroglio and eight stories on the Gillespie–Prince Kamarul standoff. The only other stories the ABC reported from Malaysia were two mentions of opposition by the Malaysian Prime Minister, Mr Mahatir, to the Seattle APEC summit and a warning to Australians visiting Malaysia to avoid contaminated seafood.

Table 4: Major story categories, Malaysia, 1993	
Sydney Morning Herald	
'Recalcitrant' affair	29
Gillespie case	16
Malaysia and APEC	11
Domestic politics	6
Military purchases	6
Malaysia's royals	5
Accident	4
Australian Broadcasting Corporation	
'Recalcitrant' affair	13
Gillespie case	8
Mahatir versus APEC	2

Indonesia

Indonesia attracted the most extensive coverage of the three countries, with the *Sydney Morning Herald (SMH)* printing 200 separate stories on Indonesia during 1993, an average of almost one story every two editions. More than a quarter of these stories (54) concerned East Timor and human rights issues linked to Indonesia's occupation of that disputed territory. Many of these stories concerned the captivity and trial of an East Timorese resistance leader, Xanana Gusmao. A further 22 stories were about Indonesia's military forces—their deployment throughout the archipelago, their involvement in maintaining law and order, promotions and retirements of senior officers, and the purchase of new military equipment—while another 18 stories were about human rights in Indonesia, mainly centred on criticisms that the Indonesian government tolerated and perpetuated violations of international standards of human rights. Other subjects that were largely framed in terms critical of the Indonesian authorities were stories on environmental problems (five), stories about Indonesia's Chinese minority (four), stories about anti-government activity outside East Timor (three) and stories about Indonesia's nuclear power program (three). Accidents and natural disasters accounted for a total of 10 stories.

But the *SMH* coverage also showed sustained interest in domestic Indonesian politics. There were 14 stories about political events and processes, several of them speculative pieces about how long President Suharto would stay in power and who might replace him. There were also seven stories about economic issues and three stories about Indonesia's relations with other countries. A major news category for Indonesia was bilateral relations with Australia, which generated 18 stories during the year.

The ABC devoted more time to Indonesia in its main morning radio bulletins—33 stories—than Malaysia or the Philippines. Ten of these were about East Timor and the trial of Xanana Gusmao and another two concerned the activities of Indonesia's armed forces. Three stories were about human rights concerns; two were about environmental problems. Four stories were about the Gillespie affair, centring on allegations that Indonesian military officers helped Prince Kamarul get to Malaysia with his children through Irian Jaya. Five stories concerned Indonesian–Australian relations, including a meeting between Keating and Suharto in Jakarta, and two stories were about a boatload of Chinese asylum-seekers passing through Indonesia on their way to Australia.

Table 5: Major story categories, Indonesia, 1993	
Sydney Morning Herald	
East Timor	59
Military matters	22
Relations with Australia	18
Human rights	18
Domestic politics	14
Natural disasters and accidents	10
Economic issues	7
Environmental problems	5
Australian Broadcasting Corporation	
East Timor	10
Relations with Australia	5
Gillespie case	4
Human rights	4
Military matters	2
Environmental problems	2

Comparisons

Some of the significant differences between the coverage of Malaysia, Indonesia and the Philippines were:

- a greater emphasis on Malaysian and Indonesian domestic politics (14 and six stories respectively, compared to two stories about Philippine politics);
- a greater emphasis on relations between Australia and Indonesia;
- more stories about Malaysia's relations with other nations (14 stories compared to two items about the Philippines' external relations and three about Indonesia);
- and a broader coverage of Malaysian culture and social issues (seven stories, compared to four from Indonesia and none from the Philippines).

There was also a marked disparity in the volume of the coverage of the three countries, with Indonesia generating twice as many stories as Malaysia and four times as many as the Philippines and an even higher rate of coverage in terms of the page space occupied by those stories. This outcome, however, may have been distorted to a certain extent by the high priority the Australian news media gave to their coverage of the diplomatic row with Malaysia over Prime Minister Keating's 'recalcitrant' remark (Ramanathan and Loo, 1993).

The ABC's coverage of the three countries also showed a higher priority for Indonesia. This result, however, may have been distorted to an even greater extent by the 'recalcitrant' affair, which accounted for 14 of the 25 stories about Malaysia. This means that without this exceptional and loud event, the coverage of Malaysia and the Philippines by the radio bulletin might be similar in volume and frequency. The *SMH*'s coverage of Indonesia reflected a much lower threshold of newsworthiness, influenced by Indonesia's closer proximity to Australia, its larger size in population and its greater importance as a trading partner. This coverage contrasts with that of Malaysia and the Philippines by its much greater range and depth; its greater emphasis on domestic politics and economic issues and its greater interest in issues affecting relations with Australia.

Historical comparison

In 1968 the *SMH* coverage of Indonesia chiefly reflected that country's problems of nation building. The greatest number of stories (54) concerned the army's efforts to control separatist insurgencies in several islands and provinces. The resistance movement against Indonesian control in Irian Jaya was another focus of this theme. A related group of stories dealt with the aftermath of the failed 1965 coup and the continued purging of suspected rebels and communist sympathisers from army ranks. The second largest group of stories (35) concerned Indonesia's relations with other countries. These included Indonesia's role in diplomatic efforts to resolve the dispute over Sabah between Malaysia and the Philippines, Jakarta's role in regional alliances and relations between Indonesia and its former colonial rulers, the Dutch. The next largest category (32 stories) referred to relations between Indonesia and Australia. Several of these stories described direct diplomatic contacts, including a visit to Australia by Indonesia's Foreign Minister, Adam Malik, and a trip to Jakarta by the Australian Prime Minister, John Gorton. They also described Australian aid pledges to Indonesia and 'chance' encounters between the two countries, such as an Australian yachtsman storm-wrecked on an Indonesia coast. Domestic politics was the subject of 27 stories. Most of them described President Suharto's efforts to consolidate his grip on power and his relationships with the national congress and opposition groups. Civil unrest was the general theme of the next highest (13) category of stories. This included violent anti-government protest in the capital and anti-Chinese riots and their aftermath. Natural disasters occurring in Indonesia during 1968 were only mentioned six times by the *SMH*, the same as the number of stories about accidents.

Table 6:	Coverage of Philippines, Malaysia and Indonesia by *Sydney Morning Herald*, 1968
Indonesia	193
Malaysia	149
Philippines	87
Total	429

Table 7:	Major story categories, Indonesia, *Sydney Morning Herald*, 1968
Insurgency, secessionism, military actions	54
External relations	35
Relations with Australia	32
Domestic politics	27
Civil unrest	13
Economy	8
Natural disasters	6
Accidents	6

The *SMH* Malaysia file for 1968 emphasised bilateral relations with Australia, particularly in regard to Australia's role in Malaysia's existing and future defence arrangements. Several of the 48 stories in this category described visits to Malaysia by Australian political leaders. Others described Australia's commitment to its military presence in Malaysia and its part in discussions about regional military alliances. The defence arrangement issue generated a further 29 stories that did not mention Australia. Many of them reflected Malaysia's anger over Britain's decision to end its military presence in the 'Far East', while others described multilateral attempts to form new regional defence alliances. Malaysia's confrontation with the Philippines over the ownership of Sabah dominated news from Southeast Asia for long periods of 1968, and this was reflected by the *SMH*'s inclusion of 38 stories on this subject in its news and foreign pages. The next most important category was insurgency, with 16 stories about the Malaysian government's struggle against communist guerillas. Some of these stories referred to joint actions of Thai and Malaysian troops on their common border. There were nine stories about external relations, only three describing natural disasters and just one concerned with domestic politics.

Table 8:	Major story categories, Malaysia, *Sydney Morning Herald*, 1968
Relations with Australia	48
Sabah dispute	38
Defence arrangements and Britain's withdrawal	29
Insurgency	16
External relations	9
Natural disasters	3
Domestic politics	1

The Sabah dispute was the dominant theme of the *SMH* reporting on the Philippines in 1968, providing 38 stories. Relations with Australia and natural disasters shared second place with 15 stories each on the list of top-ranking categories. However, several of the stories referring to Australia concerned one incident: a damaged Australian warship seeking emergency repairs at the Subic Bay naval base. Most of the natural disaster stories were about two incidents: a volcanic eruption by Mount Mayon and a severe earthquake near Manila. There were four stories about violent crimes, three stories about a fading communist insurgency and just two stories about domestic politics.

With the exception of Malaysia, where the Gillespie abduction and 'recalcitrant' incidents placed Australia in the centre stage of news about Malaysia in 1993, one major difference in the *SMH* coverage of the three subject countries back in 1968 was a greater focus on Australia's engagement with those countries. In 1993 the *SMH* ran 18 separate stories linking

Australia and Indonesia, just 9% of its total 200 stories on Indonesia. This compared to 32 stories out of 193 in 1968 (17%). The *SMH* made four mentions of Australia in the 52 stories it ran about the Philippines in 1993, compared to 15 stories with an Australian angle in the 87 stories it ran on the Philippines in 1968. For Malaysia the figures were 48 (all but three of them about the Gillespie case or the 'recalcitrant' affair) out of a total of 98 in 1993, and 48 out of 149 in 1968. Although there was a higher proportion of Australian-angled stories in 1993 (which must be considered an abnormal year in Australian–Malaysian bilateral relations), the total number of Australian-angled stories was the same in 1968. While there were some prominently newsworthy situations in the region in 1968—such as the impact of Britain's announced military withdrawal and Australia's concern over Indonesia's political instability—that may have raised interest in news stories with Australian angles from the three subject countries, it still seems somewhat surprising that there appear to be fewer stories today linking Australia with these regional neighbours, in the midst of a sustained campaign to persuade Australians to feel more closely connected to the region.

Table 9: Major story categories, the Philippines, *Sydney Morning Herald*, 1968	
Sabah dispute	38
Relations with Australia	15
Natural disasters	15
Crime	4
Insurgency	3
Domestic politics	2

Comparison with other countries

The *SMH* ran stories on a total of 142 different countries and territories in 1993. The United States dominated this foreign news coverage, accounting for 1,096 separate stories, more than twice as many as the next most prominent country, Great Britain, which generated 519 items. Ranked third was Russia with 377 stories, followed by Israel with 281, Indonesia with 200 and China with 172. In gauging the *SMH* foreign editors' approach to news from the three subject countries it is useful to compare the themes and issues they chose to embrace in their coverage of these countries with the subject matter of stories they chose for other countries represented in their pages. For this comparison three countries that roughly matched the three subject countries in terms of their news prominence during 1993 were chosen. China ranked one place below Indonesia on the list of countries by frequency; France ranked one place below Malaysia with 93 stories compared to Malaysia's 98; and South Korea, generating 48 stories, was just below the Philippines with 52 stories.

Table 10:	Foreign news in the *Sydney Morning Herald*, 1993—countries ranked by number of stories	
USA	1,096
Britain	519
Russia	377
Israel	281
China	172
South Africa	172
Bosnia	158
Japan	145
India	122
Cambodia	120
Somalia	115
Italy	108
Papua New Guinea	99
Iraq	98
Germany	98
France	93
New Zealand	92

   More than a third of the stories in the China file were about its diplomatic relations with other countries, the majority of those concerning negotiations with Britain over the future of Hong Kong. Almost a quarter of the stories about China dealt with human rights issues. Domestic politics in China generated 25 separate stories; accidents ranked fifth with 16 stories, just ahead of crime with 14 stories. With East Timor dominating the coverage of Indonesia in 1993, the issues embraced by other stories represented a very different news focus than was applied to China that year. External relations was almost a non-issue for Indonesia, except for 18 stories concerning bilateral relations with Australia. Human rights issues were prominent, but nowhere near as prominent as they were for China. Domestic politics in Indonesia were also considered much less important than they were for China. Economic issues also received less emphasis than in the coverage of China.

Table 11: News stories on China, *Sydney Morning Herald*, 1993	
External relations (mainly Hong Kong)	69
Human Rights	42
Politics	25
Economics	23
Accidents	16
Crime	14
Military	13
Human interest	9
Trade	7
Sport	6

The *SMH's* approach to France as a news story differed markedly from the newspaper's construction on Malaysia in 1993. There was a more even spread of subject matter in the 93 stories about France, with crime, domestic politics, trade and external relations generating similar numbers of stories. The next four categories of stories from the French file—military matters, accidents, natural disasters and economics—were also clustered in a narrow range of frequencies. In contrast, the coverage of Malaysia was dominated by two narrow issues: the 'recalcitrant' affair and the Gillespie case. The next highest category, Malaysia's engagement with the APEC forum, was also framed as a single 'one-off' issue. Domestic politics accounted for just over 6% of the total Malaysia file.

Table 12: News stories on France, *Sydney Morning Herald*, 1993	
Crime	15
Politics	12
Trade	12
External relations	10
Military	7
Accidents	6
Natural disasters	5
Economics	4

The coverage of the Philippines, with its focus on natural disasters, insurgency, vice and the shadow of Ferdinand Marcos, displayed different newsworthiness characteristics to the *SMH* coverage of South Korea for the same period. The most prominent theme for South Korea was military matters (chiefly about the on-going confrontation with North Korea). Crime came second in order of importance, followed by external relations, accidents and issues relating to nuclear energy and nuclear weapons. Domestic politics fared only marginally better than for the Philippines, with just three separate mentions.

Table 13: News stories on South Korea, *Sydney Morning Herald*, 1993	
Military	11
Crime	8
External relations	7
Accidents	6
Nuclear	6
Trade	4
Politics	3

There are several major differences in the way the three subject countries were portrayed by the *SMH*, compared to the way the same newspaper portrayed other countries with similar news salience levels. While it is difficult to draw conclusions from direct comparisons between different countries in the way they are constructed by the international news media (because of their widely varying domestic and geopolitical situations this is a bit like comparing apples with pears), a deeper analysis along the lines outlined above should demonstrate that certain countries become framed by foreign news editors' perceptions about what is regarded as conventional behaviour and consequently about how they should be described to readers in terms of which stories are selected for publication.

Conclusion

The three Southeast Asian countries studied in this investigation were presented to the Australian public in terms of a few narrow frames of reference that emphasised the problems of their conditions of nationhood and the problems of their relations with Australia. While the Western news media display a preference for bad news—derived to some extent from traditions born with the concept of Western news reporting during the war-plagued first half of the Seventeenth Century—they also have an informational and educational role, a role they manage to project in their more balanced constructions of First World societies. The United States, for example, has many natural disasters annually, some of them causing loss of life; it has violent crime of epidemic proportions, official corruption, vice scandals and problematic relations with other countries, yet the Australian news media do not report these problems to the near-exclusion of other issues. In addition they report on Hollywood and American culture, on elections and American politics, on sport and American society. In other words, they tend to present a more rounded portrait of the American nation that balances its low points against its achievements.

But their construction of Indonesia, Malaysia and the Philippines is weighted heavily on the downside of life in those countries. It describes these countries as appearing to falter in their quest for modernity, prosperity and security. The narrative on these three countries is a narrative about conflict, brutality, danger and disappointment. This negative news focus may be partly a result of habit. Insurgency, disasters, repressive politicians and sleaze have been loud themes in international news media coverage of Southeast Asia for decades. It seems difficult for media gate keepers to refocus on other issues. The innate conservatism of news production practice determines that they keep doing things the traditional way, until they are confronted with compelling reasons to look for new issues.

The Australian news media's negative and even hostile portrayal of our northern neighbours does not seem to be in step with Australia's much proclaimed efforts to enmesh with the Southeast Asian region by adopting friendlier attitudes towards the nations and societies of that region. This is not to suggest that the Australian news media should be responsible for supporting this policy. Any such assumption would run the risk of assigning the press a propaganda role. Perhaps, as some media researchers have speculated (Smith 1981), foreign news has the function of making its audiences feel better about the conditions of their own lives by reminding them that there are other societies beyond their borders with much worse conditions. Constructing our Asian neighbours as 'places worse than ours' may provide some comfort for Australian audiences when they consider their relative advantages over other nations, but it is likely to be counterproductive to Australia's long term quest for a place in Asia.

References

Almonte, J 1994, 'World Media: Help or Hindrance to International Relations', paper presented to the *Australian Associated Press Conference of Asian, Australian and Pacific Media Executives*, Sydney, 21 November.

Blood, D and Zhu, J 1996, 'Media Agenda-Setting Theory: Review of a 25-Year Research Tradition', *Perspectives Working Papers*, Department of English, City University of Hong Kong.

Boyd-Barrett, O 1977, 'Media Imperialism: Towards an International Framework for the Analysis of Media Systems' in Curran, J, Gurevitch, M and Woollacott, J (eds), *Mass Communication and Society*, Edward Arnold, London.

—— 1980, *The International News Agencies*, Constable/Sage, London.

Brooks, H 1995, '"Suit, tie and a touch of the juju"—the ideological construction of Africa: a critical discourse analysis of news on Africa in the British press', *Discourse and Society* Vol 6 No 4.

Chomsky, N and Herman, E 1988, *Manufacturing Consent: The Political Economy of the Mass Media*, Pantheon Books, New York.

Chua, S 1993, 'Reel Neighbourly: The Construction of Southeast Asian subjectivities', *Media Informational Australia*, No 70.

Dahlgren, P and Sparks, C (eds) 1992, *Journalism and Popular Culture*, Sage, London.

Dobell, G 1993, 'Laying to Rest the "Drongo-Journo" Myth', *24 Hours*, ABC Radio, April.

Evans, G 1994, 'Australia, the Asia Pacific and the Media', paper presented to the *Australian Associated Press Conference of Asian, Australian and Pacific Media Executives*, Sydney, 21 November.

—— 1992, 'Foreign Policy and the Media', *Proceedings of the University of Canberra Faculty of Communication Conference on Media Images of Asia/Australia: Cross Cultural Reflections*, University of Canberra.

Galtung J and Ruge, M 1973, 'Structuring and Selecting News' in Cohen, S and Young, J (eds), *The Manufacture of News*, Constable, London.

—— 1965, 'The Structure of Foreign News: The Presentation of the Congo, Cuba and Cyprus Crises in Four Norwegian Newspapers', *Journal of Peace Research* Vol 2, No 1.

Hamilton, A 1990, 'Fear and Desire: Aborigines, Asians and the National Imagery', *Australian Cultural History* No 9.

Hartley, J 1982, *Understanding News*, Methuen, London.

Hartmann, P and Husband, C 1973, 'The Mass Media and Racial Conflict' in Cohen, S and Young, J (eds), *The Manufacture of News*, Constable, London.

Ismail, B 1996, 'Asian News in Four US Newspapers' in Yeap, S, Mahizhan, A and Goonasekera, A (eds), *Opening Windows: Issues in Communication*, Asian Mass Communication Research and Information Centre, Singapore.

Lee Kuan Yew 1994, 'Do Australians Know Enough About Asia?', address to the *National Press Club*, Canberra, 20 April.

Lowe, B 1995, *Media Mythologies*, University of New South Wales Press, Sydney.

McCombs, N and Shaw, D 1972, 'The Agenda Setting Function of the Mass Media', *Public Opinion Quarterly* Vol 36 Summer.

Meaney, N 1994, 'The End of "White Australia" and Australia's Changing Perception of Asia, 1945–1990', paper presented at the University of London Robert Menzies Centre for Australian Studies conference on *Australia and the End of Overseas Empires 1945–1975*, 29 April, London.

Molotch, H and Lester, M 1974, 'News as Purposive Behaviour: On the Strategic Uses of Routine Events, Accidents and Scandals', *American Sociological Review* Vol 39, February.

Moores, S 1993, *Interpreting Audiences: The Ethnography of Media Consumption*, Sage, London.

Murphy, B 1983, *The World Wired Up*, Comedia Publishing Group, London.

Pillai, M 1993, 'Is Australia Ready to be Truly Asian', *Australian*, 5 May.

Ramanathan, S and Loo, E 1993, 'Australian and Malaysian Newspaper Coverage of the Gillespie Dispute', *Australian Journalism Review*, Vol 15 July.

Robinson, C 1986, 'The American Press and the Repairing of the Philippines', *Race and Class*, Vol. 28 No 2.

Said, E 1978, *Orientalism*, Penguin, Harmondsworth.

Smith, A 1981, *The Geopolitics of Information: How Western Culture Dominates the World*, Oxford University Press, New York.

Tiffen, R 1976, 'Australian Press Coverage of the Third World', *Australian and New Zealand Journal of Sociology*, Vol 12 No 1.

—— 1978, *The News From Southeast Asia*, Institute of Southeast Asian Studies, Singapore.

Tuchman, G 1978, *Making News: A Study in the Construction of Reality*, Free Press, New York.

Westerstahl, J and Johansson, F 1994, 'Foreign news: News Values and Ideologies', *European Journal of Communication* 9.

White, D 1950, 'The Gatekeeper: A Study in the Selection of News', *Journalism Quarterly* Vol 27.

Thai reporting of the rise
and fall of Pauline Hanson

Glen Lewis

The meteoric rise to public prominence of the independent Federal Australian MP Pauline Hanson in 1996, the controversy surrounding her One Nation Party in 1997 and her failure in the October 1998 federal election will likely be remembered as one of the more significant events in Australian politics in the 1990s. Hanson's highly controversial career has already spawned a minor literature, as well as sustained media coverage. This includes books aimed at the general market (Manne 1998), publications from her own camp, and numerous articles seeking to explain her significance (eg *Metro* 1997; Lewis 1997).

This article will examine one aspect of the Hanson episode not yet systematically considered—the reporting of Hansonism in Asia, specifically in Thailand in 1996–1998. This focus arises from the author's period of residence in Bangkok between June 1997 and June 1998. A comprehensive analysis of the broader Asian media's coverage of Hanson's rise and apparent fall will require further studies of the media in other Asian states. To begin with, however, Thai reporting in the Bangkok English-language press will be considered.

There are two reasons why this kind of micro-study is worthwhile. First, though Hanson was defeated in the October 1998 election, her One Nation Party reportedly still polled one million votes and, according to the *Bangkok Post*, this represented the votes of one in twelve Australians (*Bangkok Post* 12 October 1998). The issues raised by Hanson, mainly about Australian relations with Asia, Aboriginal reconciliation, and the adequacy of the traditional party system in coping with globalisation will be continuing concerns. Understanding the Asian readings of these issues is therefore important.

Second, a case can be made for more bilateral news studies between Australia and its Asian neighbours, of which Thailand is an important one. The major Australian on-going work in this area is being conducted by Peter Putnis, based on the quantitative analysis of international news flows (Putnis and Patterson). There is also the work of Boyd-Barrett (1992) and Hachten (1992). While these global studies are essential to understanding the composition of the international news map, they take time and resources to complete and have difficulty in dealing with current issues. Arguably, they need to be supplemented by analyses focussed on the present that address the comparative construction of news agendas in bilateral and regional relationships.

Previous significant research on international news reporting has tended to adapt the model of news agendas developed in the US by McCombs (1981). This model has been revised in the US itself according to the liberal (O'Heffernan 1993), critical (Herman and Chomsky 1988) or conservative predilections of particular researchers. However, in Australia, where journalism and media studies are developed on a much smaller scale, there has been little sustained investigation of international news. Notable exceptions here are Tiffen's early work on Southeast Asia (1978), his more recent studies of Vietnam war reporting (1990), Knight on Cambodia (1994), Kingsbury on Indonesia (1992; 1998), Loo and Ramanathan on Malaysia (1993) and Payne on Vietnam (1995).

This chapter aims to make a preliminary analysis of the wider question of Asian reporting about the Hanson episode by using Thai press coverage between 1996 and 1998 as a case study. The chapter will outline the Thai international news agenda in 1996 and consider reporting of Hanson's fortunes in 1996, 1997 and 1998, and last, some broader comments about the significance of Hansonism in Asia will be ventured.

Setting the Thai international news agenda

Thai newspapers are sharply divided between tabloids and broadsheets, with the quality broadsheets the main sources for international news. The quality Thai-language papers include the influential political dailies *Matichon* and *Siam Post*, and the financial papers *Phujadkarn*, *Thansettakit* and *Krungthep Thurakij*. There are also weekly political magazines, such as *Arthit* and the *Nation Weekly*. While the tabloid papers, such as *Thai Rath*, have much larger circulations (one million), they usually only devote one page to foreign news. The main English-language papers are the *Bangkok Post* (established 1945) and the *Nation* (established 1970). The *Post* is the only Thai newspaper to publish audited circulation figures, currently about 50, 000.

In broadcasting, the main official service concerned with international news is Radio Thailand, which relies on the under-funded Thai National News Agency. Although the Army-owned TV channel 5 is now launching a global network service aimed at the US, Europe and Australia, this is mainly an entertainment medium for overseas Thais (Krungthep Thurakij 24 September 1998). Historically, Thai foreign policy and international reporting are most concerned with the great powers—the US, Japan, China and Europe. Further, Thailand's continuing role as a 'front line state' in the heart of mainland Southeast Asia concentrates its attention primarily on its troubled neighbours—Indochina, Burma, and currently Malaysia (Lewis 1996).

One last rather paradoxical feature of Thai journalism vis-à-vis international reporting needs mention. Thailand traditionally has been seen by foreign correspondents covering Asia as one of the best locations. This is because there have been considerably less impositions on foreign reporting by the Thai government than in most other countries in the region. Thailand and the Philippines usually are seen by journalists as having the freest press cultures in Southeast Asia (Boonrak 1982). Recently, a journalists press freedom watchdog association has been formed between Thailand, the Philippines and Indonesia (*Nation* 9 November 98). Yet the same degree of freedom has not traditionally been part of Thai journalism. Until quite recently, stringent press laws were regularly used to control domestic reporting. The issue of domestic press freedom is not yet entirely resolved, despite the significant moves to liberalisation that have taken place since the Anand government of 1992 (McCargo 1993).

Thailand also remains quite sensitive to foreign reporting about its domestic politics and culture. No journalist, foreign or Thai, is permitted to write anything critical about the King or the Thai royal family. Anyone who does so risks incurring a charge of *lèse-majesté*, a serious matter in Thailand, which is still applied at times to those who criticise the Thai royals, either through foolhardiness or inadvertence. Second, the Thais are quite protective of their international good name. At times they have taken action against foreign publishers who have criticised Thailand—for example, when the Longman's dictionary linked prostitution with Bangkok in 1995, the Union Jack was burnt outside the British Embassy.

Lastly, when foreign news stories reflect unfavourably on Thai domestic politics, governments may retaliate against foreign journalists. During the 1996 Banharn administration, for instance, scandals took place over reports about the Thai purchase of Danish submarines in suspicious circumstances. The Banharn government, which had one of the worst records of recent Thai governments for corruption, took issue with several leading international news publications, such as *Time* magazine, for what they claimed was unfair and hostile reporting. One of the few detailed studies of Thai international journalism established that in this case foreign news reports were used by the domestic government to protect their own political position (McCargo 1996).

Given this context, what was the Thai international news agenda in 1996, especially concerning Australia? In 1996, a recurrent topic from February to May was the need for Thailand to build up its armed forces to protect itself from possible regional threats. The growth of the Malaysian armed forces was highlighted. Debates here centred on the purchase of new submarines for the Thai Navy and a possible military satellite, the latter strongly supported by then Defence Minister Chavalit. Border disputes with Burma, mainly concerning in-fighting between sections of the Karen military, also were reported (*Bangkok Post* 27 August 1996; 2 September 1996). A related Burmese issue was the controversial construction of the Yadana natural gas pipeline from Burma to Southern Thailand, which involved French and US oil companies.

The dominant newsframe, however, from mid-1996 onwards, was not international, but growing domestic concerns about the poor performance of the Banharn government, the growing budget deficit, and scandals concerning the Bangkok Bank of Commerce. In September 1996 the beleaguered Banharn resigned and was replaced by General Chavalit as Prime Minister. Foreign news was not of great concern at the time. The US strike against Iraq in September (*Bangkok Post* 4 September 1996), the North Korean famine (*Bangkok Post* 27 August 1996) and the South Korean impeachment of former President Chun Doo-hwan (*Bangkok Post* 28 August 1996) were reported, but not extensively. Some sense of the imminent financial crisis was emerging. For example, a 3 September report 'Curse of Mexico threatens economy' by the *Post*'s Paisal Sricharatchanya, but this was not followed up.

One domestic concern that distracted the Thai media from the coming financial crisis was their protracted struggle with the Banharn administration, which peaked in September 1996. Banharn had been accused of plagiarising his Master's thesis by his critics, including journalists at the *Siam Post*. Government reprisals against the paper led to the dismissal of five news editors and the subsequent resignation of 50 more editorial staff (*Bangkok Post* 3 September 1996). This issue had begun in January, when the Prime Minister's office had sued three *Post* journalists for libel. Banharn also pressured the management of Army TV Channel 5 to replace its news chief for unfavourable coverage (*Bangkok Post* 14 September 1996). This was one of the last straws that toppled Banharn, as he announced his intention to resign a week later (*Bangkok Post* 24 September 1996).

Thai reporting of Pauline Hanson in 1996

These domestic political concerns and a growing unease about the economy precluded press attention to international news. If anything, it was surprising that Thai journalists did pay the attention to Pauline Hanson's maiden speech in October that they did. Shortly afterwards, the editors of both the *Bangkok Post* and the *Nation* made a point of criticising Hanson, both in editorials and in television interviews for Australian audiences. The *Post*'s editor took an unusually interventionist position, warning that the 'White Australia' history was in danger of being resurrected. This could block Australian attempts to 'become part of Asia', as the previous Prime Minister, Paul Keating, had argued for.

As the coverage of the Hanson issue would become quite extensive over the next two years, this analysis will concentrate on the sources used, with only a limited appraisal of the stories themselves. An important point here is that, with the exception of several editorials and an occasional special report by Thai journalists, most material came from either special correspondents of the two papers in Australia, from Australians in Thailand, or through letters-to-the-editor. There was little or no use of press agency sources. To this extent, coverage of Hanson was almost like a heated discussion among Australians themselves, except this was framed by the selection, and doubtless omission, of viewpoints by the papers' editorial staff.

The usual pattern of coverage at this time was for there to be one or two special reports on the issue, which usually would be followed in a few days by several readers' letters, then perhaps an editorial. For instance, on 30 October, Canberra correspondent of the *Post*, Russ Properjohn, outlined the recent events around Hanson. His story also considered the role of the Australian media in the issue, mentioning that the *Sydney Morning Herald* had reported on its front page the criticism of one prominent Thai Australian-alumni, Mechai Viravaidya, who had called on Prime Minister Howard to resign for not opposing Hanson's views. Properjohn cited Asian immigration, funding for Aborigines and welfare payments for single mothers as Hanson's agenda, then concentrated on the immigration debate as the most central issue (*Bangkok Post* 30 October 1996).

The *Post* highlighted the issue on 1 October by printing ten readers' letters. None of these supported Hanson's views and several longer ones (about 600 words) expressed disgust with what they took to be the racist nature of Australian society. The President of the Australian–Thai Chamber of Commerce, Greg Thomas, cautiously dissociated the Chamber from Hanson's views, while not advocating 'the curtailment of individuals' rights to 'freedom of speech'. Letters by Seng Yeoh, and especially Loki Ragnarokssen (Sydney), however, went into some detail about several discreditable racist events in Australian history. Ragnarokssen, who would become a regular letter-writer on this matter, referred to 'pogroms' against the Chinese in Queensland in the 19th century and the Italians in Kalgoorlie, Western Australia in 1931.

This initial round of exchanges was typically capped off by the *Post*s editor, Pichai Chuensuksawadi, in two short commentaries on 1 November ('Howard's position must be clarified') and 4 November. Pichai, who by this time had been interviewed by Australian television speaking against Hanson, struck a generally warning note—'Asian eyes will be watching' (4 November 1996). His theme was that as Prime Minister, John Howard was obliged to take a leadership position and refute Hanson. Australian desires to engage with Asia, he argued, were not legitimate if that engagement was limited to trade and Hanson's views were not rejected. He welcomed the bi-partisan parliamentary resolution on equal rights, but warned that a divisive race row would damage Australia's regional credibility in the eyes of its neighbours.

This theme was repeated in several more stories in late 1996. Thai and Australian travel executives in Bangkok were canvassed for their opinion of Hanson's views, reassuring potential Australia-bound Thai travellers they would not meet with racial discrimination (*Bangkok Post* 5 November 1996). Later, another dire warning was sounded by an Inter Press correspondent for the *Nation* in Canberra, Kunda Dixit—'Ethnic fissures could affect Eurasian future'. This canvassed the usual set of issues associated with Hanson's rise to influence. It also cited two Asian-Australians, Ramesh Thakur of the Peace Research Centre at ANU and Dai Le, a Vietnamese Sydney television researcher, both criticising Hanson (*Nation* 24 November 1996). This strategy of using Asian-Australians as sources of public opinion would be repeated in later reports. It would also emerge that the *Nation* would be more critical and more vocally nationalist in its coverage of the Hanson issue than the *Post*.

Finally in 1996, on 1 December, the *Post* carried a feature article on 'The Great Australian Race Debate', by Deborah Parker—one of the few women reporters to write about the issue and a sub-editor on the *Post*'s *Student Weekly*, a paper aimed at teaching English to Thais. Her piece was a mostly lifestyle treatment that cited the experience of ordinary Australians with Asian partners with racism, the success of several non-Anglo Australians, such as Jenny Kee, Kate Ceberano and Pat O'Shea [sic], and the pro-Asian views of several leading Melbourne educationalists, such as Alan Gilbert, Vice-Chancellor of Melbourne University.

Thai press coverage of Pauline Hanson in 1997

After this initial creation of a news agenda about Hanson in late 1996, similar treatment of news about her in 1997 continued. In fact, there were only two periods in 1997 when the issue again received as much attention—in May, after the launch of her biography and when Prime Minister Howard finally spoke out decisively against her views, and again in August, when Australian aid was given to Thailand to cope with the effects of the Thai financial crisis. Thai attention to foreign news after its currency collapse in July was understandably minimal. Unless international events concerned the IMF and the US and Japan's economic assistance to Thailand, they received scant attention.

The publication in late April of *Pauline Hanson: The Truth*, her endorsed biography, produced new derision and criticism in the Thai press. The *Nation* noted the book's appearance, highlighting its claims that Aboriginies had cannibalised their own family members, and its prediction that in the year 2050 Australia would have a lesbian president with Chinese-Indian-cyborg parents. The *Nation* dismissed the book by making its own warning—that 'unless a mature debate on the race issue is allowed to take place, the country won't become a part of Asia' (*Nation* 25 April 1997). The paper repeated this theme in a subsequent editorial (4 May 1997), as did the *Bangkok Post* (7 May 1997), which welcomed John Howard's explicit anti-Hanson comments made on Australian radio. When Howard repeated his denunciation of Hanson a week later, at the launch of the Australia–Asia Centre in Sydney, the *Nation* headlined its story 'Better late than never, but Howard has more to do' (13 May 1997).

In the absence of new developments in the Hanson saga, the story lapsed from the Bangkok papers until August, when Australia decided to grant a US$1 billion line-of-credit as aid to Thailand. The *Nation*'s report here noted Hanson's parliamentary criticism at the time of the decision, but went on to focus on broader regional issues (14 August 1997). Two follow-up articles analysing Hanson's Australian appeal were then published—a piece by Keith Suter, a Sydney writer (*Bangkok Post* 27 August 1997) and an American view by Tom Plate, a *Los Angeles Times* columnist, in the *Nation* (31 August 1997). Both articles placed the Hanson phenomenon in an international context, identifying the pressures of globalisation and the subsequent rise of culturally nationalist anti-immigration movements in California, New Zealand, France and Russia as counterparts to Hansonism.

For the remainder of the year the issue dropped from the Thai press, except for one lifestyle report by the *Nation*'s Kulachada Chaipipat in Australia (*Nation* 19 November 1997). This article, like other lifestyle stories about how Thais/Asians in Australia were managing well enough, eg Wee Soo Cheang's 'Hanson? No hassle, say Thais' (*Nation* 20 July 1997), cited the views of prominent anti-Hansonites, both Government (Fischer and Downer) and Opposition (Sandra Nori and Peter Cook). Like the earlier Deborah Parker 1996 story, Kulachada's cited pro-Asian educationalists in Melbourne and Sydney, especially Stephen Fitzgerald, whose book 'Is Australia an Asian Country?' had been published in May. Hanson's influence was now interpreted as waning.

If this was true, and Australian public opinion polls appeared to suggest so (Blood and Lee 1997), one reason was probably the growing impact of the Australian government's tacit public relations campaign, through both positive initiatives to the embattled region and intentionally ignoring her existence. It is useful to recall one of the basic findings of earlier studies of the media–foreign policy nexus here: the established government of the day in any country has an enormous media advantage in putting its own views on foreign policy (O'Heffernan 1993). They have a near-monopoly on the provision of official information sources. Hanson, as a lone Independent MP, could express opposition to Howard's policies, such as the loan to Thailand, but did not have the resources to even formulate foreign policy alternatives. Her gross factual misstatements, for instance about the population of Malaysia at the time of her maiden speech in September 1996, indicated the depth of her ignorance in this area.

So as well as the more serious coverage Hanson received in the Thai press, there was level of reporting of other Australian foreign news in which the Hanson factor was never mentioned or just used as comic relief. These stories included Howard's position on Aboriginal land rights (*Nation* 29 November 1997: 'Australia must respect Aboriginal rights'), dealings with the PRC over human rights (*Nation* 18 April 1997: 'The dismantling of Australia's image'), and with the South Pacific's regional leaders (*Nation* 26 September 1997: 'Australia bullies Pacific Islanders'). For instance, the *Nation*'s Puangthong Rungsawsdisab's feature on the first meeting of the Thai–Australia Economic Commission (26 February 1997), reiterated the paper's theme about how Australian engagement with Asia needed to be more than just economic, but did not mention Hanson. Similarly, the Australian ambassador to Thailand, Gavin Hogue, argued that 'A fair go for all [was] the basis of society' in Australia. His letter briefly mentioned Hanson, but concentrated on presenting the positive aspects of Australian immigration and social policies (*Bangkok Post* 18 June 1997).

Thai coverage of the fall of Pauline Hanson in 1998

Two elections in 1998 saw the Thai concerns about Pauline Hanson's influence in Australia rise to a peak then fall. The first was the Queensland state election in June, when her One Nation party shocked Australian and overseas opinion by winning some 12 seats and a quarter of the votes, according to the *Nation* (18 June 1998). Growing alarm at this outcome led to unprecedented Thai criticisms of Australian society and politics, especially in the *Nation*. These dire warnings mounted until the Federal election in October 1998, when Hanson lost her own seat and One Nation managed to win only one federal seat in Queensland.

In the earlier part of 1998, apart from reports about Prime Minister Howard's visit to Thailand to honour Australian war dead from the Second World War at Hellfire pass at Kanchanaburi (*Bangkok Post* 19 April 1998), there was little Thai coverage of Australian news. In May, leading up to the Queensland election, however, coverage started up again, with a lifestyle piece by the *Nation*'s Steve Rhodes titled 'Living with the enemy' (*Nation* 3 May 1998). This profiled the experience of a Thai immigrant who had been living in Hanson's electorate for 20 years and was now convening an Indochinese community group alarmed at Hanson's rise to power. The sense of alarm in this article was fuelled by another anti-Australian letter by that tireless Sydney correspondent Loki Ragnarokssen, who warned 'Don't look south for examples of moral leadership' (*Nation* 12 May 1998). A subsequent *Nation* editorial, 'Hanson fans racism, Howard adds fuel' (5 June 1998) maintained the rage, claiming that 'Hansonmania has now become a permanent feature in the political landscape of Australia'.

Naturally, several Australians wrote in to dispute the tone of the *Nation*'s press coverage, including the new Australian ambassador, William Fisher (*Nation* 8 June 1998). The *Nation*'s editors, however, persisted in seeing the matter in a jaundiced light. In another June editorial 'Australia must slay its racist demons', they wrote: 'while there is no doubt that a majority of Australians are not racist, there has to be a recognition that a sizeable proportion are, and this number is fast growing' (*Nation* 18 June 1998). The *Nation*'s journalism here was rather long on criticism and opinion while being short on providing any sustained analyses of the complexities of the Hanson case. When these were written, they often were by expatriate Australians who were not journalists. For instance, one story by John Knox (*Nation* 2 August 1998), a Rangsit (Bangkok) University lecturer, provided a fair overview of the historical background, in contrast to the grouchy tirades by Ragnarokssen (eg, *Nation* 5 July 1998), but little new information about current events in Australia.

Ragnarokssen's pride-of-place as the Thai English-language press' leading Australian critic in the letters section, however, was replaced on 7 August by a militant pro-Hanson letter writer to the *Bangkok Post who* signed himself 'A Hanson Man'. In contrast to the majority of letters, this one argued aggressively for an end to Asian immigration to Australia. This led to media coverage in Australian, many more outraged rebuttals of the pro-Hanson views by other correspondents (eg, *Bangkok Post* 10 August; 13 August 1998) and even the claim that the letter had been the work of a 'spin doctor' aiming to divert attention from the release of One Nation's small business policy (*Bangkok Post* 14 August 1998: 'A Hanson man is really a fake'). So many letters arrived about this that on 14 August the *Post*'s letters editor declared further correspondence on the subject was closed.

The *denouement* of the coverage of Hanson in the Bangkok press came in September and October with the Australian federal election. The *Nation* again sounded an editorial dire warning if Hanson was successful (*Nation* 8 September 1998), and fell back on their Darwin-based correspondent Sonny Inbaraj for a review of the issues (*Nation* 14 September 1998). A more informative analysis was provided by Natalie Bennett, the Australian chief international sub-editor of the *Post*. Warning that 'One Nation's roots run deep', Bennett explained Hanson's political appeal in generational and class terms. She argued that older, rural, less-educated voters were the core Hanson supporters, and that the new globalised, multicultural policies adopted first by Hawke and Keating's Labor Party, then by Howard, had marginalised significant numbers of voters from the electoral process. Whatever the electoral outcome, the same core of disillusioned voters would be waiting for a new champion (*Bangkok Post* 21 September 1998).

The *Nation*'s political writers had the final Thai pre-election word. Peter Weekes canvassed Thai-Australian opinion (*Nation* 27 September 1998), interviewing among others, Surasak DouangRuana, the editor of *Thai-Oz*, a Sydney community Thai paper. He also noted the activities of the Unity Party, a pro-Asian party formed specifically to contest the election against Hanson. *The Nation*'s foreign editor, Kavi Chongkittavorn, profiled some of the Thai candidates in the Unity Party, pointing out that some 30, 000 Thais now resident in Australia mostly lived in Sydney (*Nation* 2 October 1998).

In the event, Hanson's loss of her own seat and the general electoral failure of One Nation came as something of an anti-climax for the Bangkok papers. The *Nation*, which had established a regular 'One Nation' news page on its internet site, commented editorially that 'Hanson's fall clears way for improved ties'. It pointed out that One Nation still had support of around 8%, and that remained a cause for concern. It also remarked that both major parties had not raised foreign affairs as an issue and had played down the Asian economic crisis as an electoral factor. Finally, it welcomed the election of Aden Ridgeway as the first Aboriginal Australian senator (*Nation* 5 October 1998). The editor of the *Bangkok Post*, Pichi Chuensuksawadi, recalled that he had criticised Prime Minister Howard originally for not condemning Hanson's views and repeated his claim that Howard had done too little, too late (*Bangkok Post* 12 October 1998). Nevertheless, the larger issue now was that Asia and Australia could 'move forward as partners in the region'.

Conclusions: the significance of Hansonism in Asia

This survey of Thai English-language press coverage of the Hanson episode in Australia suggests several conclusions. First, most of the coverage was by Australian special correspondents or provided by extensive letters-to-the editors. Neither the *Bangkok Post* nor the *Nation* has full-time correspondents in Australia, and to this extent their coverage often provided more of a heated discussion between Australians than any informed Thai perspective. The coverage also was invariably anti-Hanson. The divisions of opinion were rather about the nature of past and present Australia and its historical treatment of immigrants.

Second, it was likely only because of the human interest elements of the stories generated by Pauline Hanson's unusual impact on Australian political life that it received as much coverage in Thailand as it did, considering the magnitude of the economic problems faced by the Thais after July 1997. With the subsequent collapse of markets in Hong Kong, Korea and Indonesia and the Japanese economic malaise, both the *Bangkok Post* and the *Nation* were understandably preoccupied with the economic crisis. Thai relations with the IMF, the election of the new Chuan government in November 1997, and the implementation of the October 1997 constitution were the main concerns. Regionally, other larger problems were also pressing: the Indonesian forest fires and smoke haze in 1997, the election in Cambodia, on-going border problems with Burma and the Karen, and the bitter conflict between Mahathir and Anwar in Malaysia in 1998.

Third, although coverage of Hansonism in these papers was only sporadic and uneven, not always well-informed, and in the *Nation*'s case at times alarmist and censorious, there was also much positive coverage about recent changes in Australian society and its longer-term commitments to multiculturalism and engaging with Asia. It is highly likely that the Thai press took a more positive view of the affair than the media in Malaysia (Loo 1998). Newspapers there remained much more under direct government control and open to influence by Mahathir and his supporters, who are rarely friendly to Australia.

A more detailed analysis of this would require examination of the Thai-language press between 1996 and 1998 and other regional media. My impression is that the issue received far less coverage in the Thai-language media than in the English-language papers, and also less favourable coverage. Elsewhere, Hanson's influence was widely reported in Hong Kong, Korea, Japan and most of Southeast Asia. Many of these reports were more likely based on rumour and innuendo than fact, just as much of the Australian media coverage had been. To counteract this negative publicity, in October 1997 the government set up an 'Images of Australia' program in its Foreign Affairs Department, especially to aid its international education programs (*Far Eastern Economic Review* 3 September 1998: Interview with Minister for Foreign Affairs Alexander Downer).

Further, the collapse of many of the East Asian economies and the major social divisions opened up by that event, especially in Indonesia, may yet have major damaging political and security consequences. Presently, Australians seem to have reverted to their 'lucky country' status of the 1960s, as the economy so far has withstood the regional economic storm. The election rhetoric of the Howard government that refers to 'insulating the economy' from Asia, however, trigger some disturbing memories of the language previously used to justify a 'White Australia'. After the election, the Melbourne *Age* (6 October 1998) ran the front page headline: 'Asia hails Hanson failure'. This misses the point that Australian problems with its own society are rarely of sustained concern to many of its regional neighbours. Perhaps it is ethnocentric to think that they should be, or that Australia can avoid global economic problems in the long run.

References

Bangkok Post, www.bangkokpost.net

Blood, Warwick R and Lee, Paul S N 1997, 'Public Opinion at Risk' *Australian Journalism Review*, December.

Boonrak Boonyaketmala 1982, 'Thailand' in Lent, J (ed), *Newspapers in Asia,* Heinemann, Singapore.

Boyd-Barrett, Oliver and Thussu, D K 1992, *Contra-flow in Global News*, John Libbey, London.

Hachten, William 1992, *The World News Prism*, Iowa State University Press, Ames.

Herman, E S and Chomsky, N 1988, *Manufacturing Consent*, Pantheon Books, New York.

Kingsbury, Damien 1992, 'Agendas in Indonesian Responses to Australian Journalism', *Australian Journalism Review* 14 (2).

—— 1998, *The Politics of Indonesia* , Oxford University Press, Melbourne.

Knight, Alan 1994, 'Australian Press Coverage of the Cambodian Elections' *Australian Journalism Review* 16 (1).

Lewis, Glen 1996, 'Communications Internationalisation and Regionalisation in Thailand', *Journal of International Communication* 3 (2).

—— 1997, 'The Media and the Pauline Hanson Debate' *Australian Journal of Communication*, 24.

Loo, Eric 1998, 'Malaysian Media Perception of Australia', paper delivered at the symposium *A Tremendously Dangerous Time*, Australian National University, Canberra, 29 September.

Loo, Eric and Ramanathan, S 1993, 'Australian & Malaysian Press Coverage of the Raja Bahrin–Gillespie Custody Dispute', *Media Information Australia* 70.

Manne, Robert 1998, *Two Nations*, Bookman Press, Melbourne.

McCargo, Duncan 1993, 'The Buds of May', *Index on Censorship* 4.

—— 1996, 'The International Media and the Domestic Political Coverage of the Thai Press', paper at the 6th Thai Studies Conference, Chiang Mai.

McCombs, Maxwell 1981, 'The Agenda Setting Approach' in Nimmo, D and Sanders, K (eds), *Handbook of Political Communication*, Sage, Beverley Hills.

Metro 1997, Special issue on Hanson, No 109. Articles by Phillip Bell, Andrew Jakubowicz and Peter Putnis.

Nation , www.nationmultimedia.com

O'Heffernan, P 1993, 'Mass Media and US Foreign Policy' in Denton, R (ed), *Media and Public Policy*, Praeger, Westport.

Putnis, P and Patterson, C (eds) *Sources of International News: Setting the International Agenda*, Hampton Press, New Jersey (forthcoming).

Payne, Patricia 1995, *The Australian press and the Vietnam War: an analysis of policy and controversy 1962–1969*, PhD thesis, University of Sydney.

Tiffen, Rodney 1978, *The News from Southeast Asia*, Institute of South-East Asian Studies, Singapore.

—— 1991, 'The War the Media Lost' in Pemberton, G (ed), *Vietnam Remembered*, Weldon, Sydney.

Reflections on coverage of Australia's involvement in the Vietnam War

Patricia Payne

Introduction

Over recent years Australia has actively pursued, in its own perceived national interests, a deeper and more productive relationship with its near neighbours. This was evidenced in the opening statements of Australia's Minister for Foreign Affairs, Alexander Downer, in his address to the Asia–Australia Institute on 6 November 1996:

> Australia's future lies in Asia. This Government is committed to that future. That is why we have made closer engagement with Asia our highest foreign policy priority...Australia is with Asia for the long-term. (Downer 1996)

Australia's participation in the Vietnam War, which prefaced this period of intense and belated interest in Southeast Asia, illustrated at least white Australia's obsession with the need for protection from ideologies and races that seemed alien to its European and Western heritage. As Britain planned to withdraw its military presence from Singapore in the 1960s, Australia gradually replaced the dominance of British and American approval of Australian foreign policy with a more solely American approval. The change evident in foreign priorities since the 1960s, including the recognition of China, was set against a background of political change in Australia. In December 1972, a Labor Party government was elected after 23 years of a Liberal/Country Party government. Seventeen years of that political domination had been under the leadership of one prime minister, Robert Menzies. It is important not to underestimate the significance of the rapidity of change in Australian society and outlook since the 1950s in any assessment of media coverage and the challenges faced by journalists translating these domestic changes into their foreign relationship reporting context. Significant as technological change is to communication, it is encompassed by the levels of rigidity and change within the domestic societal context.

Present discussions that concentrate on how effectively the media have responded to understanding and reporting Southeast Asia highlight the constraints and complaints of foreign governments on the quality of Western reporting. Of particular importance is the use of the foreign media by some regional leaders to accentuate their national and often personal interests. An examination of the metropolitan newspapers' coverage of Australia's involvement in the Vietnam War emphasises the dominance of the domestic rather than foreign context in shaping the quality and flow of public communication on foreign issues. While Australia was involved militarily in Vietnam for ten years, there is little evidence that in the major decisions to become involved in the War, in the escalation of that involvement and in the decision to withdraw, that the aspirations of the Vietnamese, both in North and South Vietnam, ever occupied much space in Australian dailies. This was despite the fact that the Vietnam War was the longest running and most intensely reported issue in Australian newspapers during the 1960s.

The dominance of the political context of involvement

In April 1994, Labor leader Paul Keating, became the first Australian Prime Minister to visit Vietnam since Liberal Prime Minister John Gorton in 1968. Preceding his arrival in Vietnam, Keating commemorated the suffering of Australian troops during the Second World War at Hellfire Pass in Thailand. When asked by an Australian journalist if Vietnam veterans were expecting something 'special or significant' from a gesture in Vietnam, in memory of Australian troops who fought in that war, Keating replied, 'I don't think they are and frankly why should they be?'(*Australian* 1994:1). The reported response of Ernie Dabble, whose only son was conscripted and killed in Vietnam, was bitter:

> There were 40,000 Australians who fought in that war so why hasn't he got the guts to lay a wreath for those whose lives were wasted in a political nightmare?...The whole damn thing was political and it's still politics when it boils down to it. (*Courier Mail* 1994:2)

Australia's participation in the Vietnam War still evokes strong emotional response. This response is often characterised by selective attribution of blame to one or more of the key players who were perceived to have determined Australia's involvement: politicians, bureaucracy, military, public and press. The political essence of war is not always readily identified as a separate and distinguishable characteristic. It is more often camouflaged by public acceptance of a necessity forced upon a government that must act in defence of its country or the values that its citizenry deems worthy of national sacrifice. Australia became militarily involved in Vietnam in 1962 during a period of increasing fear of the extension of communism in Asia and distrust of Chinese and Indonesian intentions. The need to retain an American presence in Southeast Asia and maintain that country's goodwill were the cornerstones of Australian defence and foreign policy. As America increased its military commitment in South Vietnam during the 1960s Australia, aiming to cement an alliance between America and itself, also escalated involvement.

Australian media's coverage of Vietnam exhibited the complexity of the interwoven domestic and foreign environments that characterise the reporting of war. The Vietnamese perspective, so rarely sought or appreciated, relied heavily on the value newspapers placed on reports from specialist journalists in Asia. Such reports vied for space not only with agency reports and syndicated American commentary, but also with news reports and specialist commentary from Canberra. No Australian paper retained a correspondent in Vietnam for the duration of Australia's participation in the War. While extending resourcing of specialised coverage from various areas would have enriched Australia's understanding, not only of Vietnam but also of its own involvement, this must be weighed against the unchanging political base from which all consideration flowed, the need for the American alliance.

The 1960s were characterised by rapid social and political change in Australia. This change was politically reflected in the decay of the dominance of the Liberal Coalition parties and the tentative willingness of the press to accept Gough Whitlam, if not necessarily the Labor party by the late 1960s, as capable of being trusted with the American alliance.[1] Neither party had wavered from support for the American alliance, but the Labor party stance against conscription was falsely interpreted in press coverage as a moral affront to American sensibilities. Labor's credibility increased as it appeared more in tune with American policy direction in Vietnam and towards China in the late 1960s than the government, and as it became increasingly difficult for the government to characterise the Labor Party as communist.

Bruce Grant, who had reported from Asia in the early 1960s and was one of Australia's most adept commentators on Vietnam in the late 1960s as a columnist for the *Age,* asserted that the Cold War had resulted in an Australian press 'notably respectful' to the Australian government and those whom the Australian government favoured. Once Australia accepted the necessity for participation in military alliances Australia's independence was lost:

> This affected not only an independent foreign policy, but also an independent press. For the Government could reasonably say: 'Look, we can't talk about this in public...but you know as well as we do the seriousness of the worldwide threat to freedom. A responsible press doesn't try to embarrass a government, which is caught up in what is virtually a war.' I don't mean that governments actually said this to newspapers, although occasionally the phrasing was explicit enough. It was implicit, however, in both the atmosphere and the situation that governments could expect newspapers not to be embarrassing on the major issues. (Grant 1969:4)

---

[1] The period is bound by the election in 1961 where Labor almost won and the election in 1969 where the basis for Labor success in 1972 was laid. During the intervening years the Liberal Country party retained strong support, evidenced in the 1966 election.

According to Grant, the split in the Labor Party in 1955 had helped government parties establish the argument in the electorate that the Labor Party was 'sympathetic to the very enemy Australia was committed to keep at bay'. The debate on 'loyalty' and 'disloyalty' in respect of foreign policy had become the:

> anguished theme of a society dependent on protection and concerned to rationalise the whims of the protector into values of universal appeal. We have lifted 'consultation' to the level of diplomacy...It is because we have become so heavily dependent on the decisions of others, because we get so very little information ourselves compared with what could be given, that, in my view, we have tended to be excessively respectful to secrecy and preoccupied with the demands of loyalty. (Grant 1969:4–5)

Other factors also influenced the free flow of quality communication in this supposedly 'uncensored war'. In 1969 Warner claimed that even historians with access to all the official diplomatic, political and military secrets that Canberra had 'guarded so jealously, and often so foolishly' would find it hard to evaluate the worth of Australia's Vietnam contribution (Warner 1969:6).

Alan Wrigley's conclusions in a report to the Minister of Defence in 1990, entitled, 'The Defence Force and the Community, A partnership in Australia's defence', accentuated the awareness of the military experience in Vietnam and the determination to obliterate the negatives learnt there. He warned against the pawn-like use of Australia's military by politicians for political rather than military purposes. The report's conclusion links the importance of public and political attitudes to defence:

> If a government is to set out to involve the Australian community more in defence, two important issues need to be addressed at the start. The first concerns the state of mind of governments...The second concerns the state of mind of the community, because if people are to be involved they will want to feel that what is being done about defence makes sense and that what they are being asked to become involved with really matters.
>
> Taking what governments think first, it is important to understand that when governments make their military power more dependent on the support of the community—for dependency comes with involvement—they risk limiting their ability to use that power for political purposes. Political purpose here means the pursuit of most of the things beyond the defence of sovereignty that governments are inclined to call 'national interests'. While there can be little doubt about the community's support for the defence of sovereignty, the same cannot always be said about national interests. (Wrigley 1990:478)

Wrigley's determination to differentiate between the defence of 'national' and 'sovereign' interests encapsulates the essence of Australia's Vietnam experience and the resultant confusion that permeated interpretations about the role of government, military, press and public in that experience. Thirty years on, the *Australian* noted that the lessons learnt from Australia's involvement in the Vietnam War included: 'the need to clearly define military objectives which are achievable; the need to ensure that the objectives are consistent with the national interest and capable of being explained to and supported by the Australian people'(*Australian* 1995).[2] Analysis of press coverage during Australia's involvement suggests that political priorities overwhelmed any premise for military effectiveness. The press in Australia, particularly in Canberra, by accentuating the vital political basis of Australia's involvement, unwittingly undermined the importance of the military aspect of commitment, not in any way denigrating Australian military personnel or their achievements in Vietnam but through a failure to examine, rather than merely report, Australia's military role.

The political 'tokenism' of Australia's military commitment had been noted in Australian reports and comment from 1962. In 1969, with the announcement of Australia's intention to withdraw, the political determinant of the basis of intervention became clear. Throughout the war, the Australian military perspectives of involvement had been minimised in reportage. There were endless reports on Australian military activities in Vietnam and many features on their civic action programs. These varied in quality and substance. The relationship between soldiers and long term correspondents had often been one of mutual benefit. There were few press attempts to establish the relationship between Australian military operations and those of the wider war. This was largely the result of limitations placed on individual journalists by editors that wanted feature reports about Australian soldiers, relying on cable services, a much cheaper option, to supply daily news. Nevertheless, this press limitation reflected the political reality, effectively asserted by Frank Frost in his study of the role of the Australian task force in Phuoc Tuy province. The 'political decision to commit forces to Vietnam in the interests of Australia's perceived security and foreign policy interests did not translate readily into a coherent or effective military role on the ground in Phuoc Tuy' (Frost 1989:182).

The eventual withdrawal of Americans in April 1975 produced television coverage that shocked the world. America's humiliation and hasty retreat were depicted in the scenes of helicopters being dumped into the sea and desperate but luckless Vietnamese allies left stranded on top of the American

---

[2] The description of Australia's military effort in Vietnam continues to be described as token. Greg Sheridan, foreign editor for the *Australian,* wrote in 1995, 'The Australian contribution was more symbolic than military. Indeed the real criticism of Australian policy makers over Vietnam is that, having declared Vietnam vital to Australia's national interests, their actual effort in Vietnam was tokenistic' (Sheridan 1995:11).

Embassy when the final Allied helicopter was gone. Television also carried the pictures of Australian journalist Neil Davis, whose camera was the only one rolling to capture the North Vietnamese tank No 843 as it smashed through the gates of the Presidential Palace in Saigon on 30 April 1975 (Bowden 1987:335–346). Commenting on the decision of Davis to film this symbolic end to the Vietnam conflict, Creighton Burns, political and foreign commentator for the *Age*, who had also reported from Southeast Asia and Vietnam in the 1960s, made the following observation:

> There is, I suggest a certain symbolism in the fact that foreign pressmen stayed on in conquered Saigon after foreign soldiers and foreign diplomats had left. It makes the simple but important point that for the international press it is the reporting of the winners and losers, not the backing of them that matters. It is also a demonstration of that capacity of survival which governments and politicians and generals do not possess. (Burns 1975:13)

Few could deny the capacity of the press for survival. Less accepted, specifically by the military and government, would be Burns' claims, not only of press bipartisanship, but also that the press were 'more often right' about the war. While acknowledging that there had been some 'wildly sensational' and 'blandly irresponsible reporting out of Vietnam', Burns claimed that 'history's calm reflection' would prove:

> that the serious press got the Vietnam war more right more often than the politicians and the generals and the diplomats did. The politicians were, I believe, the worst and most dangerous offenders...Anyone who reported Vietnam in the 1960s can testify to the anguish of American diplomats and political advisers-and Australians, too—who could not get their political masters to listen to what they did not want to hear. Inevitably, the powerful men in Washington—and Canberra—got told...what they wanted to hear. The self-deception was monumental and finally fatal. (Burns 1975:13)

William Hammond, in his analysis of American military and the media between 1962 and 1968, commissioned by the American Army, supports Burns' assertion. 'It is undeniable, however, that press reports were still often more accurate than the public statements of the administration in portraying the situation in Vietnam' (Hammond, 1988:388).

Australian journalist Gerald Stone, in one of the first published Australian interpretations of the war, also attacked the communicative role of politicians. Stone criticised the tendency during 1965 for important defence decisions to be carried in British and American papers before being officially announced in Australia. He also noted the refusal of Paul Hasluck, External Affairs Minister, after a tour of Vietnam and Southeast Asia, to answer questions from reporters who had met him at the airport. 'It is this kind of contempt for public opinion, particularly for critical opinion, that may ultimately present a graver threat to Australian democracy than anything that occurs in South Vietnam,' determined Stone (Stone 1966:152–3).

While aiming to expose the deception of Australian politicians and bureaucracy in Australia's decision to become involved, Michael Sexton emphasised the responsibility of the press in assessing the lack of informed public debate before the decision to send a battalion in 1965. Sexton attacked the quality of the initial Australian media coverage of the war, and accused Australian editors of producing editorials that ignored the facts.

> When the commitment of Australian troops was announced, it took place in an atmosphere where rational debate was almost impossible. And no group had done more overall to make debate impossible than the Australian media. (Sexton 1981:135)

Rodney Tiffen's research on Australian news coverage of Vietnam is similarly critical of its role. He is succinct in linking rather than isolating the roles of press and politician in the communication process.

> Throughout, the Australian media were more a dependent than an independent variable in the process. They were primarily creatures of the Australian political environment and shared the failures of Australian officialdom for the same reasons. (Tiffen 1990:125).

Tiffen's conclusions are central to any understanding of the influence of the parameters set by the political context of Australia's involvement.

> Australia took its cue from American positions, and conformity with America was the primary political test of a policy. The role of the junior ally permitted the luxury of embracing alliance policies without the need to evaluate their costs and prospects. (Tiffen 1990:125)

Further Tiffen states that, 'in Australia it would be ludicrous even to raise the issue' of an oppositional media (Tiffen 1990:137). Despite the validity of this later analysis, the Australian media, like their American counterparts, were accused of undermining Allied objectives in South Vietnam during the war. Burns' assessment of the communicative role from military and politicians was reciprocated in their criticism of the role of the press.

This was plainly evidenced in Prime Minister Gorton's response to the death of three Australian reporters in Vietnam. On 5 May, 1968, Michael Birch, a 24 year old Australian journalist working for *AAP*, was gunned down as he called pleadingly, 'Bao Chi' to a Viet Cong commander. Birch died with three other journalists investigating a communist offensive in Cholon.[3] The National Liberation Front (NLF) took the unprecedented step of calling a

---

[3] Bruce Piggott and John Cantwell were also killed, along with English journalist Ron Laramy. Australian journalist Frank Palmos, also in the jeep when it was attacked, escaped. For his account of the incident, and his journey back to confront his foe after the war, see Palmos 1990.

press conference in Moscow to deny any responsibility for the killing of these Australian journalists. The NLF's concern to limit the damage of public outcry in Australia was unwarranted. The incident did not receive prolonged coverage. When Gorton was asked in *Question Time* if he would investigate the claim by NLF members, he said he would not because 'the reports that have been received here and throughout the world were certainly not from any source aligned against the front, but from a press coverage in Vietnam which if anything, does not support as it might, the efforts of Australians and others in that area' (*CPD* 1968:1433). Gorton's public ridicule of the 'loyalty' and partisanship of Australian journalists repeated the criticism many American journalists were also receiving from the political managers of military involvement in South Vietnam.[4] The political attacks on the 'unpatriotic' role of the press were unwarranted, as later research in America and Australia has asserted.

The attacks on the quality of press coverage are less readily dismissed, but need to be tempered by understanding that press coverage was largely reflective during the years of Australian involvement. In the vital first decision to become involved, in May 1962, editorialists raised searching questions about government duplicity, but these represented the only public challenge to political explanations on involvement. As a result, Australia committed advisers without parliamentary or public input. This silence represented not only the general acceptance of policy direction that strengthened the American alliance but also mass ignorance about North and South Vietnam and the needs and aspirations of the Vietnamese people.

---

[4] War correspondent Pat Burgess was present when the five journalists left for Cholon. He was upset by parliamentary response to the deaths of his colleagues claiming that during discussion of the incident one interjector exclaimed, 'What do they expect? If they play with fire they are going to get their fingers burned.' When Burgess returned from Vietnam he writes that he tried 'but could not find out who the backbencher was' (Burgess 1986:171). Clem Lloyd concludes his history and analysis of the Press Gallery by noting that Birch, who had briefly reported from Canberra before Vietnam, had expressed 'distaste, almost a revulsion, for the parliamentary milieu in a terse fragment of poetry:
In the present year of grace
as we face annihilation
Young reporter comes to Canberra
Came into the House and listened
Lost respect there while he listened
to the men of Parliament. (Lloyd 1988:268)
Years after the war, Gorton claimed that 'if you were ever going to fight another war...one of the first things you would need to do would be to keep the press entirely out of it, not let any journalist go along.' He did not believe however that the press reports from Vietnam should have always been positive. 'It was such a muck up, such a horribly bungled sort of war, particularly after 1969, that you couldn't go on saying what a good war it was, because it wasn't.' (John Gorton, interview with the author).

Affirmation of the value of foreign correspondents and the need for the media to prioritise a wider international perspective in the interests of the quality of Australian democracy are well evidenced in consideration of Australia's military entry in the Vietnam War.

Factors affecting quality communication during a foreign crisis

In periods of acute foreign crisis, the prime minister has considerable power to set the parameters of public debate. Issues of national importance are centralised in the political environment of Canberra. As a result the Canberra Press Gallery becomes central to the reporting of foreign issues raised in Parliament. A number of factors can accentuate the dominance of the Parliamentary environment over foreign policy debate and its reporting. Governments have always displayed a reticence to communicate developments in foreign policy, arguing that secrecy in diplomacy is often required in the national interest. If the public and the media, through ignorance or indifference, are unable to extend the political parameters of explanation and debate on policy, then the communication process will lack democratic vitality. If, through commentary and coverage from a few informed specialist journalists, the press becomes a lone voice of alternative considerations to the publicly reported government explanations of policy, it too can be hamstrung by the lack of the necessary public and/or political impetus to maintain a newsworthy stance. This is particularly evident if the government removes the issue from its public agenda with the aid of a parliamentary adjournment. If the media coalesce with the government position and choose to ignore or limit public input, the public may lack the stimulus necessary to command media and political attention for the issue to become newsworthy. In time of war, the arguments involving national honour and morality permeate policy debate and can still alternative considerations. All these determinants of the quality of democratic communication were evident in press coverage of Australia's policy development during the Vietnam War.

Fundamental characteristics of Australia's reporting of the Vietnam War remain valid for present considerations of how communication, despite the massive flow of available information, remains selective within any environment. More than anything else that selectivity will be determined by domestic, not foreign, interests, even though those domestic interests may be influenced by a foreign power. The dominance by domestic agendas also accentuates the dominance by domestic, essentially political reporters, over the input on issues involving reports and commentary from foreign correspondents. Vital perspectives of foreign correspondents and some editorials in May 1962, were quietly smothered amid the reported hype of a physical American presence in Canberra.

Commitment to a war, May 1962

The first release of public information indicating the likelihood of Australian military involvement in Vietnam came from two reports published on the same day: from foreign correspondent Denis Warner in the Melbourne *Herald* (Warner 1962:7*)* and the Canberra political reporter for the *Age,* John Bennetts (Bennetts 1962:2*)*. It is significant that both a domestic and foreign reporter shared the release of information that political sources had so selectively leaked. When the Australian government first indicated publicly, in May 1962, its intention to become militarily involved in Vietnam, the reports from foreign correspondents represented one of the few sources of specialised comment on Vietnam. However, Australian foreign reporters, although few in number, had their insights devalued by the reporting of political agendas, both Australian and American. This is not to deny that Australia's most widely published Asian foreign reporter, Denis Warner, was not in accord with Australia's involvement to secure the protection of America and also committed to the 'domino theory', the toppling of countries in Asia under an advancing flow of monolithic communism. Both these arguments were central to newspaper approval of the government's policy direction. However, Warner, like other correspondents that understood the region, raised pertinent considerations about Australia's involvement in an Asian war. They fell on deaf ears because to have heeded them would have been to deny the Australian government its opportunity to secure a hoped-for American presence in the region. Australia's orientation was to the United States, and journalists in Australia supported that priority.

Calling whose tune?

American media theorists David Paletz and Robert Entman assert that: 'foreign news reporting helps the powerful mobilise public opinion (or quiescence) behind the basic goals of policies on which most Americans have little information and less control'(Entman and Paletz 1981:233). As the introduction to this paper indicated, there are conflicting views within Australia about the role the press played, or should have played, during the period of Australia's involvement in the Vietnam War.

Political decisions and comment are invariably carried on the prominent news pages of Australian dailies.This is particularly evident when parliament is sitting. The quality of information conveyed to the reader will depend not only on the level of specialisation of the journalist, but also on the quality of the reporter's source. Also important is the reader's level of understanding of, and interest in, the information being reported. The complexity of reporting during the time of crisis is increased by perceived levels of 'loyalty', which can help to accentuate Government support in reportage. This was exemplified in the willingness of editors to raise pertinent arguments for consideration in 1962 before the decision to send advisers was finalised, with the more hesitant approach of editorials to criticise once the government decided to escalate commitment in 1965.

As Australia's defence and foreign policy became increasingly less certain, press commentary became more confident and uninhibited by 'loyalty'. Grant's assertive attitude about the press and the perception of its role in reporting foreign policy by 1969 is exemplified in the following comment:

> I have been saying that there has been a breakdown in the former assumptions, the conventional wisdom, which used to govern discussion of foreign affairs in Australia. The role of the press in these circumstances is not to feed on the discomfiture of officialdom but to take part in the forging of new policies. It's not sufficient for the Australian press to complain after policy has been decided. It must be informed and alert about developments in foreign policy before they reach the point of decision. (Grant 1969:19)

The importance of his concern was illustrated in the significant first decision to commit Australian advisers in 1962. Despite the warnings from Southeast Asian correspondents Denis Warner, Richard Hughes and John Williams, who demonstrated so amply that only specialist understanding of Asia will allow for the posing of the right questions, it was the politicians' perspective offered and reported to an uninformed and uninterested Australian community that dominated. At this vital time of policy initiation, Asian correspondents and editorialists raised pertinent questions, but these were lost in the dominance of political agenda setting. The influence exerted by the American government at this time is worthy of note.

Setting the press agenda

The American government was definite in its setting of the Australian press agenda in 1962. In the euphoria of Coral Sea celebrations, a reminder to Australia of its debt to America in the Second World War, Dean Rusk (American Secretary of State, present for an ANZUS conference) stood with the Commander of the Seventh Fleet, Admiral Harry Felt; the announcement of an Australian military commitment to South Vietnam was auspicious. The trouble to which Rusk went to highlight his chosen public agenda displayed the importance he placed on the press in the political acceptance of the message. 'It was the first taste of the American machine in action,' claimed press gallery journalist for the *Courier Mail* Wallace Brown. Rusk flew into Canberra in Airforce II and, having invited journalists to view the aeroplane, exhibited his coloured telephones, one giving direct access to the President. A few days before his arrival messages were sent from the American Embassy to organise a briefing with Rusk of Australian editors at a press conference at the American Embassy. Brown recalls this unprecedented event:

> He summoned editors to the American Embassy...I got a message from the American Ambassador, 'Rusk will be here...he wants to brief all Australian editors on the war. Can your editor be here, or sort of *will* your editor be here?' This came to everyone...Editors came from all over Australia, at very short notice...to hear Rusk, Secretary of State...to get a briefing from them on the war. And they were impressed of course, the US Secretary of State was summoning them to the US Embassy. That was a big event. (Wallace Brown, interview with author, 1994)

The briefing was evidently as memorable as the invitation. Brown described it as 'impressive' and 'professional':

> Journalists were confronted with Rusk's public relations staff, screens, blackboards and Rusk in rapid fire manner reeling off statistics, and American policy, and everybody blinded by science by this man that had this amazing grasp on world affairs. This was the softening up, undoubtedly. He was the President's emissary and was treated as such. Whether an American President could do it now I don't know. He was a real 'pro'. It had a big influence. (Wallace Brown, interview with author, 1994)

This influence is difficult to gauge, as some editorial response represented the strongest of public warnings for restraint of government initiative in Vietnam in May 1962. Brown's commentary suggests he too balanced the American public relations 'machine' in assessing public disclosures during and arising from the ANZUS conference. Removed from the front page agenda by Rusk's concentration on Vietnam was the government's approval to allow the establishment of an American military base at West Cape and the approval of the continuation of American nuclear testing in the Pacific.

The release of information from political players, and the comments of Rusk, whose high public profile assured publication of his views, indicated careful orchestration of public information. Rusk remained central to continuing press coverage of Australia's possible intervention in Vietnam. In his address at the State Dinner held in Canberra on 9 May 1962, Rusk pleaded for a 'helping hand' in South Vietnam (*CNIA* 1962:12–19). Rusk's plea received very prominent coverage in Australian dailies on 10 May. While he claimed that Australia was helping in 'significant and growing ways', there was still more for all to do (*CNIA* 1962:19). The war that Communists called the 'war of national liberation' was 'a gangster war of horror and assassination. The stakes are greater than South Vietnam itself. The dependence of all peoples of South East Asia is involved' (*CNIA* 1962:19).

The *Daily Telegraph* (1962:1) chose to headline its story with the words, 'Gangster war in S-E Asia.' However sensational the heading appeared, it accurately represented the words of America's Secretary of State. It was an emotive and simplistic interpretation of the war by a high ranking American official who knew that his words would be carried through the press the following morning.

Emphasis in most newspaper summaries of Rusk's speech was on the request for a 'helping hand'. The language in Rusk's speech appeared calculated. The headlines to the reports on 10 May illustrate the point. The *SMH* heading read, 'More For All of Us to Do'. 'Rusk calls for Aid in Vietnam' read the heading page one in the *Canberra Times*. The *Advertiser* headed its story, 'Call By Mr Rusk: 'Helping Hand' Needed for South Vietnam.'

Press interest in reporting Rusk's request for a 'helping hand' owed much to Barwick's announcement, made three hours after Rusk's address, of the decision to send Australian military experts to South Vietnam if requested. An examination of the press coverage on 10 May of Barwick's announcement suggested a hurried and poorly thought through decision, or in hindsight, a calculated attempt to misinform the Australian public about the extent of the proposed commitment. One clear government objective of public disclosure of its intention was related to Rusk's presence in Australia. Had the government not intended the gesture for America then Barwick's claim that it was a SEATO initiative, owing nothing to American pressure, would have been more readily sustained if not made at the final press conference of the ANZUS meeting. As the *Age* reminded its readers:

> the timing of events could leave an impression that a new Australian commitment in Vietnam is being considered as a gesture of support to Washington. A more solid basis for such an extension of our foreign policy is required and it is the Government's duty to the public to provide it. (Bennetts 1962:2)

The *Age* wrote critically of government performance and intention in its proposal of military involvement in Vietnam. It warned that the public presentation of government policy needed a credible interpretative base.

The information that emerged during press coverage of the decision illustrated Australia's self interest as a motivation for commitment. The American context of all deliberation, both press and official, was evident. The political determinant rather than military of Australia's commitment was recognised but the implications not yet fully realised. The official response from the Vietnamese Ambassador that South Vietnam did not need combat troops initiated no response; nor did journalists press for proof of a Vietnamese request required under SEATO provisions. Oversimplified comment on the nature of the conflict was being partly balanced by the copy of Southeast Asian correspondents. The views of an individual journalist rate low against the need to publish widely and prominently the views of political individuals with the democratic power to direct policy. The lack of any public reaction, save one small report, significantly entitled 'Protest', the publication of one article by an Australian academic in the *Daily Telegraph*, and three published letters, indicated that the Australian public had not responded to Australia's decision to become militarily involved in Vietnam.

The reportage of Australia's first commitment illustrated that South Vietnam was the new element involved in Australian foreign policy. It had received little press coverage due to a perceived or real lack of public and or press interest. This was accentuated by the lack of interest in Australia for the Asian context of the decision and therefore the ability of foreign correspondents to attract or maintain newsworthy attention through commentary and reportage. This created a perfect situation for political dominance in setting the agenda for the flow of public information. The need for press vigilance in the publication of political announcements in a context devoid of supportive or alternative comment is vital when viewed from the examination of Australia's decision to become militarily involved in Vietnam in May 1962.

The official decision concerning Australian involvement was announced in a press release on 24 May by the Minister for Defence, Athol Townley. It indicated that the handful of advisers, 'three or four', was now 25. The information was released three days after Parliament had risen, when Barwick and Prime Minister Menzies had already left the country for overseas commitments. Perhaps because of the departure of two key spokesmen and the parliamentary adjournment, little coverage of the decision was given in Australian dailies, though it had dominated the interest of political reporters during the ANZUS conference, where the suggestion of help had been publicly realised. Once committed, the *moral* argument, which fluctuated in public explanation from the need for Australia not to falter in its alliance commitment to SEATO to the need to support America in her lone stance against creeping communism in Asia and that asked American youth to die for the protection of Australian interests, became paramount in all consideration by the press of Australia's commitment. More than any other argument it was this that sustained press compliance with government policy for the crucial years of escalation. By the late 1960s, when the Labor Party appeared more clearly than the Coalition to echo the American moves towards withdrawal, the moral argument that intrinsically linked Australian involvement to American involvement in the war could support Australian withdrawal. By 1969 the *Age* had joined the *Australian* in that demand.

Gallery journalist Alan Reid asserted years after the war that despite many political journalists' being opposed to involvement in the war, they supported the government in their reports and commentary. It was 'a moral judgement, rather than a military or political one—a broad one...the moral issue had already been thrashed out and decided in favour of the morality of the war and its expediency. It was a loose feeling, it wasn't totally thought through (Alan Reid, interview with author, 1984). It was a moral dilemma, which, for the decisive years of escalation, pushed the press into a limiting, and with hindsight, untenable position.

Warner had always asserted that the major reason for Australia's participation in the Vietnam War was that America was in Vietnam. He had always maintained that the war was unwinnable. His comments by December 1969 explicitly defined the totality of Australia's consideration in sending military assistance to Vietnam:

> Canberra paid great heed to its responsibilities as an ally of the United States: it is not easy to believe that it regarded the war itself as a serious threat to the security of Australia. (*Courier Mail* 1969)

The point was reiterated in a slightly different way by Grant. 'The survival of the Thieu Government is not, however, a vital Australian interest' (*Age* 1969b:6).

When Gorton announced Australia's decision to withdraw, the cartoonists depicted a pathetic picture of Australian foreign policy. Atchison's cartoon in the *Advertiser* portrayed Gorton as a little mimicker, trumpeting his message from the base of the bigger American trombone (*Advertiser* 1969). Bruce Petty's cartoon depicted Gorton shuffling out of Nixon's office in his pyjamas, carrying a big note on which was written 'You can go'. The President was calling after him, 'Sorry to have wakened you!' (*Australian* 1969:2).

Grant concluded that realistic appraisal of the situation required withdrawal of Allied forces from South Vietnam, where Australia's intervention had already 'destroyed the assumptions of our policies in South-East Asia'(Grant 1969b:5). Warner was insistent on making the basis of Australia's intervention clear in December 1969, despite the fact that he had always claimed that it was the American alliance. Warner claimed that Australian policy from the fall of Dien Bien Phu in 1954 had been the maintenance of an American presence in Southeast Asia. Also spurred to comment on American Senator Fulbright's 'barbed' attack on Australian participation in the war, Warner acknowledged that 'the Australian tactic of maximum applause with minimum participation was bound eventually to excite unfavourable comment, if not be self defeating'(Warner 1969:6). Echoing past fears that Warner now saw as realised, he adopted a pessimistic view of the future for Australia in Southeast Asia:

Today the consequences of American failure will be immeasurably greater. Better not to have tried at all than to have tried and lost, for Vietnam is now of major importance and the consequences of defeat, in South-East Asia and elsewhere will be horrendous. (Warner 1969:6)

The warnings carried in reports in 1962 that questioned the danger of being identified with a 'white man's war' were by 1969 being acutely felt, as the withdrawal of Britain and America from Asia left Australia exposed to an environment that it had proclaimed as threatening. The fear of China as an immediate threat had virtually dissipated in coverage in Australian newspapers by December 1969. Reports indicated that America was moving to a less hostile stance against China, partly because American businessmen were tired of being denied the value of Chinese markets for trade (eg Salisbury 1969:5). The change in Australian attitude, although not universal, was evidenced in an editorial in the *Age* encouraging the Australian government to move in advance of American initiatives. 'Since we live on the fringe of Asia and already maintain commercial relations with China, our own foreign policy makers have an opportunity to lead, rather than follow, the mighty but perplexed ally' (*Age* 1969a:2). The demand for initiatives that did not rely on American direction could equally have been seen as a novel departure for the press itself.

'a face to face meeting...'

Throughout the war Vietnam too often remained an abstraction to which the differing political sides attached their own symbolism and whose complexities were largely ignored. This was accentuated by political reporters weighing issues related to Vietnam against the survival and/or success of Government and Opposition leaders. The superficiality of domestic reporting of the Vietnamese context is well illustrated in the visit to Australia of Air Vice Marshall Nguyen Cao Ky in January 1967.

Ky's visit received saturation coverage from the Australian press. It was a strange media event. Newspapers that had decried the stupidity of Prime Minister Holt in allowing the visit to proceed suddenly embraced Ky with a fervour tempered slightly by ambivalent editorials, which left an indelible image of South Vietnam's Prime Minister and his wife in Australia. Whether the image that emerged of Ky was genuine or just the result of a brilliant public relations exercise became irrelevant. Ky produced in less than a week what years of reporting had failed to—a flesh and blood Vietnamese leader, a seemingly acceptable and likeable one at that.

Ky's proposed visit to Australia in January 1967 was met with virtually unanimous criticism in the editorial columns of Australian newspapers. Bruce Grant, correspondent for the *Age*, wrote that Holt's decision to allow Ky to visit Australia was 'singularly inept', an action 'to provoke and irritate the Australian community'. He conceded that Ky as the man 'in charge' at the time was the logical representative 'if someone had to be invited' (*Age* 1966a).

The Melbourne *Herald* on 6 January stated that the visit was 'premature and provocative' and Holt should consider calling the tour off. Whatever his personal attributes, the paper advised, Ky was not 'a chosen representative of the Vietnamese people' and his group did not 'symbolise the purpose of our war effort in Vietnam'(*Herald* 1967).

Arthur Calwell reacted vehemently to Ky's visit, and promised to lead demonstrations against Ky in every capital city he visited (Barker 1967:3) to demonstrate to Ky 'that he is not a welcome guest in this democratic country and to show to the government that his visit does not have the support of the Australian people' (*SMH* 1967:1). Press focus on Calwell's distain for Ky and his visit owed something to the emotive invective, but it also provides an example of the use by political reporters of Australia's political leaders to represent the case for and against involvement in Vietnam. Calwell's response to Ky, as on so many other occasions when Labor policy was interpreted by the media as dangerously disunified, was also linked to domestic party politics:

> Left-wing forces in the Federal A.L.P. hope the visit to Australia of the Premier of South Vietnam...will influence the outcome of next month's vital caucus vote for the party leadership. Senior Labor men said last night the left-wingers saw...Ky's visit as an opportunity to embarrass the Federal Deputy Leader (Mr. Whitlam)—a leading contender for the leadership after Mr. Calwell retires. (Barker 1967:3; see also *Age* 1967a:5)

'Calwell again calls Ky a little butcher' read the headline of the Canberra Times on 11 January (*Canberra Times* 1967a:1). It was a headline that carried a damning image of South Vietnam's Prime Minister. Calwell referred to Ky in stinging, emotional invective: a 'little Quisling', 'gangster', 'dictator', 'murderer'—all duly reported in the press. When questioned on the validity of his claims, Calwell reportedly answered, 'if anything, it played down the truth of this miserable little butcher'(*Canberra Times* 1967a). (They were descriptions Ky was to apparently casually note as those used by Communists against him back home.) On 11 January the Australian claimed that Ky was 'virtually uninvited and certainly unwanted by 40% of the community, perhaps more' (*Australian* 1967). The *Financial Review* wrote that the itinerary for Ky's visit had allayed fears of government embarrassment by assuring that he would hardly be sighted by the Australian public (*Financial Review* 1967).

Ky arrived in Australia on 18 January 1967. The virtually complete turnaround of the Australian press to favourable pronouncements of Ky and the political success of his visit for Prime Minister Holt illustrated the correct warning from two Australian reporters in Vietnam, Geoffrey Murray and Nicholas Turner, that the image presented in the Australian press might not be sustained after Ky's visit. Turner claimed that Ky's reality and image were mismatched (Turner 1967). Murray also asserted that Ky would not fit the 'tarnished reputation' that had been 'unfairly given' (Murray 1967). These two reports on Ky and his performance in Vietnam as Prime Minister were lost in the voluminous domestic reports and commentary that their views challenged.

It was the speech Ky gave to the National Press Club luncheon in Canberra that provided considerable impetus for wide media approval of the Prime Minister of South Vietnam. The 'Marshall Ky hits back at his critics: Beat the Press' headline on page one of the *Age* succinctly exemplifies the broader political press response to Ky. 'It was a first-class performance', began Sturt Sayers' report from Canberra (Sayers 1967:1). The *Daily Telegraph* editorial proclaimed that once 'again Australians have discovered that a face to face meeting is the best answer to the lies of propaganda' (*Daily Telegraph* 1967). The televised press conferences set the portrayal of Ky across Australia. In a reflective commentary on Ky's address, John Graham in the *Canberra Times* was a little more circumspect, but reported that the applause for Ky was a 'tribute indeed' from 'Canberra's cynical press corps'. Graham questioned whether Ky's favour had been earned because of a 'professional performance' or because 'the sincerity of the Prime Minister's argument...It was probably a little of both' (Graham 1967). Graham noted that there had been doubt about whether the visit was an 'exercise in domestic politics or a genuine attempt to inform the Australian people of the situation in Vietnam'. Coverage and commentary evidenced the usual desire for political issues to be defined within the parameters of domestic political influence.

Though it is not possible in the scope of this paper to present the detailed perspectives that emerged about Australian coverage of the visit, it is important to note that Ky's visit provides a significant illustration of domestic factors that influenced Australian coverage of Vietnam. Coverage assessed, and emphasised in headlines and photographs, the value of the visit in political terms for Calwell, Whitlam and Holt. In this instance, as in so many, Calwell's response and invective left the commentators loudly proclaiming the 'brilliant casting' of Ky. 'But, in fairness, Mr Calwell is not alone responsible for the twist of circumstance in the past few days. Premier Ky's behaviour in Canberra has been a significant factor in exploding Calwellian logic and amplifying the Prime Ministerial ego' (*Age* 1967b) Under the heading, 'Why Mr Holt is smiling', the chief political reporter for the *Age*, John Bennetts, noted that Prime Minister Holt was smiling as he strode into the Hotel Canberra for dinner with the Prime Minister of South Vietnam. Reportedly, Holt called to journalists: 'It's turned out nice again'. Bennetts asserted that the Prime Minister had reason to be pleased because within 24 hours of Ky's arrival: 'it was clear the gamble had come off...Organised demonstrations had attracted little support. And in the contest for public attention and sympathy the younger amateur politician from Saigon was points ahead of the old professional from Melbourne, Mr Arthur Calwell.' The article ended by forecasting a further three years for Holt as Prime Minister. 'The confidence Mr Holt exuded last week seemed well founded' (Bennetts 1967:5).

From the past to...?

A positive result of the Vietnam experience has been Australia's increased respect and willingness to respond to the region. Vital and positive changes have been wrought in Australia's relations with Asia. Nevertheless, at times it seems attitudes to foreign policy and its formulation from both sides of the political spectrum indicate little has changed. This is despite political claims that Australia's future lies with and in Asia.

On 3 May 1996, a *Canberra Times* page one report read 'Downer looking at more US bases'. The report from the paper's foreign affairs reporter, Ian McPhedran, stated more accurately the words, if not the intent of the new Minister for Foreign Affairs:

'The Government would look at how it could allow the US military to establish a greater presence' in and around Australia. Before the election, the Coalition committed itself to 'reinvigorating' Australia's alliance with the United States to encourage the US to remain actively involved in the Asia–Pacific region. (McPhedron 1996)

The report indicated that the Howard Government was keen to establish closer ties with the United States. It also noted that Ed Perkins, the US Ambassador to Australia, and Sheila Widnall, Secretary of the US Air Force, 'questioned how Australia could possibly be any closer to the US' (McPhedron 1996).

Paul Dibb, Head of the Australian National University's Strategic and Defence Studies Centre, reportedly asserted that 'America's allies, including Australia, would have to do more to contribute to 'alliance burden sharing', but modified the Government's stance by stressing that 'Asia's security environment would be shaped in the future more by the strength of the large Asian powers than by the US and its allies. "It is far from certain that the American alliance system in Asia will decay, but American's alliance partners

perceive that they will need to do more militarily for themselves"'
(McPhedron 1996).

In December 1995 Paul Keating, then Australia's Prime Minister, signed
an undebated agreement between the Government of Australia and the
Republic of Indonesia on maintaining security. It was ratified by the President
Suharto on 24 June 1996 with the comment: 'It is intended only to establish a
foundation for consultation about things which might affect security'
(*Financial Review* 1996). It is prudent to question Keating's justification for
the total lack of public and parliamentary consultation before the signing of
the agreement. His own defence of such secretive diplomacy was that the
public could not have been trusted with the information as it may have
harmed the discussion in Australia and in Indonesia. Keating's argument
indicated that such fragile diplomacy is best left to political leaders who have
all the facts.

As this publication went to press, the security of Australia's relationship
with Indonesia and the United States that both Downer and Keating worked
towards was being severely challenged. Australia's determination to support
the right of the East Timorese to be independent has seriously affected its
relationship with Indonesia.

A *SMH* editorial welcomed and rued Indonesia's abrogation of the 1995
agreement on Maintaining Security. 'The strain in Australia's relations with
Indonesia which the abrogation reflects is to be greatly regretted. But those
relations will improve. And they will do so more readily in the absence of this
strange and shadowy artifact of personalised international relations' (*SMH*
1999:14). The United States' reluctance to respond immediately and more
determinedly to Australia's call for help in defending East Timorese rights
increased Australia's vulnerability. That vulnerability has always been
defined by the level of comfort afforded Australia by ties with stronger allies.
Australia's The decisions in relation to East Timor have the potential to
redefine Australia's understanding of an *Australian* foreign policy.

So what has changed in the formulation and basis of foreign policy over 40
years? The slow, tenuous attempts to realise an Australian nation, to recognise
its regional influence and the balance between national interests and those of
our neighbours, appear to have a very long way to go. Keating's close
development of security arrangements with Indonesia and Downer's early
public reiteration of stronger ties with the United States evidence the
perpetuality of political secrecy in the formulation of foreign policy and
Australia's continued perceived need for strong defensive alliances. In 1961
Warner asked if the lessons of Dien Bien Phu had been forgotten. In his
autobiography, written much later, referring to the same period and comment
he noted, 'they had not been forgotten. They had never been learned' (Warner

1995·299). Perhaps the lessons of Australia's Vietnam experience have also still to be learned. The part the media will play in that learning remains unclear, but the strength of media contribution will depend on maintaining specialist journalists in political and foreign reporting. Those with experience in both will have much to offer. Nevertheless, quality coverage and a challenge to political agenda setting will depend on the use of insights from both the domestic and foreign environments to extend the parameters of news coverage, commentary and debate in the Australian media.

References

Advertiser 1969, Adelaide, 17 December.

Age 1967a, 'Mr Calwell's promise', Melbourne, 17 January.

—— 1967b, 'Brilliant casting', 21 January.

Australian 1966, 'Bring Ky to Australia', Sydney, 28 December.

—— 1967, 'Ky's visit calls for restraint', 11 January.

—— 1969, 17 December.

—— 1994, 'Vets, Coalition slam PM's Vietnam stance' 11 April.

—— 1995, 29 April.

Barker, G 1967, 'Ky visit influence on Labor leadership, Mr. Whitlam's silence', *Age*, 17 January.

Barwick, G 1964, 'Australia's Foreign Relations', in Wilkes, J (ed), *Australia's Defence and Foreign Policy,* Australian Institute of Political Science, Angus and Robertson.

Bennetts, J 1962, 'Frank talks when Anzus delegates meet', *Age*, 7 May.

—— 1967, 'Why Mr.Holt keeps smiling', *Age*, 23 January.

Bowden, Tim 1987, *One Crowded Hour, Neil Davis Combat Cameraman, 1934–1985*, Collins, Sydney.

Burgess, Pat 1986, *Warco, Australian Correspondents at War,* Heinemann, Sydney.

Burns, Creighton 1975, *Age*, 3 May.

Canberra Times 1967a, 'Calwell again calls Ky a little butcher', 11 January.

—— 1967b, 'Impressions Of Premier Ky' 23 January.

Courier Mail 1969, 17 December.

—— 1994, 'Veteran slams PM over wreath', 11 April.

Commonwealth Parliamentary Debates (*C P D*) 1968, House of Representatives, Volume 59, 15 May.

Current Notes on International Affairs (*CNIA*) 1962, Volume 33 No 5, May.

Daily Telegraph 1962, 'Gangster War in S-E Asia', 10 May.

—— 1967, 'Australia's message to Marshall Ky', 23 January.

Dixit, K 1996, 'Development Journalism', paper delivered to the conference *Intersections with Asia, the Future of international Journalism*, International Media Centre, Sydney, 11–12 November.

Downer, Alexander 1996, 'Australia's commitment to the region', *The 19th Asia–Australia Institute lecture*, University of New South Wales, 6 November.

Evans, Gareth and Grant, Bruce 1992, *Australia's Foreign Relations: In the World of the 1990s,* Melbourne University Press.

Financial Review 1967, 12 January.

—— 1996, 5 July.

Frost, Frank 1987, *Australia's War in Vietnam*, Allen and Unwin, Sydney.

Grant, Bruce 1966a, *Age*, 18 December.

—— 1966b, 'The Role of the Foreign Correspondent', in *The Australian Press and Foreign news,* Second Summer School of Professional Journalism, Canberra, February.

—— 1969a, 'Foreign Affairs and the Australian Press', *20th Roy Milne Memorial Lecture*, Sydney,   The Australian Institute of International Affairs, 7 August.

—— 1969b, *Age*, 17 December.

—— 1972, *The Crisis of Loyalty: A Study of Australian Foreign Policy*, Angus and Robertson in association with the Australian Institute of International Affairs, Brisbane.

Graham, John 1967, 'Marshall Ky: the urbane visitor', *Canberra Times*, 20 January.

Hammond, William 1988, *The US Army in Vietnam, Public Affairs: The Military and the Media, 1962–1968*, Government Printing Office, Washington, D C.

—— 1989, 'The Press as an Agent of Defeat: A Critical Examination', *Reviews in American History*, 17, 2, June.

Herald 1967, Melbounre, 6 January.

Lloyd, Clem 1988, *Parliament and Press, The Federal Parliamentary Press Gallery 1901–88,* Melbourne University Press.

McPhedran, Ian 1996, 'Downer looking at more US bases', *Canberra Times*, 3 May.

McNeill, Ian 1984, *The Team: Australian Army Advisers in Vietnam 1962–1972*, University of Queensland Press in association with the Australian War Memorial, St. Lucia.

Murray, Geoffrey 1967, 'Australians will meet a quiet Premier KY', *Canberra Times,* 7 January.

Paletz, D and Entman, R 1981, *Media, Power, Politics,* Free Press, New York.

Palmos, Frank 1990, *Ridding the Devils,* Bantam Books, Victoria.

Salisbury, H 1969, *Age,* 22 December.

Sayers, Stuart 1967, 'Beat the Press: then on to drinks' *Age,* 19 January.

Sexton, Michael 1981, *War for the asking, Australia's Vietnam secrets,* Penguin, Ringwood.

Sheridan, Greg 1995, 'Why the Vietnam War was just and winnable', Australian, 19 April.

Stone, Gerald 1966, *War without Honour,* Jacaranda Press, Sydney.

Sydney Morning Herald 1967a, 'Ky protests by Calwell in four capitals' 14 January.

—— 1967b, 'The Ky to it all', 17 January.

—— 1999, 'The end of an agreement', editorial, 18 September.

Tiffen, Rodney 1978, *The News from Southeast Asia: the Sociology of Newsmaking,* Institute of Southeast Asian studies, Singapore.

—— 1983, 'News Coverage of Vietnam', in King, P (ed), *Australia's Vietnam,* Allen and Unwin.

—— 1990, 'The war the media lost', in Pemberton, G (ed), *Vietnam Remembered,* Weldon, Sydney.

Turner, Nicholas 1967, 'What manner of man?' *Age,* 11 January.

Warner, Denis 1962, 'Australia and US in plain talk on our aid to Asia', *Herald,* 7 May.

—— 1969, *Sydney Morning Herald,* 30 December.

—— 1995, *Wake me if there's trouble: An Australian correspondent at the front line—Asia at war and peace 1944–1964,* Penguin, Ringwood.

Wilkes, J (ed) 1964, *Australia's Defence and Foreign Policy,* Australian Institute of Political Science, Angus and Robertson.

Wrigley, A 1990, *The Defence Force and the Community. A partnership in Australia's defence,* Report for the Minister of Defence, Australian Government Publishing Service, Canberra, June.

Cambodian news media[1]

John Marston

The outcome of the 1991 Paris Agreements was the 1993 Cambodia election, supported by a major UN mission. An uneasy political agreement worked out after the election survived for four years before succumbing, in July 1997, to a coup. Most recently, in July, 1998, there was another national election, whose contested results led to massive demonstrations and their violent suppression. Throughout this time, power in Cambodia still lay largely in the hands of the same party and the same political leaders, and Cambodia is far from a liberal democracy. The most cynical position is that changes in the county have amounted to very little; nevertheless, it would be hard to deny that there have been basic changes in the Cambodian economic system and that the nature of contestation has changed. It is especially in relation to these two features that we see the Cambodian media so completely transforming themselves from what they were in 1991. This transformation is still in process, and it remains difficult to say what exactly the media are transforming into. On the most superficial level, there has been a shift away from the state-owned and party dominated media of the 1980s to media more often privately controlled, dependent on advertising, and, among at least the larger media institutions, more and more links to systems of regional and global corporate media. This private media, enmeshed in personal and political networks and profoundly vulnerable to harassment and corruption, are far from the ideal of a fourth column or from contributing to the enlightenment ideal of the public sphere. Despite all this, they remain, in their own incongruous way, one of the most important loci of contestation in Cambodia and continue to serve as a marker of larger processes of social change.

The most dramatic turning point for the Cambodian media was the 1992–93 period of the United Nations Transitional Authority in Cambodia (UNTAC). Whatever other transformations may or may not have taken place

[1] This chapter is adapted from Marston 1996 and a chapter in my dissertation (Marston 1997a). It draws on my experience on the staff of the UNTAC Information/Education Division and on later research assisted by a grant from the Joint Committee on Southeast Asia of the Social Science Research Council and the American Council of Learned Societies with funds provided by the Andrew W Mellon Foundation, the Ford Foundation, and the Henry Luce Foundation. My thanks also to the Cambodian Ministry of Culture and the College of Archaeology of the Fine Arts University for their sponsorship during my 1993–4 research period. I would also like to express my thanks to Susan Aitkins of UNESCO for her help during the 1993–4 period and during a 1995 visit to Cambodia, and to Yin Luoth for his help during a 1998 visit to Cambodia.

in Cambodian society during the UNTAC period, the media formed unquestionably a very different kind of body when UNTAC left than when UNTAC arrived. The media changed rapidly and dramatically, and this change was itself an influence on the political climate of the time: it gave the public a sense that a more general change was taking place. While the institutions of media that emerged were often still far from perfectly free, balanced, or effective, the new media nevertheless represented shifts in the ways Cambodians could observe the events unfolding in their country and see themselves in relation to it. Fundamental changes were occurring in the economy of what could be said, by whom, and under what circumstances.

During the 19 months that UNTAC was present in Cambodia, the media developed in several specific directions. Political factions and parties that had never before been permitted to function in Phnom Penh established a media presence there along with the media of State of Cambodia (SOC). Soon after that a non-state/non-party media arose that attempted to function within the framework of a free-market economy. Although there were some significant developments during 1992, such as the emergence of a range of political party bulletins, it is in particular the five months between the beginning of 1993 and the May elections that stand as a watershed period during, which in a great rush of activity and many new, independent organs of media appeared. At the same time, the political changes taking place during the UNTAC period accelerated a shift away from the influence on the media of Soviet bloc countries (and Vietnam) and toward, on the one hand, nationalism, and on the other hand, the influence of ASEAN countries and the West.

The new independent organs of media fell into two very different categories: small Khmer media enterprises and independent institutions of media funded by foreign corporations based in ASEAN countries. Together with the state media and the media of political parties, this meant that now at least four different kinds of institutions were operating simultaneously. The convoluted developments in the media in the post-election period are perhaps best seen as a process of working out the new social reality of the media as these institutions interacted with each other, with the state bureaucracy, and with political power brokers. A new political reality meant a need for media institutions to try find new ways of defining a public stance of neutrality; but the changing society also meant coming to terms with a changing social framework of personal networks and patronage, which in Cambodian terms often meant covert political patronage. The years since 1993 have seen the party in power during the 1980's (Cambodian People's Party—CPP) reassert its dominance over the media—private media, as well as the state media it had traditionally dominated and new media explicitly affiliated with the party. The nature of this dominance had changed, however, simply by the fact that it was now more often dealing with private media, and that even state and party media were commercially oriented. Its dominance had also changed because of the persistent presence of independent newspapers, which through the shifting politics of the years since 1993, despite harassment, have continued to nip at its heels.[2]

Cambodian media before UNTAC

Toward the end of 1992, at the time that the UNTAC Information Division initially attempted to create a media association, the most conspicuous obstacle to its formation was the fact that there was little that could be called 'independent' media. The existing institutions of media were situated firmly within the administrative framework of one or another political party or faction. Despite the Paris Agreements, the factions remained hostile to each other, and there was not even sufficient neutral ground for an association to elect officers. Individual journalists, however much on one level they might want to, could not sufficiently forget the political networks to which they were bound to work together for common goals as journalists. While there were communities of common reference and a common sense of a public as it related to the private, there was no public sphere in the sense used by Habermas, that is to say, no realm where there could be exchange of ideas free of political domination.

The media in Phnom Penh at this time still primarily consisted of the State of Cambodia organs of press, radio and television. Political divisions still to some extent followed geographical lines. The Khmer People's Liberation Front (KPNLF), National United Front for an Independent, Neutral, Peaceful and Co-operative Cambodia (FUNCINPEC) and the Party of Democratic Kampuchea (PDK) had radio facilities broadcasting from Thailand or near the Thai border, and FUNCINPEC was still publishing a bulletin from the border.

---

[2] Journalists and Ministry of Information officials interviewed for this article include:
1993–94: Chhay Sinarith, Chhim Van Sithay, Sara Colm, Dith Monti, Michael Hayes, Khieu Kanharidth, Khan Sok, Khieu Sengkim, Khun Heng, Khuon Sodary, Mao Ayuth, Meas Boret, Nguon Noun, Nima Rasidee, Om Chandara, Pen Samitthy, Pin Samkhon, Pol Ham, Prach Sun, Prum Nhean Vichet, Sam Borin, Sieng LaPresse, Som Sophatra, Sum Mean, Tat Ly Hok, Thung Punthouern, Touch Chattha, Ung Tea Seam, Vann Seng Ly, Vann Sun Heng, Vun Sothan, You Bo.
1995: Chan Rattana, Chhay Simarith, Chum Kanal, Sue Downing, Stephen Pak, Keo Phen, Pichai Chand-Aium, So Naro, Som Chhaya, Tat Ly Hok, Thang Sarak.
1998: Ek Mongkul, Keo Phan, Mam Sonando, Om Chandara, Pen Samitthy, Phan Tith, Phuong Monti, Rath Sandalo, Tat Ly Hok.
For the basic chronology of evens during the periods I was not in Cambodia, I have relied on wire service reports, *Phnom Penh Post*, and occasional packets of Khmer-language newspapers bought for me by friends visiting Cambodia.

This represented a continuation of the situation of Cambodian media from 1979 until the 1991 Paris Agreements, which pitted the socialist media based in Phnom Penh against the media of the tripartite resistance based on the Thai border.[3] The media of the People's Republic of Kampuchea (PRK, which after 1989 would be called State of Cambodia—SOC) were socialist in that all media were controlled by the state. They were also socialist by nature of the degree to which their existence was dependent on political and economic links to a group of countries that identified themselves as socialist: to the Soviet bloc countries, and, in particular, to Vietnam—through the membership of its journalists in a Soviet-dominated journalists' association, through the fact that Vietnam and other countries sent experts to provide training and technical expertise, and through the fact that Cambodian journalists were sent to socialist countries for political or journalistic training. The state news agency, SPK, was originally designed to be part of an interlocking system of socialist bloc news agencies, but this plan fell by the wayside as Soviet influence disintegrated. By the time UNTAC arrived the Soviet Union no longer existed and Vietnamese troops and advisors had left, but the media were still shaped by these systems and identified with them in the public mind.

The Cambodian media were also socialist in that, following a Leninist model, they had since 1979 fallen under the direction and review of the Commission for Education and Propaganda of the Central Committee of the Revolutionary People's Party of Kampuchea and its successor, the Cambodian People's Party (CPP). Party members sometimes referred to the Commission as functioning as the 'brain' of the party. It was the branch responsible for generating and promoting the party's political philosophy. The Commission had a regular weekly meeting in Phnom Penh with representatives of the media to discuss goals. Editors who worked with the Commission now say it did not engage in a *priori* censorship. The heads of the various branches of media were responsible in the eyes of the party for guiding their institutions along the lines that the party directed. However, because of the weight of this responsibility, politically sensitive materials were at least sometimes sent to the Commission for approval prior to publication or broadcast, and major

---

[3] In describing the PRK/SOC media as based in Phnom Penh, I don't meant to imply that they were only in Phnom Penh. A more detailed description of the media would take into account regional radio and television stations set up in several provinces in the late 1980s, as well as a long-time program of loudspeaker programming functioning in many provinces. A fuller description of the media on the border would also include mention of a United Nations Border Relief Operation-funded newspaper printed there, which came to have a circulation as great as any of the newspapers published inside the country—in itself a comment on the strange economics of the border camps.

programming decisions were only made with the approval of the Commission.[4]

Most media cadres now recall that disagreements rarely arose at the meetings between the Commission and media representatives. If true, this is one indication of how seldom the consensus of what could be said was ever questioned. At its worst, the Phnom Penh media in the 1979–91 period fell back on slogans, perpetually repeated political formulas, and a dry litany of the who, what, when and where of official meetings. This is the image that most Cambodians call up when asked to recall the media from the socialist period. It is hard to get a sense of the times when the media from this period might have been effective or interesting At least two contexts reported by the journalists who participated stand up under further investigation. In the early 1980's, surprisingly moving anti-Pol Pot songs were recorded and broadcast by radio arts teams, at a time when the population's memories of the DK regime were still fresh and when there was still energy and excitement about reviving radio in the country. The quality of radio arts declined as the surviving pre-75 equipment deteriorated and as artists left for greener pastures—some of them to the camps on the border. There was also an exciting period for Cambodian newspapers in the late 1980's, when for a time the party espoused a policy of self-criticism, and daring articles and political cartoons began to appear, particularly in *Kampuchea* newspaper. However, this led to repression when the party decided that criticism was going too far.

During the period between the signing of the Paris Agreements and the official arrival of UNTAC, there was significant reshuffling of staff between the Commission for Education and Propaganda and the ministries it regularly dealt with. This aimed at streamlining the Commission and assuring that the party would still be in a position to wield influence once UNTAC assumed authority. The Paris Agreements mandated that UNTAC should have direct control over the field of information in order to ensure 'a neutral political environment for free and fair elections'. However, the Commission was never dissolved during the UNTAC period, and it continued to exert its authority over the SOC media even though the state and the party were, by the Agreements, to be separate. The SOC media would maintain a clear editorial slant in favour of the CPP and its leaders throughout the period leading up to the elections.

In April 1992, shortly after UNTAC was established, most of the national media institutions that had fallen under the jurisdiction of the Commission

---

[4] In 1990, for example, the radio arts division consulted the Commission about whether it could begin broadcasting recordings of the wildly popular pre-1975 balladeer Sin Sisamut, long avoided because of his association with previous regimes.

were joined into a newly formed Ministry of Information. Dith Munty, the head of the CPP Commission, while continuing to serve in that role (and in his role as a representative to the Supreme National Council), also assumed the newly created position of Minister of Information, a move that would assure him of having a continuing influence over the Ministry even if it were forced to separate from the Commission.

Later that April, the SOC parliament passed a media law. Accounts vary as to who wrote the law, but it seems to have been drafted by the SOC Journalists Association in conjunction with the Commission for Education and Propaganda and then channelled through the Ministry of Justice. The law immediately drew fire from the other factions in the Supreme National Council, who perceived that it attempted to pre-empt UNTAC's position in relationship to the media and leave SOC in a position to exert its control. It is not true, as has sometimes been claimed, that the law was 'communist'; the media as defined by the law are free-market, and the law made no provision for the role of the Party, an essential aspect of a Leninist system. But the law would have given existing SOC administration considerable restrictive power over the media, and in effect the power to block the creation of opposition media. (In general we can say that it was not SOC policy to adhere to institutions that functioned along classic Marxist/Leninist lines so much as to ensure a system where order would be maintained and its own figures would maintain their positions of power.)

The media of the armed opposition

Arising alongside and in opposition to the socialist media were the media of resistance groups. In 1982, after the formation of the Coalition Government of Democratic Kampuchea, FUNCINPEC and KPNLF radio and print facilities had been established in Thailand and along the Thai border. According to a KPNLF official who is now in the Ministry of Information, the facilities and training of staff were funded by what was called the 'ASEAN Working Group', with money from Thailand, Singapore, Malaysia and the United States. The two factions set up separate AM stations on the Thai border that could broadcast into the adjoining provinces; eventually, a joint FUNCINPEC–KPNLF FM station, Voice of the Khmer, began broadcasting into Cambodia from Chiang Mai, Thailand. Some staff were sent to Bangkok or Singapore for technical training. Broadcasts were very political in nature and aimed as much at the population within the country as at the Cambodians in their own zones. It was not any more 'free' than the media being produced inside the country. (A FUNCINPEC information official, recalling the broadcasts, said that all programming had a political agenda. The radio station might play sentimental songs from the Sihanouk era, but this was done with the political goal of reminding people of their life in that time.) Bulletins published by the two factions, and, for a short period, a slick jointly produced magazine, were sent to Cambodian supporters overseas as a way of raising funds. According to a FUNCINPEC official, Khmer-language bulletins were also brought into the country to be distributed by guerrillas. The information teams operating on the border also made videos of military activities to be sent overseas to generate contributions.

FUNCINPEC and KPNLF AM radio broadcasts continued up until the time of the elections, but in December 1992 the FM broadcasts from Chiang Mai were discontinued because the countries that had been supporting the station were under pressure to maintain a stance of neutrality with respect to the elections. The KPNLF had by this time organised itself into two separate political parties, the Buddhist Liberal Democratic Party (BLDP) and the Liberal Democratic Party (LDP), and since LDP was in a position to take over the AM station on the border, BLDP effectively lost its broadcasting capacity in the country. While a single small station of this kind would perhaps have had only a negligible effect on their standing in the election, BLDP leaders sometimes hold this up as an example of the party's lack of access to the media, which they blame for its relatively poor showing.

The arrival of UNTAC and the Cambodian media

In response to the SOC Press Law, the UNTAC Information/Education Division began preparations for what was to be a 'Media Charter', which would provide a legal framework for a free press that would be operative in the administrative zones of all four factions during the UNTAC period. As such it would take precedence over the SOC law. In the process of meetings with journalists, political representatives, and UNTAC legal staff, the Media Charter ended up becoming a watered-down set of 'Media Guidelines,' which did not claim to have the force of law, but did serve as a basis for Information/Education Division discussion with the media about what was and was not appropriate. Legal issues were further complicated when an UNTAC Penal Code and an UNTAC Electoral Code were passed (with little or no consultation with the people who had been working on the Media Guidelines), both with measures pertaining to the media. On a given issue, it might have been difficult to say precisely what the law actually was. It is fair to say that in practice the SOC media law was ignored, and, during the UNTAC period itself, the more restrictive measures of the UNTAC Penal Code were never acted on. This meant that there began to be room, in ways that there hadn't before, for independent media to exist.

The BLDP had been the first of the factions from the border to set up a bulletin in Phnom Penh. The *KPNLF Weekly Bulletin* was founded in January

1992 after meetings in the Supreme National Council in which the four factions had agreed in principle that a free press should be allowed to exist in the country. The *Bulletin* was about 20 pages in length per issue, photocopied on regular-sized typing paper, stapled in the corner. It was printed and sold at BLDP headquarters in Phnom Penh. Editorials took a strong anti-SOC stand, and it included reports of human rights abuses sent to the party by its members in the provinces. These reports, while not a paradigm of careful reporting, represented a breakthrough in the possibility of Phnom Penh press speaking openly about the darker sides of the SOC. In March 1992 the *Bulletin*'s editor was shot and wounded while riding a motorcycle in what many believed was an attempt to intimidate the paper and the activities of the party. Throughout 1992 the *Bulletin* continued to be subject to pressures by local authorities and had difficulty bringing issues to party offices in the provinces. On occasions when its copy machine broke down, it was unable to find any shops willing to do printing for it, and Cambodians expressed fear of being identified by agents if they went to BLDP offices to buy the paper. (It was only in early 1993, accompanied by UNTAC information officer Susan Manuel, that BLDP staff were able to bring a small printing press from the Thai border by truck. This enabled the BLDP to print the *Bulletin* and party campaign materials more cheaply.)

By late 1992 other larger political parties had also begun distributing political party bulletins in Phnom Penh: FUNCINPEC, the LDP, and the Democratic Party. Perhaps because of the SOC reactions to the strident *KPNLF Weekly Bulletin*, the other party bulletins were less confrontational in tone and tended to focus on providing basic information about the parties and their leaders. They had limited circulation. Sometimes, even in the case of the *FUNCINPEC* bulletin, there were not enough copies issued to distribute to all the party offices in the provinces. In practice, these bulletins tended not to be something that people sat and read in their homes but something to be posted on notice boards outside of the party offices that were opening up throughout the country. The contents sometimes seemed less important than the mere fact that the existence of a journal legitimised a party. Even so, they had impact on the more traditional field of the media by demonstrating that a multiplicity of political voices was now possible.

By the end of 1992 the few publications that could be called independent still occupied a peripheral position for the average Cambodian. *Sânthepheap* (Peace), a weekly journal started in March by a long-time writer and deputy editor at the SOC newspaper *Kampuchea*, is significant in that it did not have any overt ties to a state or political organisation. However, its independence did not mean it was neutral. It maintained a militantly pro-SOC/CPP position, and sometimes took extreme stands, which prominent SOC/CPP figures supported but did not want to be linked to officially. (It tells something about its relationship to the party that in January, 1993 it was seen posted in a more conspicuous position on bulletin boards outside the CPP office in Siem Reap province than were the official SOC and CPP newspapers.) *Sânthepheap* was similar in format to the *KPNLF Weekly Bulletin* and may have been conceived of as a response to it. The summer after it began publication it began featuring political cartoons drawn by Em Sokha, who came along with the editor from *Kampuchea* newspaper. While similarly scathing cartoons had sometimes appeared in *Kampuchea* before the Paris Agreements, they were now given a large format and placed on the front or the back cover to dramatic effect, becoming the *Bulletin*'s trademark. The editor of *Sânthepeap*, who after the May elections became CPP's officially designated Deputy Secretary of State for Information, continues to insist that the paper was genuinely independent and funded by income he was receiving from rental property. (A rumour often repeated among Cambodian journalists holds that a high-ranking CPP figure had given him the villa with the understanding that he would put out the paper in return.)

Perhaps more truly economically independent were the two English-language newspapers, the *Phnom Penh Post* and *Cambodia Times*, both for-profit institutions that started publication in July 1992. The *Post* was the personal investment of its American editor, a former Asia Foundation official. The *Times* was a Malaysian corporate venture by a firm dominated by the Malaysian-Chinese businessman Dato Dr Chen Lip Keong, although it had at least some Cambodian shareholders. Both newspapers ended up being printed overseas and shipped by air to Phnom Penh (the *Post* from Thailand, the *Times* from Malaysia), a move that protected them from censorship and dramatically increased the quality and range of print-styles available to them. The status of the *Post*, and perhaps the *Times*, would have been questionable under the April 1992 SOC press law, which prohibited foreign ownership. (The *Post*, which was already in the process of negotiating to set up the newspaper when the law was passed, regarded this provision as a slap in its face—although officials denied that the measures were drafted with the paper in mind.)

The *Cambodia Times* began publishing a Khmer-language edition in November 1992. (The Khmer edition had the same English name, transliterated into Khmer.) This Khmer-language edition, more slickly edited than the other Cambodian newspapers, and using colour photographs, attracted a lot of attention when it first started (although this waned in the months before the election as other newspapers appeared on the horizon and the paper's willingness to tote a pro-SOC line became increasingly obvious). When the Khmer edition first started, the paper was in a position to offer salaries that attracted journalists and computer staff away from other papers. This was a cause of distress among the editors thus abandoned. The pattern that *Cambodia Times* set—of an internationally financed newspaper that was able to attract staff, readership and advertisers—and which turned out to be less neutral with regards to the election than it initially seemed—would be repeated when *Reaksmey Kampuchea* (Light of Cambodia) came on the scene.

Meanwhile, UNTAC was also beginning to generate its own broadcast programming. In the second half of 1992 the UNTAC Information and Education Division began producing video news clips and dialogues to be broadcast on SOC television, and it also set up its own radio studios to produce materials for broadcast over SOC facilities. Eventually it would also set up its own radio station, thereby assuming a role that the UN had never taken on previous missions (a decision that has far-reaching implications). UNTAC radio would increasingly have an impact on the political mood.

Despite UNTAC's mandated control of the field of information, it in practice often found that access to antennas and to television air time involved a process of negotiation with SOC. Some of the more controversial television programming, dealing with human rights abuses, was never broadcast on SOC TV.

The 'Control Unit' of the Information/Education Division, as part of UNTAC's mandated 'direct control' over the field of information, was also in dialogue with the media as it wrote and tried to implement the Media Guidelines, which aimed to promote principles of a free press and set up the conditions for a 'neutral political atmosphere' in preparation for the elections. Information staff monitored the media and started regular visits to the offices of newspapers, radio, and television.

UNTAC formally requested access to Party of Democratic Kampuchea (PDK, that is to say, the Khmer Rouge) radio facilities but was never allowed to visit them. The PDK station, the Voice of the Great National Union Front of Cambodia, continued to broadcast inflammatory programming that attacked SOC, made allegations of the presence of Vietnamese forces in the country and accused UNTAC and its leaders of sabotaging the Paris Agreements. The PDK ignored all communications from UNTAC asking it to stop making racist and inflammatory remarks about the presence of Vietnamese civilians in the country and about Westerners and others in UNTAC.

Early 1993: the period of media transformation

The media began to change rapidly in early 1993: there was a consolidation of the FUNCINPEC media; a new television station and a newspaper, both Thai-financed, were set up; and small independent newspapers began to proliferate. These trends were perhaps the natural outgrowth of the economic and political developments taking place, especially the conversion to market economy and the establishment of a multi-party political system, which were at least the stated goals of all the political parties. Although the emerging media outlets were indeed independent in ways that the institutions that preceded them hadn't been, they were nevertheless haunted by political interest and the influence of power brokers. Many of the independent media (both small-scale Cambodian ventures and internationally financed institutions) often had political agendas or were allowed to exist because of agreements to tote a political line.

All of the 20 registered political parties had some access to the media during the period leading up to the election. This was because UNTAC systematically provided air time on both television and radio for each of the parties during the official campaign period, as was mandated by the Paris Agreements. But it is only FUNCINPEC that can be said, by the time of the elections, to have created a media network in any way comparable to that enjoyed by SOC. In addition to its more cut and dried bulletin, FUNCINPEC started a newspaper and two youth bulletins in the weeks preceding the elections. More importantly, it began broadcasting an FM radio station in February, and, after the start of the official campaign period, in late April, launched its own TV station. Both the radio and television stations operated out of the complex of buildings where Prince Ranariddh was living, on Street 214 in Phnom Penh. Not too surprisingly, SOC officials claimed that the stations were unauthorised, and they held up FUNCINPEC television equipment at the airport for a period of time against the protests of UNTAC. Although these stations did not have the broadcast range of SOC stations, and the television station, in particular, could not be picked up outside of Phnom Penh, their existence (quite apart from the content of the broadcasts) made a powerful statement about FUNCINPEC's importance and potential for influence.

For many months, the *KPNLF Weekly Bulletin* was the only media outlet produced in Phnom Penh that dared to take a stance directly in opposition to SOC/CPP. It would be naïve to say that FUNCINPEC did not attack SOC/CPP; but it did so with a certain strategic finesse. For a period of time FUNCINPEC's attacks on SOC were in large part limited to its press releases (a branch of journalism in its own right). The actual media organs of the party maintained a stance of detachment. As SOC attacks on FUNCINPEC became increasingly acrimonious, however—in particularly focussing on the allegation that FUNCINPEC was linked to the Khmer Rouge or to criminal activity—the FUNCINPEC media began responding in kind. They sometimes made their attacks more indirect by the technique of broadcasting letters that had been written to FUNCINPEC FM. their attacks often focussed on allegations, similar to the ubiquitous attacks in PDK radio broadcasts, that the Phnom Penh government was the puppet of the Vietnamese.

Many of the opposition political parties had strong anti-Vietnamese tendencies and to one extent or another espoused positions similar to the anti-Vietnamese stance of the PDK as manifest in its regular broadcasts from the border. This evidenced itself early on in inflammatory articles in the *KPNLF Weekly Bulletin*, although the *Bulletin*'s contents were toned down after UNTAC objected to them. (They surfaced again in *Utdomkate Khmaer* [Khmer Conscience], a small newspaper that was published by a high-ranking BLDP figure, but which had no official connection to the party.) As the campaign progressed, some material of this kind also appeared in the FUNCINPEC youth bulletin *Sâmleng Yuvachon Khmaer* (Voice of Khmer Youth).

The independent media that arose after the beginning of 1993, both internationally financed enterprises and small-scale Cambodian ones, were very much subject to political pressure. In conversation, at the time, Cambodians often complained that new newspapers would start up that seemed politically neutral, and then, after a few issues, would begin assuming inflexibly the SOC political line. In the period of time leading up to the election there seems to be some validity to this charge, at least in the case of the largest of the new newspapers, *Kâh Sântepheap* (Island of Peace) *Reaksmey Kampuchea*, and the Khmer edition of the *Cambodia Times*. Other papers no doubt also modified their editorial positions to some extent in response to pressure or bribes, although it is hard to distinguish between a genuine political position and one produced by bribes; there was certainly variation from paper to paper, as well as from issue to issue.

The Thai-financed IBC TV, which began broadcasting in early May, during the official campaign period, had a clear pro-SOC position from the very beginning, leading some to conclude that this stance was part of the agreement by which the station was allowed to open. There was some speculation that the television firm specifically had links to CPP figure Prince Norodom Chakrapong, who was often featured in its programming.

The new print media

Small-scale independent Khmer newspapers began appearing in Cambodia with the publication of *Kâh Sântepheap* and *Toek Dey neung Manuh* ('Territory and Man') in late January 1993. *Kâh Sântepheap*, the more significant of the two newspapers, was edited by Thong Uy Pang, a journalist who before 1975 had worked for a popular paper of the same name. Its style and subject matter were to set a model for many of the small newspapers that would follow it. Its front page layout was a crazy-quilt of pictures and headlines in a variety of sizes and print-styles that, though hardly reader-friendly, somehow, much like Phnom Penh traffic, evoked the anarchic mood of the time. It was splashed with lurid pictures of dead bodies and recently captured thieves, perhaps following the example of the popular SOC police newspaper *Nokorbal Prâcheachon* (The People's Police). And it had a nitty-gritty knowing attitude toward the topics it wrote about, displaying this, for example, in tersely worded poems about the rich and the poor and the abuse of power. A Cambodian who visited the newspaper office regularly reported that most of the editorial staff carried guns, suggesting an atmosphere at the newspaper of paranoia or hard-nosed realism. It was one of the papers about which people complained that it started out neutral and then began assuming the SOC line.

In the months that followed—before and after the elections—many similar small newspapers would be formed, some with experienced journalists working for them, some without. Some folded after only a few issues, and it was often hard for Cambodians, as well as foreign observers, to keep track of the papers and their different political lines. Journalists might end up working for a whole series of different newspapers, or for more than one newspaper simultaneously. The best of the newspapers had a vivid colloquial style that was different from anything that appeared in the traditional SOC media. They tended to be a venue for opinion rather than news, although it was perhaps those papers who were most often able to provide real news that tended to survive. Because the small independent newspapers operated on a shoestring, they were particularly susceptible to bribes and intimidation—as evidenced by their sometimes rapid fluctuations of editorial opinion. Unable to survive by advertising or the sale of the paper alone, these papers in effect relied on either overt or covert patronage. They very much existed within a traditional Cambodian world of personal networks.

The emergence of an independent print media represented a real change in the way the media worked. Although SOC newspapers were available for sale in Phnom Penh in a couple of government stores, they had over the years primarily been distributed through government offices to state employees. The growth of independent print media in Phnom Penh corresponded to an amazing proliferation of news-stands throughout the city. This was said to be reminiscent of the large numbers of news-stands that had existed in the Lon Nol period of the Khmer Republic. The actual sale of the independent papers was often essential for their continued existence in a way that it had not been for the state organs of media for many years. Reports on crime (which had made the SOC police newspaper *Nokorbal Prâcheachon* so popular) and sensationalistic love stories (sometimes pornographic) were standard fare in the new newspapers. This may have had more to do in determining which newspapers sold well than their political positions. Some of the new smaller newspapers assumed the names of newspapers that had existed prior to 1975, thus underlining the notion that the new era represented a return to the past.

Although some Cambodians complained that the political bias of the new newspapers was no better than the bias that had come before, there was in fact a significant difference simply in the fact that, because they were nominally independent, the new newspapers could cover events involving a number of parties. This contrasted with the situation as late as the end of 1992, when journalists associated with SOC, on the one hand, and the opposition parties on the other, were saying that they did not feel they could even enter the state or party offices of the opposing faction to conduct interviews in the course of their journalistic work. They feared this would be interpreted as political betrayal. Whatever the degree of bias of the new independent newspapers in the period leading up to the election, or the degree to which they were persuaded to have a certain bias, they had a certain freedom that allowed some kinds of news to be covered that had not been covered before. And, in fact, there was increasingly a range of opinion in these newspapers.

The foreign-owned corporate media

These small Khmer enterprises contrasted with the corporate media institutions represented by *Cambodia Times*, IBC TV and the daily newspaper *Reaksmey Kampuchea*. The last two came on the scene at about the same time that many small newspapers were appearing, in the weeks before the election. They and *Cambodia Times* were all owned by foreign-based firms who hoped that the venture would pave the way for other corporate media investment in the country, or other investment more generally. An indication of the complexity of the corporate relations involved is seen in the situation of *Reaksmey Kampuchea*, which was a joint venture between the Thai-based media firm Wattachak and a Sino-Khmer businessman, Theng Bun Ma, born in Cambodia, who had citizenship in both Thailand and Cambodia and is recognised as one of the largest landholders in Cambodia and a figure deeply involved in corporate investment in the country. *Cambodian Times* was also run by a foreign media firm linked to interests involved in a variety of kinds of investment in the country.

The three foreign-financed institutions were the only media outlets in Cambodia that could be said to have had a corporate structure by the time of the elections. Together with the *Phnom Penh Post*, they were also the only media outlets deriving a significant portion of their income from advertising. It is not clear to what extent, or for what period of time, the institutions may have operated at a loss in order to establish a niche in Cambodia. The three tirms have all at one time or another been subject to rumours of having shady dealings with government officials. This is part of the reality of what it means for corporate institutions to operate in Cambodia. When they were written about in the pages of the small independent newspapers these corporations were personalised, depicted as run by bloatedly rich, self-centered individual men, a far cry from the (perhaps ultimately more sinister) dry, business-as-usual atmosphere of corporate power that greets the visitors to these institutions. This personalised image perhaps illustrates how Cambodians are likely to perceive corporate institutions more generally.

When the Thai-financed newspaper *Reaksmey Kampuchea* began in April 1993, it had a strong impact on the rest of the print media. It was published six times a week, used colour, had a more sophisticated layout than other papers, had more pages, and yet, as Cambodians often pointed out, was being sold for the same price as other newspapers. The editor, Pen Samitthy, one of the more talented Cambodian editors, came from the CPP municipality newspaper *Phnom Penh*. *Reaksmey Kampuchea* was able to pay much higher salaries than a government newspaper, and some of his staff at *Phnom Penh*, as well as experienced journalists from a number of other newspapers, left their jobs to join the paper. *Phnom Penh* was already in difficult financial straits (and, like most state offices, unable to pay its employees a living wage). Pen Samitthy's departure was in effect the death knell of the paper. Its first and second deputy editors would go on to edit their own small newspapers.

Other newspapers also complained that it was difficult to compete with the new newspaper. The impact was particularly dramatic in the case of the SOC bi-weekly police newspaper *Nokorbal Prâcheachon*, which for many months had grown in popularity because it was the most politically daring of the SOC newspapers and because as a police newspaper it was in a position to cover salacious crime stories that attracted wide readership. Circulation fell drastically when the new *Reaksmey Kampuchea*, less closely identified with the state, began covering the same themes on a daily basis.

Although, like *Kâh Sântepheap* and the Khmer edition of *Cambodia Times*, *Reaksmey Kampuchea* was initially perceived as neutral, it took a pro-CPP stand during the election campaign and after the elections supported CPP allegations that the elections were not fair. Although some Cambodians complained in conversation about the bias of the paper, it continued to be widely read. Its editor objected strongly to the paper being called 'pro-SOC'—to the point of breaking off business relations with Agence-France Press when they refused to issue a retraction on this point. It is indeed true that the newspaper's links to SOC at the time of the election were never as straightforward as the links between SOC and, say, Pen Samitthy's previous newspaper *Phnom Penh*. *Reaksmey Kampuchea* is not a socialist paper in the old mould, but a corporate newspaper. However, it is one that was linked through corporate interests as well as personal connections to SOC and its leadership. The three corporate media institutions tended, not so much to favour one party over another as to take what appears at the time to be non-controversial stance. This often meant supporting what they perceived to be the position of the powers that be.

The arrival on the scene of *Reaksmey Kampuchea* was similar to the arrival on the scene of the Khmer edition of *Cambodia Times*. It was in a position to dominate the scene because of the investment funds backing it from overseas and technological advantages it had in being printed overseas. For whatever reason, perhaps because its editor was talented and Khmer, or because it came out more frequently, *Reaksmey Kampuchea* appeared to be more widely read and talked about than *Cambodia Times* during the year after the election, when I was in Cambodia. On the other hand *Cambodia Times* (perhaps because of its link to an English-language edition of the paper) continued to have more pages of advertising.

IBC-TV, also Thai-financed, became popular very quickly, although it never acquired the clear dominance over the field that *Reaksmey Kampuchea* did over the print media. IBC-TV primarily drew its staff from Thai-speaking Cambodians who had returned from refugee camps on the border—which meant it wasn't competing with TV Kampuchea for staff. (There was no evidence that the predominance of staff from the border affected the political stance of the station.) TVK officials, however, were sensitive to the fact that the new television station was able to attract advertisers that they were not. IBC TV programming did not break drastically from the patterns set by TV Kampuchea.

Although no corporate-financed radio station opened up during the period prior to the election, the argument could be made that Radio UNTAC took on a role that was in some ways parallel to that of a foreign media corporation like IBC-TV and *Reaksmey Kampuchea*—it represented a sudden infusion of foreign capital and technical expertise. During the weeks preceding the election, when Radio UNTAC began broadcasting live, it became extremely popular. At great expense, UNTAC set up relay stations so that its broadcasts would reach throughout the country. The international technical expertise of the broadcasts was no doubt an element of what generated a mood of excitement about the radio and made it more attractive than its competitors (along with, of course, the content of its programming and what that represented as a departure from the past and an opening up of new kinds of discourse).

During the actual elections all broadcast media, in accordance with electoral regulations, refrained from political broadcasting, and in the wake of tho oloctions the stations allied to SOC or FUNCINPEC never returned to the pitch of acrimony that had been reached during the campaign period. For various reasons, many smaller periodicals stopped publishing at the time of the elections, and some of them never reopened, although other similar papers would open in their place. All the political party bulletins that started in the period before the election stopped publication, but eventually a few small newspapers would open up that were loosely affiliated with some small parties that had stood in the election.

After the 1993 election

Although FUNCINPEC won the election by a plurality, it needed to form a coalition with CPP in order to form a government, and, especially after the threat of secession by several eastern provinces, CPP was able to manoeuvre into a strong position of power-sharing with FUNCINPEC. An agreement was worked out where there would be two prime ministers. Prince Norodom Ranariddh, of FUNCINPEC, became First Prime Minister, Hun Sen, of CPP, the Second Prime Minister. The arrangement in effect acknowledged the fact that FUNCINPEC had won the elections, while also recognising, in *real politik* terms, CPP's preponderant control over the military, the police and state apparatus at the local level.

The degree to which, over the next four years, FUNCINPEC ever enjoyed more than symbolic power, is open for debate—although one should never underestimate symbolic power. CPP's political organisation stayed intact, and in many ways it consolidated its power. It shrewdly manipulated to its advantage splits in FUNCINPEC and BLDP (the only other party that won a significant number of seats in the National Assembly). One of the most prominent figures in FUNCINPEC, Sam Rainsy, a particularly confrontative politician who had taken strong stands against corruption, was expelled from the party and would eventually form his own party. By the time of the 1998 elections it would totally eclipse BLDP.

In 1997 Hun Sen seized power in a coup, apparently a response to FUNCINPEC attempts to manoeuvre into a stronger position in relation to elements of the military loyal to it, as well as to negotiate for the support of Khmer Rouge's defecting to the central government. The post-coup government, led by Hun Sen, was isolated diplomatically and suffered from severe reduction of foreign aid and investment. Ranariddh was allowed to return and stand in elections held in July 1998. According to the official results, Hun Sen's CPP won a majority of seats in the National Assembly, although in terms of popular vote he only received 41%. The opposition vote was split between FUNCINPEC and the Sam Rainsy Party. Elections were followed by large-scale demonstrations against perceived balloting irregularities; only after a violent crackdown on demonstrators and another two months of negotiations was a new government formed.

In terms of the media, the period from 1993 to 1998 was one in which the state developed bureaucratic and legal mechanisms for interfacing with a post-socialist, non-state media. At the same time it was a period in which international organisations, smaller NGOs and human rights organisations, and funding agencies associated with the governments of Western countries, worked to encourage the creation of journalists associations and to promote standards of journalistic professionalism, as conceived in terms of the ideals of civil society in relation to liberal democracy. However, given the shaky position of the Cambodian court system and the tentativeness of the very idea of rule of law, Cambodian journalists had little legal recourse when they were subject to harassment, just as, in fact, individuals had little recourse when they were subject to libel by the press.

The distinctions between corporate, party and state media, which seemed fairly clear at the time of the 1993 elections, blurred more and more with the formation of joint ventures and the success of CPP in consolidating its power in relation to state institutions. Even before the 1997 coup, CPP had managed to dominate most of the large-scale media institutions in the country, and, after bringing FUNCINPEC radio and television into its camp at the time of the coup, was clearly the dominant player from then on. Immediately following the coup, many opposition journalists fled to Thailand. Most came back in the months before the 1998 elections, and many opposition newspapers were available in the run-up to the elections. There was, nevertheless, fear among opposition journalists and widespread speculation that if Hun Sen succeeded in dominating the political scene after the elections, opposition newspapers would once again be extremely vulnerable.

Broadcast media

Radio has long been recognised as the most important single medium in Cambodia and the only medium that truly reaches to all parts of the country, as well as to all segments of the population, regardless of degree of literacy. It was for this reason that UNTAC placed so much emphasis on creating its own radio station and helped organise a project, with Japanese support, to distribute secondhand radios throughout the country. Television continues to have a much more restricted audience, although anecdotal evidence suggests that television ownership has increased rapidly since the 1993 elections, especially in rural areas where there was once very little television.

Soon after the 1993 elections, FUNCINPEC FM and FUNCINPEC TV officially became private stations, although this was primarily a cosmetic difference, and the general public would still identify the stations as

'FUNCINPEC', (One radio official said the decision was made so that FUNCINPEC wouldn't seem like the opposition party: FUNCINPEC was the government.) With the closing of Radio UNTAC, FUNCINPEC Radio emerged as the most popular radio station. This was less because of its editorial standpoint than the quality of the music it played and the effectiveness of its live format. (It was an example of a media success achieved on a modest budget, without an inpouring of international corporate funds.) The old SOC radio, like the state news agency and the police newspaper, changed its name to one that was regarded as more politically neutral. In general the broadcast media tended to exercise caution, perhaps unsure where their bread would be buttered in months to come.

Gradually, language with a socialist ring to it was decreased on state television and radio. There was some innovative programming, such as broadcast fora in which government officials answered questions put to them by citizens, an innovation of Sieng LaPresse, a new BLDP ministry official. (A similar program initiated by IBC, which used figures from NGOs instead of merely government officials, proved more controversial, and was eventually shut down.) In general, however, broadcast media were much less likely than print media to push the limits of public etiquette. The downside of the efforts to make a broadcast media that would be inoffensive to all parties was that it was very cautious, bland programming that avoided or ignored the most far-reaching political tensions in the country. State media, during the 1993–94 period when I was in the country, chose to downplay reports of demonstrations. Perhaps simply because of technical considerations, there was surprisingly little broadcast coverage at the time Khmer Rouge and government forces were struggling for Pailin. At the time of a June 1994 coup attempt it would be government policy to remain silent. Radio and television policy at this time was that, in reporting news, political affiliation of politicians would not be announced—meaning that the stance of neutrality was not (as it might be, say, with BBC) one of a detached, God-like observation of political parties that one could assume would be in conflict, but one of ignoring political differences and presenting opposing camps as though they, and the stations themselves, were part of a single party with common loyalty to the king.

However, there gradually began to be a process of repoliticisation of the broadcast media, as new stations were created, almost all of them allied with CPP. The numbers of private and semi-private stations increased dramatically. Thai-owned IBC TV eventually, in 1995, sold out to a joint venture between another Thai company and the Ministry of Defence. Earlier, the municipal radio station, which during the 1980s had specifically been a Party station, formed a joint venture with a Thai company and in effect became a commercial venture, later expanding into television as well. All the new television stations and all but two new radio stations were affiliated with people with strong links to CPP. The new Apsara television and radio were explicitly linked to the CPP in ways that directly paralleled the role of FUNCINPEC radio and television; the new Bayon television and radio were owned personally by Hun Sen. Eventually, there would be six major television stations and 14 radio stations broadcasting from Phnom Penh with power of ten KW or more, as well as a handful of low-scale state-run provincial TV and radio stations. All broadcasting media, including state and party institutions, now relied on commercial advertising to a much greater extent than had ever occurred before IBC opened the first private TV station.[5]

The pattern of CPP domination of the airways no doubt related explicitly to an attempt to dilute and counterbalance the effect of FUNCINPEC TV and radio and to dominate sources of information in the country. It also related to the fact that government bodies, including those that formed joint ventures in media, were still dominated by CPP, and that investors attempting to establish a foothold in the country and advertisers could be convinced that it was more realistic to ally themselves with CPP than FUNCINPEC. Beginning in 1997, the Ministry of Information repeatedly denied permission for Sam Rainsy to operate a radio station on behalf of his newly formed party.

Earlier in the period, there still seemed room for occasional adventurous news programming, as in the television fora with public figures on state television and IBC-TV, mentioned above. During a 1995 visit to Cambodia, I heard a radio talk-back show on a new radio station where listeners could criticise social problems; it seemed to me a daring and refreshing radio format. When I met the director of the radio station, he made it clear that he considered himself allied with Hun Sen. A program of this kind was possible, perhaps, because the new station made clear its loyalty to Hun Sen. What was striking, perhaps, was that at this point in time once a media institution's primary loyalties were clear, there could be latitude for social criticism at a local level. When I visited Cambodia in 1998, though, Cambodians spoke of such programming as a phenomenon of the distant past.

At the time of the 1997 coup, the FUNCINPEC radio station and a small BLDP radio station were trashed. At this time, FUNCINPEC TV (Television 9) also began assuming a pro-CPP stance, which meant that all television in the country was pro-CPP and all radio except for the small Sbok Kmum (Beehive) station. A Television 9 official interviewed at the time of the 1998

---

[5] Television and print advertising, for example, increase by 300% in the first half of 1997 compared to the previous year. Tobacco advertising, in this period, constituted US$2.6 million (AP 1997).

elections seemed at first very much in the CPP camp: he insisted that we avoid the word 'coup' and use the official euphemised phrase 'the events of July 1997' instead. Perhaps a hint of his real sympathies was peeking through, however, when he told me that even though the programming on TV9 was the same as on all the other channels, audiences continued to turn to it because it still in some ways symbolised the opposition.

In general, there have been many fewer incidents of violence and harassment of broadcast media journalists than of print journalists. One such incident was an attack on a popular FUNCINPEC radio announcer, Ek Mongkul, in February 1996, when he was shot in the chest and neck while riding from work on his motorbike. Ek Mongkul recovered and continued to work for FUNCINPEC radio until the time of the 1997 coup. In some ways the most disturbing interview I had at the time of the 1998 elections was with Ek Mongkul—not because he was still being threatened but because the interview appeared to show that someone who had been subject to violence might later take a pragmatic approach to political risk. Poised, smiling, alert, everything that he told me about his background, his philosophy, and his experience of violence would have led me to believe he would continue to be pro-FUNCINPEC and anti-Hun Sen—and yet at the time of the coup he sought out the personal protection of a high-ranking FUNCINPEC politician who had decided to compromise and work out an agreement with Hun Sen. A year later Ek Mongkul continued to live in this man's house and was standing as a candidate in the politician's small newly-formed party, seemingly a testimony of the power of force to eventually influence the behaviour of public figures.

Not all violence has been directed against the media of FUNCINPEC or other opposition parties. A hint of the struggles over the control of the airways in the weeks preceding the 1997 coup is indicated by the fact that in March 1997, Ranariddh, still First Prime Minister, threatened to use tanks against the Ministry of Information if the state media did not give him and his party more air time. In May, a regional television station was attacked by seven armed men with rocket-propelled grenades, in an incident Ministry of Information officials attributed to CPP refusal to cede air time to FUNCINPEC. One television technician was killed and two other persons wounded.

At the time of the 1998 elections, the only non-CPP radio station was the Beehive station, started in August 1996 by Mam Sonando, an overseas Khmer who had returned in 1991 after 30 years in France. The radio was originally the outgrowth of Mam Sonando's discotheque, and specialised in a mixture of Western and Cambodian music. Sonando also always used his station as a forum for his musings about Cambodian history, culture and society, and over time he became a well-known public personality. These musings were only political in a vague way, although definitely nationalist, perhaps populist, in tone. He emphasised in an interview that he was prohibited from any political broadcasting by the government, and had been reprimanded when once on the air he questioned the neutrality of the National Electoral Commission. Nevertheless, sentimental and self-dramatising, and representing the one station that was not CPP, Mam Sonando and his station were spoken of fondly by Cambodians I knew. The station also had a popular free service to match job seekers with prospective employers, and claimed to have found jobs for 560 people. Finally, Mam Sonando formed his own small political party, which never gained a great deal of momentum. With a sort of inevitability, soon after the post-election demonstrations, the station was closed down.

Electoral law for the 1998 elections prohibited political advertising on commercial stations and restricted campaigning to a strict format on the state television and radio station, seemingly modelled on the way parties were allowed to present their platforms on UNTAC radio and television programming, which gave each of the parties a short time slot with equal time. This policy was much criticised by opposition parties, who claimed it did not give them sufficient opportunity to counterbalance the dominance over the media that CPP already wielded.

The question of how, during the 1993–1998 period, actual day-to-day programming changed remains to be fully explored. Watching Cambodian television in 1998 after a three year absence, I observed that variety programming was much more sophisticated and the commercial nature of television more firmly entrenched. It was also clear to me that, more generally, programming tended to be dominated by films and soap operas from other Asian countries, particularly Thailand.[6] A major issue associated with television in Cambodia is the extent to which, for merely financial reasons, programming tends to be non-Cambodian, an issue which perhaps has become more noticeable as there are more stations with time to fill up competing for quality programming. IBC, the first commercial station, was totally Thai owned, and was sometimes subject to criticism that it was promoting Thai cultural imperialism. In response to such criticism, government review of the station's programming intensified. This ensured that all programming was dubbed in Khmer (the station could no longer fall back on Thai music programming) and there was review of such matters as

---

[6] In 1994 a much greater percentage of programming was devoted to kung-fu type series. In 1998 it was much more common to see romantic soap operas. When I asked one viewer about this, he told me that the change from kung-fu to romance had occurred at about the time of the 1997 coup, but could offer no explanation as to whether this may have been caused by government policy, popular sentiment or changes in movie rental prices related to the Asian economic crisis.

whether women announcers were dressed in an appropriately Khmer fashion. All indications were that IBC did everything it could to co-operate. It tried to increase the percentage of Khmer staff, and made a point to include more Khmer films and other cultural programming. It aired statements that emphasised its commitment to Cambodian traditions. (After newspaper articles appeared that commented on the fact that television advertising made parents subject to unreasonable demands from their children to purchase the products, IBC even broadcast a short that showed a child asking his mother for a toy, and his older brother castigating him for making unreasonable demands that didn't take into consideration the family's finances.) IBC Thai staff I talked to in 1995 pointed out that its Khmer staff was given full control over news programming.

As early as 1993, the Ministry of Information declared a temporary moratorium on new foreign-owned media in Cambodia, and when IBC sold out its Cambodian station in 1995 there were no longer any exclusively foreign-owned broadcasting stations in Cambodia. Even so, the issue of cultural imperialism continued to be problematic. Most Cambodians I talked to in 1998 simply found Thai movies and soap operas they watched on TV to be better of quality than comparable Khmer productions—but intellectuals also expressed dismay over the obvious influence of Thai hairstyles and the influence of popular Thai entertainers on the performance style of Cambodians; they pointed to the fact that sometimes, where there was a Cambodian and Thai version of the same story, Cambodians were becoming more acquainted with the Thai version because of television (see Chea 1998).

In 1998, a television program caught my attention on Channel 9, the former FUNCINPEC station, which seemed to be dramatising the Pol Pot period. As I continued watching, however, the drama showed the protagonists converting to Christianity, and I realised that it was programming that had been prepared by a missionary group. When I asked a Cambodian university student in the home where I was staying about this, he told me, with some cynicism, that this kind of thing was happening more and more often, and showed that the stations would do anything for money. Later, an official with the station assured me that the owners of the station were not themselves Christian. Quite apart from the question of the degree to which any religious group should promote their philosophies on prime time, the story points to the degree to which, merely because there is a shortage of Khmer-language materials to be broadcast, major cultural influences may be determined merely by the question of what is made readily available to television programmers—the same issue lying behind the overabundance of Thai programming.

Radio programming broadcast into Cambodia from overseas, such as Voice of America and BBC, continue to be widely listened to and respected, as they have been at least since the socialist 1980's—perhaps another example of how non-Cambodian media can come to fill the gap when local products are limited in quality or heavily censored. When I was travelling around the country in 1992–94, Cambodians often told me (an American) that they listened to VOA, and it was clear that many of these persons knew specific Khmer-language VOA announcers by name and identified with them as personalities. The impact of these foreign radio broadcasts on political developments should not be underestimated. A recent *Phnom Penh Post* article describing post-election 'Democracy Square' demonstrations, for example, cites Sam Rainsy as complaining in a speech to demonstrators that VOA had underestimated their numbers. Later, as it goes on describe demonstrators attacking a monument, the article quotes a rally participant speculating excitedly to the reporter that the crowd's actions would be reported on VOA the next day (Eckardt and Chea 1998). For good or bad, in a situation like this, VOA comes to be perceived, more than other news sources, as the viewpoint of the wider world, and in at least some situations, political action is played out explicitly in relation to broadcasts of this kind. It is not yet clear how much influence will have the more extensive Khmer-language broadcasts of Radio Free Asia, another US-funded radio, which started broadcasting in Cambodia in September 1997.

In August, 1997, Khmer Rouge Radio, a constant media presence in Cambodia since the 1980s, stopped broadcasting, apparently as a result of the increasing disintegration of the guerrilla movement (Reuters 1997).

The state and the media

After the 1993 elections the idea that the state should be politically neutral in relation to the media came to have some currency, in direct contrast to the Leninist idea that state media should serve state and party goals. Underneath the surface neutrality, however, it was always clear that struggles for power were taking place. In the period leading up to the 1997 coup, it became increasingly evident that CPP was winning these struggles. Nevertheless, it is fair to say that the state had a much less direct relation to the media than it did prior to UNTAC, in that it was now primarily interfacing with private media instead of state media, and had to evolve new mechanisms to do so. These mechanisms sometimes worked to reduce tension and sometimes provoked it.

When the constitution was passed and Sihanouk re-crowned king, BLDP figure Ieng Mouly replaced CPP Minister of Information Khieu Kanharidth, a move that was announced as one that would give the ministry a neutral position with regards to FUNCINPEC and CPP. At this time, Khieu

Kanharldth was given the secondary position of Secretary of State of Information and continued to exercise authority in many situations. It was a compromise situation similar to what was being put into effect in other ministries. While this did in some ways help effect neutrality, it sometimes served to paralyse the everyday operations of the ministry (as similar compromises were doing in other ministries). There were few actual staffing changes in the state media, despite FUNCINPEC calls for giving its people more jobs. In 1994 I learned that, several months after ministry staff said that the decision had been made to make a FUNCINPEC figure the head of national radio, the decision was still bogged down in political bureaucracy. It is difficult to gauge the degree of political infighting over control of state broadcast media, but it was obviously taking place. By 1995 a split would occur between a faction of BLDP led by Ieng Mouly and another led by Son Sann. Hun Sen would come to the aid of Ieng Mouly and Ieng Mouly would come to be seen as in the pocket of CPP; this was typical of the pattern whereby CPP came to extend its domination in ministries that were technically headed by the opposition.

However, despite the continuing presence of state radio and television, the more general trend was for state media to yield to the many new non-state institutions opening up. After the 1993 elections, the print media that had once been associated with the SOC government became increasingly peripheral to the media scene. *Phnom Penh* closed down. The police newspaper *Nokorbal Prâcheachon* (now called *Nokorbal Cheat* [The Nation's Police]) became increasingly lacklustre. A year after the elections, its editor said that the pressure from the two different parties controlling the Ministry of Interior made it increasingly impossible to write anything but the blandest articles. Soon afterwards it closed down. *Kampuchea* newspaper survived the changes somewhat better, but still had a much more modest role than in its hey day. Under the editorship of Tat Ly Hok, who returned to the paper after several years in radio, it acquired some momentum. It continued to be published and distributed to state employees, but was not sold at news-stands. Thus it came to have something of the character of an in-house bulletin. It was still publishing in 1998, but staff were clearly discouraged by lack of funds, which had forced the paper to come out less and less frequently. Staff at the state news agency, now called AKP, said a year after the elections that one of their previous functions, to write official state-sanctioned editorials, was now impossible. They complained that they lacked direction from the Ministry, and that their division was increasingly being ignored. The CPP party newspaper *Prâcheachon* (The People) (which for some time had primarily supported itself from the income from its printing press and its computer school) declared itself an independent newspaper during the year following the 1993 elections and revised its format so that it was more like that of the newer small newspapers. It came out less often and no longer carried the status of the newspaper of record of the Party in a socialist state. However, it continued to be distributed for free among state employees (as were some other small independent newspapers that had the funds to do so).

The emergence of an independent Cambodian media has meant a need to redefine the relationship between the media and the state in several ways. It has meant the emergence of bureaucratic institutions within the Ministry of Information that had never existed before. It has meant a process of re-negotiation of the way the role of the media is defined in law. It has resulted in the formation of new journalist associations, which have had to work out their role in the country.

Starting in the period of the Provisional Government, immediately after the 1993 elections, the Ministry of Information created a press department that would have responsibility for supervising the independent media. (There had been no need for such a department in SOC because there hadn't been an independent media.) This office was to be responsible for monitoring the media and informing relevant officials about what the media were saying; it also played a role in mediating disputes between the media and individuals who had grievances with them.   During the year after the 1993 elections, the Ministry sometimes held informal meetings with journalists when it felt they were engaged in objectionable practices. It, for example, asked newspapers to stop printing pictures of dead bodies on their front pages. It also had meetings with newspapers asking them to be less harsh about the issue of the discrepancy between government employees' salaries and the amounts parliament had voted to give its members, which had proved to be an explosive issue. Sometimes government officials would make the point that the press should not depict the country too negatively because it would scare away foreign investment. Although these Ministry suggestions did not have the force of law, and different newspapers chose to follow them or ignore them in varying degrees—one still sees many dead bodies on the front pages of Cambodian newspapers—they did have a noticeable effect on the overall style of journalism in the country. A state-affiliated Communications Institute started in 1995 with funding from Australia, Denmark and France, the goal of all to professionalise journalism in Cambodia.

Media law became an extremely controversial issue. Since the April 1992 SOC media law was never really put into practice, the question of what law was in effect over the press was not clear when UNTAC left the country. There was considerable uproar in the press when, in late 1993, the Ministry of Information announced that the April 1992 SOC press law was operative. The consensus of the press at that this time was that the law was a repressive, 'communist' law. In response to the uproar, the Ministry of Information attempted to draft a new law in conjunction with the Council of Ministers. In May 1994, when a draft law that was to be brought before the National Assembly was circulated to the press, journalists again objected strongly to several measures, including one that would allow the government to close down newspapers, and one that would require news-stands and printing presses to have government authorisation. The newly formed journalists association was able to lobby to have the law rewritten. (In the meantime, it was the 1992 media law that was invoked as the legal basis for the shutting down of the newspaper *Prum Bayon* on 7 June 1994.) Drafts of the press law continued to be shuttled back and forth between the Ministry of Information and the Council of Ministers, and pressure was mobilised by international journalists associations and human rights organisations. The press law passed by the National Assembly in July 1995, with provisions calling for fines and imprisonment for journalism affecting national security, was far from pleasing to the journalists affected, but at least did represent a process of active negotiation.

Direct, repressive state action against specific newspapers began with the March 1994 imprisonment of Ngoun Noun, and increased during the period leading up to the 1997 coup. It is still difficult to detect a clear pattern to state interventions during this period, except that, whereas print journalists seemed to genuinely be allowed a great deal of latitude in everyday matters, they put themselves at risk when they attacked personalities wielding particular power or symbolising the state in a particularly powerful way: Hun Sen, Ranariddh, the King or national chief of police, Hok Lundy. Most offences for which newspapers were closed or journalists arrested seem trivial by Western standards, such as when newspapers compared political figures to animals, but may have greater force of insult in a Cambodian cultural context. Arrests and newspaper closings were certainly arbitrary and politically motivated, but issues were complicated by the fact that many of the newspapers in question were indeed guilty of irresponsible reporting or, as in the case of Ngoun Noun, viciously provocative. (Pro-CPP papers that were just as irresponsible or provocative never faced the same legal problems.)

Government action against newspapers tended to coincide with incidents of harassment and violence against the same newspapers, leading observers to suspect that the same authorities were responsible for both, and harassment and violence against journalists could be called state issues insofar as the perpetrators of violence were rarely brought to justice. Some government interventions were against journalists associated with FUNCINPEC, such as Ngoun Noun, but, increasingly, they tended to focus on a group of six newspapers loosely affiliated with Sam Rainsy and his party.

For the record, it is useful to list some of the cases of government action against journalists:

- March 1994. Imprisonment of Ngoun Noun, editor of *Dâmnoeung Pel Preuk* for two days.
- 17 May 1994. Confiscation by police of print run of *Sakâl* (Universe) newspaper.
- 7 June 1994. Banning of the newspaper *Prum Bayon*.
- 8 July 1994. Rearrest of Ngoun Noun in connection with articles about the attempted coup. This time he was imprisoned for a month.
- 11 July 1994. Letter from the Minister of Information to the Phnom Penh Municipal Court asking them to investigate the issue of whether the newspapers *Sakâl* and *Kolbot Angkor* were 'badly affecting social order and national security'.
- December 1994. *Monaksika Khmaer* (Khmer Conscience) ordered to suspend publication for two weeks.
- 14 January 1995. *Sâmleng Yuvachon Khmaer* and *Sereypheap Thmey* (New Liberty News) suspended.
- 26 February 1995. Chan Rotana, editor of *Sâmleng Yuvachon Khmaer* imprisoned briefly.
- 19 May 1995. *Utdomkate Khmaer* (Khmer Ideals) ordered closed.
- 20 May 1995. Editors of *Sereypheap Thmey* and *Utdomkate Khmaer* found guilty in court.
- November 1995. Unregistered and highly critical newspaper, *Plech Dâmnoeung*, ordered closed after three issues.
- 28 June 1996. Chan Rotana's prison sentence upheld and he is imprisoned (released after one week with the intervention of the King).
- 23 August 1996. Hen Vipheak, of *Sâmleng Yuvachon Khmaer,* imprisoned (also released after a week).
- 10 September 1997. Opposition newspaper *Prâyut* suspended for 30 days for allegedly inflating casualty figures in reporting about government forces fighting resistance.
- 15 October 1997. *Chakraval* warned for printing headlines insulting to the King.
- 15 October 1997. *Antarakum* suspended for 25 days for practising 'psychological warfare' against government when it printed a doctored photo.

- 10 January 1998. Six opposition newspapers suspended on grounds of defamation of country's leaders and threat to national security (decision reversed five days later).

- 10 September 1998. *Monaksika Khmaer* suspended for publishing article derogatory to the King.

Perhaps just as significant as the government interventions against journalists is the fact that many were soon reversed, pointing to active public debate on these issues. The cause of imprisoned journalists was championed by overseas Cambodians, human rights groups and international journalists associations. Surprisingly, given his record with journalists in the 1950s and 1960s, the King was also a strong advocate of journalists' rights.

Journalists associations

The issue of the creation of a journalists association has always been linked to the discussions about media law. The underlying conception of UNTAC's unsuccessful attempts to form a politically neutral journalists association was that such an association would help provide a tradition which in which journalists could regulate themselves without state interference. The idea of a journalists association continued to be discussed and meetings among journalists began taking place in September 1993. Debate about the association focussed on the issue of the degree to which it would be linked to the government. Finally, at the end of 1993 the Khmer Association of Free Journalists was formed, later to be called simply the Khmer Journalists Association (KJA). The issue of the press law was one catalyst to the Association's finally being formed. Journalists hoped that by developing their own code of ethics they could preclude government intervention and preserve greater freedom than they would otherwise have. Pin Samkhon, the editor of *Khmaer Ekreach* (Independent Khmer), a small newspaper with ties to the small Democratic Party, was elected president. There was general consensus among the journalists forming the Association that they didn't want the president to come from either the state media or from *Reaksmey Kampuchea*. Pin Samkhon, a recent returnee from France, was new to journalism, but obviously intelligent and politically astute. Soon after the Association was formed it created an ethics committee that wrote a code of ethics. The Association became officially affiliated with the International Federation of Journalists in April 1994.

The KJA always had some basic weaknesses, and some papers notably refused to join it from the beginning. But it had a significant success in its ability to mobilise opposition to the early drafts of the new media law. It always faced the risk of being co-opted by the government. Pin Samkhon was out of the country in March 1994, at the time that the editor of *Dâmnoeung*

Pel Preuk was arrested. He would later say in conversation that he had expressed disapproval of *Dâmnoeung Pel Preuk*'s violations of journalistic ethics in meetings with the Ministry of Information; this, he speculated, may have been interpreted as a green light for the arrest to be made. Both a May 1994 draft media law and a later Ministry of Information statement showed that there was tendency for government officials to conceive of the Association's code of ethics not as a voluntary act of consensus, but as something that needed to be enforced. The May draft of the press law would have made the Association the sole agent for providing credentials to the press—in effect turning it into a government agency. This measure was eliminated in a later draft of the bill, but it is characteristic of the precariousness of the situation the Association found itself in. It was trying to protect the rights of the press, but was also being manipulated into being an agent for controlling the press.

Similarly, Cambodian journalists may have found it difficult to conceive of the organisation as one of journalists voluntarily joining together to control their own destiny. They may have conceived the organisation more as a form of patronage for journalists—which, given the fact that it was largely funded by outside sources, it largely was. A non-Cambodian who worked closely with journalists associations in Cambodia told me that journalists were reluctant to serve on an ethics committee unless they were paid.

In July 1995 a new association was formed, the League of Cambodian Journalists. The break reflected genuinely dissatisfaction within KJA, but also reflected a pattern whereby CPP successfully exploited political divisions within parties and organisations in order to create new organisations that clearly supported it. The new association, headed by *Kâh Sântepheap* writer Chum Kanal, was openly supported by Hun Sen, and the newspapers that joined it tended to support CPP. One officer of the KJA told me about specific pressures he had experienced to join the KJA.

In September 1995, when I visited Cambodia, I was told that the handful of newspapers identified as 'opposition'—they would become more and more explicitly identified with opposition leader Sam Rainsy and his new Khmer Nation Party—had been denied permission to form their own association. Soon afterwards, they informally formed the Association of Independent Journalists. All this represented a tendency for journalists to ally themselves once more along political lines that precluded them having a unified voice.

At the time of the 1997 coup a large number of KJA and Association of Independent Journalists members fled to Thailand. Many of them would return before the 1998 elections, but no effort was made to revive the associations. Pin Samkhon was one of the journalists who did not return, and, according to Tat Ly Hok, since 1995 co-president of KJA, he is now working for Radio Free Asia.

One reason the associations were never revived was that they had been heavily dependent on US funding, and all non-humanitarian US aid was cut at the time of the coup. The League of Cambodian Journalists still had a functioning office in 1998, but a deputy director of the league told me that, lacking funding, they now had virtually no activities.

Print media

The Cambodian print media continued to be dominated, in terms of numbers, by small independent newspapers squeaking out a living by personal patronage as much as by sales of newspapers or advertising. Newspapers are very much a phenomenon of Phnom Penh, with distribution rarely extending far from the city. By 1998 the official list of newspapers had increased to 79 (not counting foreign-language newspapers printed in Phnom Penh), although the numbers of papers available at a given moment could fluctuate widely. John Brown has shown statistically that numbers of newspapers available tends to increase in times of political tension (Brown 1998). This may be because sales are greater when people need to know what is happening, or because during these times people of power are more willing to make contributions to newspapers to promote their positions. Newspapers tend to be strongly editorial in content, to the extent that, in the 1998 elections, many were distributed by political parties and might be better thought of as political flyers than as newspapers.

An official of one of the journalists associations made the argument to me, in 1995, that the distinction between pro-government papers and opposition papers was false. All the newspapers, he said, sometimes criticise the government; on the other hand, every newspaper was dependent on at least one person in power for support and protection, and would never criticise that person. From this perspective, what we have is not a situation of newspapers representing contrasting ideological positions so much as newspapers linked to personal networks in different ways, links that sometimes shift dramatically. It is these shifts that ultimately give the newspapers their individuality and prevent one from thinking them slaves to their patrons.

On the other hand, pressure on these newspapers, such as the pressure to join the CPP-affiliated League of Cambodian Journalists, or the legal action and harassment against the newspapers associated with Sam Rainsy, have tended increasingly to push them into well-defined camps. Their are seemingly no papers that are neutral, and very little evidence of the ideal of objectivity in reporting.

Just as we can make a list of state interventions against the press, we can make a list of incidents of violence against the press since the 1993 elections:

- March 1994. Bombing of the office of *Antarakum* (Intervention) newspaper.
- 11 June 1994. Unexplained death of the editor of *Antarakum*.
- 7 September 1994. Assassination in broad daylight of the editor of *Sâmleng Yuvachon Khmaer*.
- 8 December 1994. Drive-by shooting of *Kâh Sântepheap* reporter Chan Dara. (His alleged murderer would later be acquitted.)
- 7 September 1995. Grenade attack on *Dâmoeung Pel Preuk*.
- 23 October 1995. Villagers from site of Hun Sen-sponsored public works ransacked offices of *Sereypheap Thmey* after the newspaper made disparaging remarks about the village.
- 8 February 1996. FUNCINPEC radio announcer Ek Monkgul shot and seriously wounded.
- 18 May 1996. Thun Bun Ly, editor of *Utdomkate Khmaer* gunned down in Phnom Penh. (Editors of two other opposition papers threatened at the same time.)
- 3 January 1997. Leng Samnang, editor of *Komnith Kaun Khmaer*, gunned down and seriously wounded.
- 26 March 1997. Kry Sothy, reporter for 'Public Opinion,' stabbed in front of newspaper office, seriously wounded.
- 1 April 1997. At least one journalist killed, 14 wounded, when grenades were thrown into a Sam Rainsy rally.
- 5 May 1997. One killed, two wounded, in firebombing attack on television station in Sihanoukville.
- 14 October 1997. Ou Saroeun, reporter for *Sâmleng Reas Khmaer*, shot by security guard at a market where he was investigating corruption.
- 16 October 1997. Grenades thrown into the home of Thong Uy Phang, editor of *Kâh Sântepheap*.
- 8 June 1998. Thong Uy Pang, editor of *Kâh Sântepheap*, shot and wounded at a Buddhist temple on the outskirts of Phnom Penh.
- 21 August 1998. Khmer driver for Kyodo News Service killed in a grenade explosion apparently directed at political figure Sam Rainsy.
- 8 September 1998. Un Sokhon, editor of *Prâyut*, beaten by police during period of post-election unrest.

One should note, again, that the newspapers that are subject to violence tend also to be those that are subject to state interventions, although the pattern is not clear cut. At least some violence against journalists relates to the simple fact that guns and grenades are readily available in Cambodia and that journalists, even more than other Cambodians, are vulnerable to chance incidents of violence, since they tend to be present at controversial political events, and to personal vendettas, because they investigate sensitive issues—as well as, perhaps, because in Cambodia journalists have sometimes committed libel and blackmail with impunity. In 1995 I tried to learn about the recent grenade attack on the offices of *Dâmoeung Pel Preuk*. I also heard stories about an unnamed newspaper that had made metaphorically graphic allusions to the promiscuity of another editor's wife. It was only when I left Cambodia and began comparing notes and newspaper accounts that I realised that the newspaper in question was *Dâmoeung Pel Preuk* and that the two incidents had occurred in close proximity. This is not to excuse the violence or to underestimate the degree to which, on many occasions, *Dâmoeung Pel Preuk* and its editor have indeed been harassed for an oppositional political stance, but does point out some of the complexity of violence in a country where there is no assurance of legal recourse.

Journalists associated with *Kâh Sântepheap*, as the above list shows, have been repeatedly subject to violence even though it is a pro-CPP newspaper and has never been subject to government shut downs or arrest of journalists. In the case of the attacks on editor Thong Uy Pang, this may relate to the fact that the newspaper has been extremely aggressive in its personal attacks on public figures, and has enjoyed impunity in doing so. The fact that a colonel accused of killing Chan Dara was acquitted, even though *Kâh Sântepheap* is a pro-CPP paper, merely tells us that he was more powerful than Chan Dara. On the other hand, a graphic Amnesty International report about the torture of a FUNCINPEC official accused of the attack on Thong Uy Phang illustrates how severely the state can act against those who target pro-CPP media (Amnesty International 1998).

In the year following the 1993 elections, when small independent newspapers were flourishing, there were frequent print wars in which newspapers attacked each other viciously, but which in no way followed political lines, perhaps starting when *Dâmoeung Pel Preuk* in an early issue made sharp attacks on many of its competitors. Some said the wars were designed to increase circulation, and they certainly did this, but the acrimony went beyond the point of collusion, resembling the cock fight of Geertz's famous article, with the drama for the readers linked to their awareness or speculation about the personal networks behind the warring newspapers. In early 1994 a particularly vicious media war started between *Reaksmey*

Kampuchea and *Kâh Sântepheap,* supposedly both pro-CPP papers, with *Reaksmey Kampuchea* accusing *Kâh Sântepheap* of corruption and *Kâh Sântepheap* accusing *Reaksmey Kampuchea* of covering up publisher Theng Bun Ma's 'Mafia' links and, in general, being the lackey of Thai interests.[7] Eventually the two newspapers 'made up' over beers in meeting of Phnom Penh journalists arranged by Secretary of State of Information, Khieu Kanharidth, which was reported in the press. It is worth pointing out that *Reaksmey Kampuchea*'s vitriolic response to attacks by *Kâh Sântepheap* were a departure from the newspaper's usual style—a sort of slipping away of the corporate mask—whereas *Kâh Sântepheap*'s attacks were very much in keeping with the style associated with the paper.

In this same early period, Em Sokha, the talented artist who had drawn political cartoons for *Sântepheap,* freelanced for a number of the small newspapers. His cartoons were made to order, and based on ideas provided by the editorial staff of the different newspapers, and they in no way reflected a consistent political position. But ubiquitous as they were, they helped stamp the newspapers with a common look. While this style was not linked in a simple sense to any specific group or stance, it did seem to reflect an unsettlingly dark, menacingly hierarchical world view, and often reflected the same sense of direct conflict that was revealed in the media wars (see Marston 1997a).

Throughout the period, different kinds of pressure were exerted on independent journalists, on the one hand, to force them to follow the government line and, on the other hand, to professionalise them. While violence against journalists and arbitrary government interventions against them are very different from the creation of media law or a Communications Institute, and very different from the creation of journalists association, or the training of journalists through those associations, all in some ways represented attempts to tame journalists, to teach them 'capitalist discipline,' perhaps, or a more personal discipline exacted by more personalised kinds of power. This trend has a kind of inevitability and, in the case of formal training of journalists, is probably good, although some of the initial excitement

---

[7] The tone of these attacks was harsh by the standards of any country. A 23 January 1994 *Reasmey Kampuchea* article entitled 'If You're Not Shit, Don't Shit,' said, 'The thing I want to say is that shit has soiled *Kâh Sântepheap* from its head to its foot. Who doesn't know that this is the foundation on which *Kâh Sântepheap* began publication? Ho, ho! The car that they drive every day doubtless comes from 'ritual offerings' made to it; and the building they use as an office every day no doubt comes from another kind of offering to the spirits. And that's not all—the printing press, the computers are gifts to the church as well.' *Kâh Sântepheap* published a cartoon in its 25–27 January edition that showed Theng Bun Ma in increasing ecstasy as two dogs licked first his feet, then his legs, and then his genital area.

caused by the very unconventionality of the independent journalism that arose at the time of the 1993 elections has been lost.

By 1996 you rarely saw political cartoons in small independent newspapers, and Em Sokha was focussing on conservative illustration work for his home newspaper *Kampuchea*. Many would say there was still a great deal of freedom among the independent newspapers, but opposition followed more predictable patterns, and was more clearly divided into camps. One photographer for a Sam Rainsy newspaper, wounded in a 1997 grenade attack on a Rainsy rally, who fled to Thailand at the time of the coup, would tell me at the time of the 1998 elections that at that particular moment his paper enjoyed a great deal of freedom. While there seems to be room for small independent newspapers to assume the oppositional stance of a political figure whom authorities allow to work in the country, it is less clear, as seemed possible when independent newspapers first began appearing in the country, whether a Khmer paper in Cambodia can be truly non-aligned and merely objective or neutral in relation to events. One long-time Cambodian journalist, well acquainted with the philosophical issues surrounding alternative styles of journalism, told me in 1998 that one Cambodian editor had told him he would specifically avoid hiring journalists trained at the Communications Institute because their ideas of objective reporting did not meet the partisan requirements of a working newspaper in Cambodia. While I suspect that this was an apocryphal story, intended to provoke me, the point of the incompatibility of journalistic training is well taken.

While less often written about, the period has also seen the emergence of periodicals devoted to business or, for example, popular entertainment, of a sort that could never have existed during the socialist period, representing the growth of consumer culture. Could any of these publications eventually evolve into something with serious cultural impact? It is still difficult to imagine.

Several French and English publications opened up in the years following the 1993 elections. Perhaps the most important one of these was *The Cambodia Daily*, created in 1994 by Bernard Krisher, a journalist with close ties to Sihanouk. *The Cambodia Daily* was formed as a Non-Governmental Organisation, which enabled it to accept donations of wire service reports by various news agencies and other funding available to non-profit organisations. It included pages in Japanese and Khmer. Like *Phnom Penh Post* it came to be widely read by Cambodian intellectuals. Both newspapers were often used in special English classes, where students would study the language by the teachers' close translation of articles. Both newspapers came out of a Western tradition of objective reporting, and whatever their occasional flaws, have come to be a major source of information for many Cambodians. It is significant that it almost seems necessary for a newspaper to be non-Khmer, or published by non-Cambodians, for it not to be subject to the pressures of personal and political networks—for it to make some pretense of being neutral and objective.

Reaksmey Kampuchea remains the premiere Khmer-language newspaper. In mid-1997, publisher Theng Bun Ma bought out the interest of Thai partner, Wattachak, at the time that the newspaper finally set up equipment for publishing in Cambodia.[8] It continues to be widely recognised as a 'pro-government' newspaper and Theng Bun Ma's notoriety in the wider world has received more and more media attention. Nevertheless, it remains one of the few Cambodian newspapers where one can find useful news about Cambodia.

Rather than falling in a separate category as a corporate newspaper, *Reaksmey Kampuchea*, despite its use of colour, abundant advertising, and greater number of pages, increasingly seems like other Cambodian newspapers, perhaps because, with huge ads taking up one-third of the front page, it no longer has such a neat format, or because sensational pictures of dead bodies more and more frequent the front page. Reading the paper in 1998, I found myself thinking that it had declined—because of the pictures of dead bodies, because my favourite column, of humorous social commentary, had disappeared, and because I intuitively felt that there was less that was new or surprising in the paper. Pen Samitthy, in 1998, was evasive about the disappearance of the column, but finally said it was no longer being published because the writer of the column sometimes said things that were not true. He defended the pictures of dead bodies, which he said was a way of bringing home to authorities the realities of what was happening in Cambodia, an argument which has some validity, even as it points to the ultimate subversive nature of more patently sensational newspapers like *Kâh Sântepheap*. He pointed out an article about kidnapping in Phnom Penh, which he said the Ministry of Interior would have preferred not appear. All this it to show that even pro-CPP publications, especially those with staff as intelligent and professional as those of *Reaksmey Kampuchea*, do not necessarily slavishly serve their patrons. No one could say that *Reaksmey Kampuchea* is merely a mouthpiece for Theng Bun Ma in the way that some of the smaller Cambodian newspapers serve other figures. It is the degree of autonomy that a newspaper like *Reaksmey Kampuchea* has been able to attain, however imperfect it is, that ultimately seems like the hope of Cambodian journalism.

---

[8] *Cambodia Times* closed in 1997. Although there are still significant business publications and foreign-language newspapers owned by foreigners, there appears to no longer be any major print Khmer-language provider of news that is foreign-owned.

Conclusions

It is, of course, impossible to predict the future of Cambodian media. The most recent agreement between CPP and FUNCINPEC to jointly form a new government will probably mean, once again, immediate suppression of media associated with Sam Rainsy and more long term movements to undermine the media position of FUNCINPEC. The most optimistic scenario would be that, as political realities force Cambodian political parties to live with each other, corresponding media institutions will also learn to live with each other.

The difficulty in understanding Cambodian media is the difficulty in understanding what, in Cambodian terms, social formations of corporation, party and state mean as they work in relation to more personal networks of the sort that are will exemplified by the small independent press. No one can doubt that such personal networks play a significant role in corporation, party and state, just as they did in the different kind of party and state that existed under socialism. In some ways the shift away from socialism has made personal networks stronger or more visible, just as new kinds of commercial social formations serve to re-arrange the sources of power they depend on, at the same time they call these personal networks into question in new ways. Will the future see a media increasingly serving the interests of the impersonal bureaucracies of state, party and corporation, or will the personality of strong political figures, like Hun Sen, come to dominate the workings even of these bureaucracies? It is still hard to say.

In the immediate future, it is difficult to imagine is how a media truly independent of political affiliation, or the affiliation of some kind of powerful person, can evolve. Perhaps the most discouraging aspect of Cambodian media is the fact that when something new or surprising appears—the cartoons of Em Sokha, the satirical column in *Reaksmey Kampuchea*, the eccentric radio programming of Mam Sonando, it does not last long, whether it appears in CPP-affiliated media or opposition-affiliated media. The general excitement about Cambodia when it first left the socialist mould has long gone.

References

Amnesty International 1998, 'Cambodia: Rule of Law Ignored as Cambodia Prepares for Polls', news release, 24 July.

Associated Press (AP) 1997, 'Ad Spending in Cambodia Increases,' 12 August.

Brown, John 1998, 'Through the Eyes of the Khmer Print Press', paper presented at EuroSEAS, 6 September.

Chea Sotheacheath 1998, 'Khmer Culture Drowning in Flood of Thai TV', *Phnom Penh Post*, 16–29 January.

Chheang Sopheng 1997, 'Battle Waging on the Airwaves', *Cambodia Times*, 6–12 January.

Eckardt, James and Chea Sotheacheath 1998, 'Diary of a Demonstration', *Phnom Penh Post*, 4–17 September.

Fontaine, Chris and Chea Sotheacheath 1998, 'CPP Rules the Television and Radio Waves', *Phnom Penh Post*, 27 February–13 March.

Jennar, Raoul Marc 1997, *Cambodge: Une Presse sous Pression*, Reporters sans Frontiers, Paris.

Marston, John 1996, 'Cambodian News Media in the UNTAC Period and After' in Heder, S and Ledgerwood, J (eds), *Propaganda, Politics, and Violence in Cambodia: Democratic Transition under United Nations Peacekeeping*, Armonk, New York and M E Sharpe, London.

—— 1997a, *Cambodia 1991–94: Hierarchy, Neutrality and Etiquettes of Discourse*. Ph.D. dissertation, University of Washington.

—— 1997b, 'Em Sokha and Cambodian Satirical Cartoons', *Southeast Asian Journal of Social Science,* Vol 25 No 1.

Mehta, Harish 1977, *Cambodia Silenced: The Press under Six Regimes*, White Lotus Press, Bangkok.

Reuters 1997, 'Cambodia's Khmer Rouge Radio Fails to Broadcast', 7 August.

Zhou Mei 1994, *Radio UNTAC of Cambodia: Winning Ears, Hearts and Minds*, White Lotus, Bangkok.

The Malaysian media:
prescribed loyalty, proscribed practices

Eric Loo

KEDAH (northwestern state of peninsula Malaysia), 23 April 1995: Dr
Mahathir lambasted an Australian Broadcasting Corporation (ABC) reporter
when asked if Malaysia was a one-party state:

'Why can't you tell the truth for once? Why do you care about our
elections? It is none of your business. You never tell the truth. You come here
to record this, then you go and tell lies. You know I have never had any good
recording from you, you are going to twist it.' (ABC *News*, 7pm)

SYDNEY, 24 April 1995: Max Uechtritz, then ABC acting network editor,
in replying to Mahathir's scorn said:

'The ABC always has and will continue to report the facts...it is a
regrettable outburst but not that surprising. Perhaps Dr Mahathir has trouble
grasping the idea that the ABC is an independent organisation and not an arm
of the Government.' (*Australian*)

Mahathir's censure of Australian media coverage of Malaysian affairs is
one of a series of periodic standoffs that date back to 1975, when the late
Prime Minister Tun Abdul Razak, while on an official visit to Canberra, was
harassed by student demonstrators protesting the detention of Malaysian
political activists. Other media standoffs stem from Bob Hawke's labelling of
Malaysian laws as 'barbaric' after the hanging of two Australians in Penang
for drug trafficking in 1986, the alleged misrepresentation of Malaysian social
and cultural values by the ABC television series *Embassy* (1991) and the
movie *Turtle Beach* (1992), and the media run on the child custody dispute in
November 1992 between Raja Bahrin, a nephew of the Sultan of Terengganu,
and Jacqueline Gillespie, an Australian freelance television journalist from
Melbourne.

Mahathir's government was often framed as 'anti-Western' and a law unto
itself when Malaysia downgraded its commercial relations with Australia and
threatened to adopt a 'buy-Australia-last' campaign in retaliation to Prime
Minister Paul Keating's 'recalcitrant' remark of 24 November 1993 (See Loo
and Hirst 1995). Then there was coverage of Malaysia's boycott of British
goods and companies on 25 February 1994, following British media claims of
corruption in Anglo–Malaysian trade[1]; the government's ban on the allegedly

---

[1] The *Sunday Times* in London reported on 23 February that a British construction firm,
Wimpey International, was prepared to offer a US$50,000 bribe to Dr Mahathir's government
to win a £615m contract for the Pergau Dam project in 1985. The allegation was tied in with
Britain's £234m development aid with arms sales and other trade. Dr Mahathir flatly denied the

pro-Jewish movie *Schindler's List* on 23 March 1994; and Mahathir's bid to exclude Australia and New Zealand from his proposed East Asian Economic Caucus, a regional trade group of Asian nations (*Australian* 4 July 1995).

Continual media spats between Malaysia and Australia are reflective of the rhetoric over a new world information order in the early 1970s, when Western news agencies were seen to be ritually negative, perpetually conflict-driven and covertly 'conspiratorial' in their coverage of Third World issues. 'Responsible reporting' was defined from two culturally absolutistic frames. Third World leaders framed it in terms of appropriate media contents supportive of national development efforts. Western news agencies framed it in terms of 'Kantian obligationism' (Merrill 1974:5), with its overt journalistic emphases on professional duty and objective rationalism. Premised in Mahathir's rationale is that Western journalistic standards and news values are not, nor should they be seen to be, universal. Instead, he said, news values and practices should be tailored to work in different cultural and political systems.

Mahathir's theoretical explication of the media's role in society can be better understood within the context of Malaysia's politico-cultural environment. First, respect for the Prime Minister and overt moral support for the government are obligations that Malaysian journalists tacitly acknowledge are central to their prescribed role in forging a sense of national pride and morality. This journalistic ethos was perhaps reflected when 100 Malaysian journalists reacted to British media comments on the subservience of Malaysian media in investigating allegations of government corruption by declaring that they 'make no apology for being supportive of the government elected by the people—a position we have adopted at our own free will'. They said in the joint statement that the Malaysian media had fully supported Mahathir's decision to refuse government contracts to British companies 'so long as this campaign of slander and falsehood against our leaders continues' (AFP/Bernama wire copy, 23 March 1994).

Second, since the race riots in May 1969, in which allegedly more than 900 civilians were killed, Malaysian media contents and practices have been reoriented to maintain racial harmony and political stability in a nation where close to 55% of the 19.6 million population are Bumiputeras,[2] 35% are Chinese; and the rest are Indians or from other ethnic groups. The

---

allegation. The arms deal and the agreement to fund the dam followed successful efforts in that year by Margaret Thatcher, then Prime Minister, to improve relations with Dr Mahathir after his 'Buy British Last' policy (*Independent* 1994:1).

[2] Literally translated, *Bumiputera* means 'Prince of the Earth'. The term is used interchangeably with the ethnic descriptor 'Malay' in public discourse. Generally, Muslims of Malay descent are officially referred to as Bumiputera.

Dumiputeras are further segmented into various communities such as the Malays, Melanaus, Bajaus, Kadazans, Ibans and Meruts. The Chinese have their subgroups based on clan identities such as Hokkien, Cantonese, Teochew, Hakka and Hainanese. Subgroups in the Indian community are the Malayalees, Punjabis, Tamils and the Sikhs. Other minority groups are the Eurasians and Sinhalese. With the influx of migrant labourers over the last decade, about 1.75 million foreign labour were reportedly in the country in 1996, about million of them illegally. Of the 750,000 legal workers, 306,000 are Indonesians, 117,500 Bangladeshis, 32,500 Filipinos, 24,000 Thais, and 3,500 Pakistanis (the *Star*, 13 October 1996), most of them mainly clustered in the state of Selangor.

In view of the heterogeneity of Malaysia's population, the late Prime Minister Tun Abdul Razak wrote in 1969: 'If the events of May 13 are not to occur again, if this nation is to survive, we must make sure that subjects which are likely to engender racial tensions are not exploited by irresponsible opportunists. We can only guarantee this by placing such subjects beyond the reach of race demagogues' (Lent 1977:34).

In 1971, the government ruled that printing permits were to be issued under conditions that there would be no 'distortion of facts relating to public order incidents', and that 'presentation of facts related to public order incidents in Malaysia should not be in such a way as is likely to inflame or stir communal hostility' (Lent 1977:34). Amendments to the Sedition Act of 1948 at about the same time ruled that mass media may not, among other things, promote feelings of ill will and hostility between different races or classes of population and may not discuss the principles behind the four sensitive issues of Bahasa Malaysia language policy, special rights of the Bumiputeras, citizenship policy toward non-Bumiputeras, and the privileged position of the Sultans. The sensitive issues are also protected by the Federal Constitution (Part 3, Articles 152, 153 and 181). The race riot in 1969 was the watershed for the introduction of numerous government bodies to promote racial understanding, such as the National Goodwill Councils, Department of National Unity, and the National Consultative Council . A New Economic Policy (NEP) was also declared as the primary tool to restructure Malaysian society so that commercial and economic domination by one racial group will be eradicated.

Coercive legislation on how the media should carry out their responsibilities was also put in place. President of the Federation of Malaysian Consumers Association (FOMCA), Hamdan Adnan, listed 47 items of legislations which circumscribed what journalists can or cannot report (1988). However, the government deemed that coercive legislation alone would not help the country achieve its superordinate goals of national unity. A national ideology was needed. Called the Rukunegara, it conceptualises the kind of society that Malaysians should envisage and dedicate themselves to: achieving a greater unity of all her peoples; maintaining a democratic way of life; creating a just society in which the wealth of the nation shall be equitably shared; ensuring a liberal approach to her rich and diverse cultural traditions; and building a progressive society that shall be oriented to modern science and technology. To achieve these objectives, Malaysians are urged from primary school, to pledge themselves to the five principles of the Rukunegara: belief in God; loyalty to King and country; upholding the Constitution; upholding the rule of law; and building good behaviour and morality.

To date, scarcely can one locate any systematic studies that examine whether tenets of the Rukunegara have actually permeated through the fabric of Malaysian society. But what is commonly theorised is that the Rukunegara has provided the media with a salient ideological framework and philosophical foundation to work from, as is reflected in the Malaysian 'Canons of Journalism', which state that the Malaysian media:

1. Acknowledge their role in contributing to the process of nation-building.
2. Recognise their duty to contribute fully to the promotion of racial harmony and national unity.
3. Recognise communism, racialism and religious extremism as grave threats to national well-being and security.
4. Believe in a liberal, tolerant, democratic society and in the traditional role of a free and responsible press serving the people by faithfully reporting facts without fear or favour.
5. Believe that a credible press is an asset to the nation.
6. Believe in upholding standards of social morality.
7. Believe that there must be no restrictions on the entry of Malaysians into the (journalism) profession.
8. Believe that the press has a duty to contribute to the formation of public policy.

Malaysian media culture

The crash of the Malaysian ringgit early 1998, followed by public disaffections against Dr Mahathir's sacking of his deputy, Anwar Ibrahim, from his ministerial perch on 20 September 1998, led to some hard soul searching by Malaysian journalists regarding their 'peacemaking' function in times of political and economic uncertainties. Amid the political and economic uncertainties on the home front, the Malaysian government unashamedly resorted to direct the local media to 'talk up' the economy. The government's sentiment was that there is no room for those who are not team players.

By 30 September 1998, those who had 'resigned' from the team were two editors from the national dailies, one director of operations at TV3 and two top brass from the Central Bank. Media discussions on Anwar's sacking and the editors' resignation were restrained if not completely self-censored. The 'media clampdown' may not be new to foreign journalists who see their Malaysian counterparts as excessively intimidated by the government. Regardless, to Dr Mahathir Mohamad, the foreign media are 'a pack of liars' who have persistently portrayed him as anti-Western, authoritarian and 'recalcitrant' and his government as repressively nationalistic. With the occasional factual and contextual errors committed by foreign journalists reporting on Malaysian affairs, Dr Mahathir could be excused for his snide retorts.

Malaysia's fragile inter-ethnic and religious sensitivities amidst current political and economic uncertainties plaguing the home front have been cited to have vindicated the compliant nature of the local media. The *modus operandi* among Malaysian journalists is that they are there primarily to report on 'safe' issues to avoid inciting racial strife or propagating salacious promiscuity. This underpins two forms of self-censorship in the Malaysian context: salient censorship, in which information and images deemed offensive to public taste and morals are omitted; and proscribed censorship in which information that is not in line with governmental discourse is unthinkingly spiked by both newspapers and the electronic media alike, both of which have enjoyed steady growth since the last 'media clampdown' in 1987.

In 1995, there were an estimated 60 dailies and weeklies published regularly—22 in Chinese, 17 in the national language Bahasa Malaysia, 14 in English and fewer than 10 in Tamil. More than 250 magazines titles, mostly imported, are on public sale. The mix of newspapers has continued to advance. Chinese newspapers are now using more national news through their subscription to the national news agency, Bernama, which was established on 20 May 1968 as a statutory body. Compared to a few decades ago, when vernacular newspaper contents catered mainly to the competing claims and interests of respective racial groups, the newspapers now have a greater balance of news in terms of Chinese, Indian and Bumiputera interests.

Likewise, the Bahasa Malaysia newspapers have to cater to the broader interests of Chinese and Indians, since Bahasa Malaysia is widely spoken and read by the two ethnic groups. In this respect, Bernama has been instrumental in circulating what it considers to be 'national news' to foster a national identity among the Malaysian media. Bernama was 'corporatised' in January

1997, with the equity wholly owned by the Ministry of Finance. The agency will maintain its exclusive rights to receive news from foreign agencies for broadcast until 2007, when it will be privatised through a public float of shares (Bernama wire copy, 20 December 1995).

Malaysia's focus on the intregrative and development-oriented function of the mass media is often argued to be vindicated by the fragile racial relations in the country. The primary role of broadcast programs, according to the charter of Radio Televisyen Malaysia (RTM), is to promote national consciousness and racial harmony. Asmah (1985) notes that by using English, Bahasa Malaysia, Mandarin and Tamil, RTM operates to acquaint the public with all the cultures of the country. Development-oriented programs and multicultural programming are most noticeable around the school holidays and religious festivals. How far these programs have impacted on strengthening national unity is debatable. Although the bulk of each of these programs is kept in the national language to symbolise unity, renderings in Mandarin, English and Tamil are included.

Within this cultural context, Malaysian media academics (Sarji 1982; Lowe 1982; Syed Arabi 1986; Asmah 1985; Sankaran 1985; Adnan 1989) have suggested that the 'neo-colonialistic' paradigmatic perception of the Malaysian press system is theoretically misplaced. Embedded as they are in clearly defined historical, cultural, political and economic frameworks, Malaysian media practices can be understood from varied perspectives. The first is through the eyes of the law. The second is through the eyes of the government, which sees the media as a facilitator of national unity, national development, political stability and economic growth. The third is through the eyes of the journalists who, despite the legal and political parameters, believe they are able to carry out their public responsibilities 'unhindered'.

Self-censorship has been built into the Malaysian media production process through political bureaucrats continuing to contain the diversity of discourse and ideological positions on public issues, either through the invocation of the array of media laws, or surreptitiously through their close personal interaction with journalists. The communication pattern, reflective of the 'paternalistic' political structure, is characterised by a largely one-way flow of information from the leadership to the masses, with government information officers at various levels as gatekeepers. Thus, for many Malaysian journalists, the real threat does not come so much from professional sanctions but a learned cautiousness against expensive defamation suits, sackings, and unannounced arrests for any 'mishandling' of information. This learned apprehension is extended to the , as where critical information on 'sensitive issues' is generally withheld from the media.

It is not surprising then that Malaysian newspapers tend to offer their readers a daily diet of mainly business news and social features and ignore the more fundamental issues of environmental degradation, poverty, public corruption, public health, illegal immigration or the activities of opposition political parties. This format has led to a retired newspaper editor, Samad Ismail, to lament over the media's hesitation to test the limits of 'press freedom' compared to the 1960s and 70s, when journalists were detained without trial under the Internal Security Act[3] for alleged journalistic subversion. Samad, former editor of the *Straits Times* (now *New Straits Times*), was a detainee in the 1970s for his critical reporting of communal politics.

Likewise, group editor of the *New Straits Times*, Kadir Jasin, admitted that many Malaysian media practitioners today, being young and inexperienced, are unsure of the true limits of their freedom. He added that press freedom in Malaysia was determined by the business nature of the media industry, the multi-racial and multi-religious environment in which it operated, and the laws that had bearing on the media. 'Given these constraints, it can be said that the Malaysian press is relatively free. Any sign that it is not free is due partly to the reluctance of the Press itself to extend the envelope of freedom.' (*New Straits Times*, 21 November 1996).

The autonomy of the Malaysian press was viewed apprehensively in a survey conducted by Freedom House in Washington (The Economist 18–24 May 1996). It indicated that out of 32 countries, Malaysia was among the top five where the press was judged to be least free, after China, Indonesia, Turkey and Singapore. The survey gauged press freedom by assessing the impact of laws, administrative decisions and economic or political influences on the content of both print and broadcast media.[4] Commenting on the survey, Azman pointed out that beyond the predictable assessment, the Malaysian media should be judged not by Western standards but by the political parameters that Malaysian journalists have to work with. This parameter can be gleaned from Mahathir's speech at the World Press Convention in Kuala Lumpur in 1985. Often wary of foreign correspondents, Mahathir said:

---

[3] The Internal Security Act (ISA) of 1960 clearly states that taboo subjects to be avoided by the press are: criticisms of the position of the rulers; the privileged position of Bumiputeras, the status of Malay as the national language; and citizenship rights of non-Malays. Similar ISAs are also applied to the media in Singapore and Brunei. The taboo subjects are also covered variedly in the Sedition Act and Printing Presses and Publications Act.

[4] Countries scoring 0 to 30 in the numerical rating are reckoned to have a 'free' press; those scoring 31 to 60 have a 'partly free' press; those rated 61 to 100 have a 'not free' press. This produces some strange results: South Korea's press is supposedly 'freer' than India's far more unruly one. All the same, two-fifths of the world's population, the survey notes, live in the 58 countries in which the press is not free.

Just as they are right in saying that a government has no monopoly on
constructiveness and wisdom, the media must recognise that they too have no
monopoly on constructiveness and wisdom. Just as the public servant must be
prepared to accept criticism, so too must the media be prepared to accept
criticism. Just as government is not above the law, the media too are not above
the law. It simply will not do if a public is subject to the laws on state secrets
but in the name of freedom others are not...Just as the government cannot be
allowed to have the freedom to do exactly as it pleases in society, so too the
media cannot be allowed to do exactly as they please in society...so long as
the press is conscious of itself being a potential threat to democracy and
conscientiously limits the exercise of its rights, it should be allowed to function
without government interference. But when the press obviously abuses its
rights, then democratic governments have a duty to put it right.

Mahathir's explication is critical of the libertarian concept of the press
where it has cast upon itself the role of a 'watchdog' of governments on the
theoretical assumption that all governments are necessarily corrupt, and
therefore, must be kept in check. The consequence of this adversarial role,
from Mahathir's rationale and that of many Third World leaders, can only
lead the press to naturally focus their resources on unearthing contentious
issues while real development policy achievements are overlooked. As Idid
(1996:18) notes, the Malaysian media 'watchdog' is 'free to bark...so long as
it knows its role, and does not bite too hard, it is allowed to roam around the
compound of the house'.

Implicit in Mahathir's criticism are the theoretial concerns voiced by many
Third World governments. Why should the press always see contentious news
of government activities as 'investigative scoops' and news supportive of
government policies as 'government propaganda'? Is this contentious
journalistic operational framework the most effective mode to gather the news
and inform the people? Why should the press feel it must be a natural
adversary to the government? Why shouldn't the press work together with the
government for the common good? These questions hark back to the
partnership-in-development journalistic genre of the early 1960s, when
journalists Juan Mercado and Alan Chalkley floated the idea of 'development
journalism', which was vaguely defined then as a form of journalism that
deals with the process of development in developing countries. Asian scholars
from India (Chanchal Sarkar, Amithaba Chowdury, Pran Chopra, Narinder
Aggarwala, et al), the Philippines (Nora Quebral, Cesar Mercado, Juan
Mercado, Gloria Feliciano, Victor Valbuena, Juan Jamias, Crispin Maslog, et
al) and Indonesia (Mochtar Lubis, Jacob Oetama, Edward Sinaga, Abdul
Razak, et al) have contended that alternative conceptions of news are
necessary to reporting in an Asian (Malaysian) setting.

Despite the dichotomistic views of media practice by Malaysian media and their Western counterparts, their professional cultures do share the inherent characteristics of what makes news[5]. Human curiosity and demand for 'news' and information transcend culture and politics. Where Malaysian media and their Western counterparts do diverge are in their interpretation of their social, economic, political and cultural role in the society they are reporting for[6]. Western journalists will commonly articulate their operational values in terms of: 'we report the news as it's happening, we don't take sides, a good story—that's all that matters; we're independent, we let the facts speak for themselves, and we know what interests our audience'. While not disputing the market-oriented, altruistic democratic values of Western journalism, Malaysian journalists, and not least their Southeast Asian peers, have imbibed the value of using the press as a catalyst for education, economic growth and national development—a value not necessarily shared by journalists trained in the Western libertarian tradition.

As Lee Hsien Loong, Deputy Minister of Singapore, remarked at the Singapore Press Club in February 1988: 'You must educate Singaporeans—not just with facts, but also in terms of national education and values. One way or another, the press moulds the perceptions of Singaporeans. It should do so constructively—both supporting national campaigns and also day to day, in the way the news is presented, analysed, emphasised' (Birch 1993:20). Likewise, Lee Kuan Yew, after winning a libel case (together with Lee Hsien Loong and the Prime Minister, Goh Chok Tong) against the International Herald Tribune in early August 1995 said that press freedom in the Western tradition was not only unwelcome but was also responsible for the decline of Western countries, namely the United States. He said: 'I have explained to American correspondents that perhaps one of the problems that America faces, one of the problems that political leaders in America face is that their credibility is destroyed by scurrilous (media) allegations, which do not have to be proved...say we do not subscribe to that system' (*Time* 7 August 1995:43).

---

[5] One of the most succinct explanations of news values is by Johan Galtung and Mari Ruge (1973). They said that events would be more likely to be covered if they fulfil any of the following criteria: Frequency, amplitude (the bigger the better, the more dramatic); unambiguity (the more clear-cut, uncomplicated the events, the more they'll be reported); familiarity (that which is ethnocentric, of cultural proximity, relevant); correspondence (the degree the events meet our expectations, predictions, consonance); surprise; continuity (that which already has hit the headlines, news peg); composition (the need for a balance in a news-spread leads the editor to feed in contrasting elements—some home news if the predominant stories have been foreign; a little good news if the news has generally been gloomy).

[6] For a glimpse into one of several studies on a cross-cultural interpretation of news values, see Masterton (1992).

As far as taking a more assertive role in their interactions with the government is concerned, Malaysian journalists would generally defer to the indirect and allusive style of criticism rather than the direct confrontational streak. Azman alluded that Malaysian journalists, for instance, differ from their Western peers in that the former knows when to throw its punches and when to pull them back. This throw-and-pull momentum marks a unique Malaysian approach to reporting and writing in-between the lines. Journalists depend on the readers' ability to read beyond the text. Since the press is ambiguously regarded as a 'partner' in national development, it is assumed that journalists do not only report and interpret the facts but also promote them to the readers and help the government open the public's eyes to possible solutions to problems facing the country—an antithesis to the Western tradition of dispassionate reporting. It may be overly simplistic to attribute the style of Malaysian journalists as a culturally determined. In view of the coercive controls on the media, it is hard to see how Malaysian journalists could have operated otherwise. For instance, one of the new signs of increasing restraints on Malaysian journalists is the compulsory issuing of press cards to both national and foreign journalists by the Minister of Information, Mohamad Rahmat, since January 1993. Requests for a press card, which is valid for only a year, should be made to the police. Temporary permits are given to special correspondents sent to cover specific events. Rahmat explained that the new measure was to reinforce security after government investigations into the media revealed 'the possible existence of pressure groups whose aim is to use the media to weaken the government' (RSF 1994:25).

Working definition of Malaysian journalism

A working definition of Malaysian journalism can start at its variance from Western liberal tradition—that is, the former is guardedly contentious, constructively adversarial and critically supportive. Journalism in Malaysia, as qualified by Mahathir, should be constructive, consensual and development-oriented. Mahathir's perception diverges from that of his former deputy, Anwar Ibrahim. Speaking to an assembly of the Confederation of ASEAN journalists in Kuala Lumpur on 20 March 1996, Anwar reminded journalists that they should serve as a 'vehicle for the contest of ideas and cultivate good taste...Asian societies are at a state of development where they are in greater need for a vigorous journalism. We still have to root out corruption and abuses of power in its many forms'. He continued to criticise, although in covert terms, the country's media laws and the nebulous notion of 'Asian values', as promulgated by Singapore's Senior Minister, Lee Kuan Yew, as an excuse for the government's authoritarian excess and limitations on press freedom.

Anwar was an activist student leader once detained under the Internal Security Act for 22 months in 1974 for leading student protests in the state of Kedah against corruption and abuse of power in the government. Journalists do anticipate a watering down of existing government controls over the media if Anwar ever becomes Prime Minister. In an interview with *Time* Australia (10 June 1996), albeit before his 1999 trial and imprisonment, Anwar said:

> I have a minority view [about press freedom] here [in Malaysia]. My principle is an informed citizenry is a responsible citizenry. We want a responsible citizenry, so there must be respect for the freedom of the press...I reject the notion that a free press is alien to Asian society. All the great sages of the past were great because they were able to write and publish freely. All our great freedom fighters...were able to be great because they believed in freedom and they were able to use the media to articulate their positions.

Whether the Malaysian media have actually served as a 'vehicle for the contest of ideas' or will move towards 'a vigorous journalism' is hard to gauge from past and current trends. An instance of tempered reporting is reflected in the media coverage of the dire straits of Perwaja Steel, a joint Japanese–Malaysian venture established by Mahathir in 1985 as part of his 'Look East' industrialisation plan. In 1987–95, the company ran up an operating loss of more than US$2 billion. As the Finance Ministry indirectly owns about 80% of the company, Anwar, then the Minister of Finance, had ordered a full audited report of the company. However, in-depth media analyses of Perwaja Steel's operations were conspicuously lacking.

As Perwaja Steel is a state-owned company, media access to detailed documentations on the company are protected by the Official Secrets Act (OSA)[7]. The Act defines that any information entrusted to a public official in confidence by another official is 'secret', which effectively covers all government activities. Thus, the loan scandals of Bumiputra Malaysia Finance (BMF) in Hong Kong and Bank Rakyat in Malaysia in the late 1970s were prevented from media scrutiny. The scandals remain, until today, a matter of intellectual conjecture among journalists and the educated citizenry who tend to rely on foreign publications, and lately the Internet, for alternative information, such as that available from 'malaysianet' (www.malaysia.net), a forum group administered from Sydney, and an independent site (www.geocities.com/CapitolHill/3939) established by the main Opposition

---

[7] The Malaysian Official Secrets Act is modelled on the British Official Secrets Act 1911. In March 1986, after a series of media exposes of financial scandals and political crises among Mahathir's cabinet ministers, the government moved to amend the definition of an 'official secret'. The amendment removed the judicial review of what constituted an 'official secret' and imposed mandatory imprisonment in the event of conviction.

party, Democratic Action Party[8] DAP leader, Lim Kit Siang, remarked in Parliament on 27 March 1984:

> It is a sad commentary on the state of press freedom in Malaysia that Malaysians have come to expect and depend on foreign publications and magazines for information and news about Malaysia. Thus, the first press to break the story of the BMF scandal was the Asian Wall Street Journal, which carried several articles of expose of the BMF dealings reeking with impropriety as far back as the end of 1982, but which were ignored by the local press. (Lim 1986:140)

While the extent of self-censorship by the local media is not documented in systematic studies, anecdotal evidence of the banning of foreign publications in Malaysia does provide a perceptual framework . The *Far Eastern Economic Review*, *Asian Wall Street Journal* and *Asiaweek* have records of being banned in Malaysia for reporting critically on the government using 'unauthorised' information. In 1987, three national newspapers—the English-language tabloid the *Star*, the Chinese language broadsheet *Sin Chew Jit Poh* and the Malay-language biweekly tabloid *Watan*—were banned for their 'vigorous' reporting on racial issues implicit in the political conflict between UMNO and MCA. In June 1994, Thootan, a national Tamil biweekly magazine, had its publication licence withdrawn for publishing reports on a stock market scandal involving the national company Maika-Telekom. Maika is an investment arm of the Malaysian Indian Congress (MIC), which is part of the ruling party.

Besides the OSA, Malaysian journalists are also oriented to exercise dubious self-censorship by the Printing Presses and Publications Act 1984, which empowers the Minister of Home Affairs, who is also the Prime Minister, to revoke or suspend a printing or publishing licence if he is 'satisfied that any printing press is used for printing any matter which is prejudicial to public order, morality, security, pulic interest or national interest'.[9] This Act requires a media operator to apply for a new publishing

---

[8] The DAP home page mission statement reads: 'Malaysia is building a MultiMedia Super Corridor (MSC) to take a quantum leap into the Information Age. Our communications policy however still belongs to the Pre-IT era—where newspapers, radio and television remain highly-regulated and alternative Malaysian voices cannot be heard in the official buzz. Let us open up the Malaysian space. This site is one such effort. Read what Parliamentary Opposition Leader, Mr Lim Kit Siang, has to say about the Malaysian situation'. The site contains the media releases of Lim, which are not normally published in the local papers. Alternative sites on Malaysia have reduced the significance of press freedom, as issues once considered to be taboo by the local media are becoming more difficult for the government to monitor on the internet.

[9] The Print Presses Act was first enacted in July 1948, a month after the armed insurrection of the Malayan Communist Party, as part of the armoury of extraordinary powers the colonial government assumed to deal with an extraordinary situation following the declaration of the first Emergency in June 1948. At the same time, the Sedition Act was also passed. The struggle

permit every year. An appendage to the Act is the need by publishers of newspapers, magazines, journals and periodicals to apply for a permit or licence from the Home Affairs Ministry (KDN), which could be issued for a period of one year or less. Experienced journalists know that when publications approach the dates of renewing their KDNs, they are particularly cautious in their reporting.

Media commercialism and political alignment

Government 'control' of the electronic media is built into the system where the Information Minister alone decides who can own a broadcasting station, and the type of television service suitable for the Malaysian public vis-a-vis the Broadcasting Act of 1988. The Act was originally legislated to prevent the 'commercialisation' of the broadcasting industry. But since the government's 'deregulation' of the media industry in the mid-1980s, commercialism has been penetrating Malaysian living rooms via two public broadcast channels (TV1 and TV2), two free-to-air private commercial stations (TV3 and MetroVision TV4), five cable channels (Mega TV) and another 22 satellite television and eight digital radio channels by ASTRO (All Asia TV and Radio Company), which is owned by the Malaysia East Asia Satellite (MEASAT) Broadcast Network Systems. The 'deregulation' is part of a privatisation drive under the concept of Malaysia Incorporated, an initiative of Mahathir's driven by his dissatisfaction with public enterprises, which he believes are unprofitable and inefficient, and indirectly, as a means to improve the Bumiputeras' position in the commercial sector.

Sistem Televisyen Malaysia Berhad (STMB), which has operated TV3 since June 1984, and Mega TV, have broken the state monopoly on television broadcasting once exclusively dominated by RTM. Others have joined the competition since then: the second commercial station, MetroVision (TV4), and the country's first cable television service, Mega TV, which came on stream in November 1995. Mega TV now carries five channels: sports programs (ESPN), documentaries (Discovery Channel), international news (CNN), cartoons (Cartoon Network) and movies (HBO). The country's first satellite pay-TV, ASTRO, beams from its Asia Broadcast Centre in Kuala Lumpur into a potential market of 30 million living rooms in Southeast Asia

---

during the Malayan Union days and the question of citizenship rights of non-Malays, who were mainly contract workers, were among the issues highlighted in the newspapers then. Clause 7 (1) of the Printing Presses and Publications Act 1984 empowers the Minister of Information 'if satisfied that any publication is in any manner prejudicial to or likely to be prejudicial to public order, morality, security, the relationship with any foreign country or government, or which is or is likely to be contrary to any law or is otherwise prejudicial to or is likely to be prejudicial to public interest or national interest' he may in his absolute discretion prohibit it with or without conditions.

and the northern part of Australia. Information Minister, Mohamed Rahmat was reported as saying that ASTRO will beam programs direct to users almost at real time without any censorship of its contents 'because the programs would be merely concerned with news, sports and entertainment' (Bernama wire copy, 11 March 1996). However, Rahmat later issued several warnings to Mega TV that its licence would be cancelled if it did not conform with the government's anti-VHC policy (violence, horror and counter-culture) (the *Star* 16 October 1996).

The galloping growth of broadcasting stations in Malaysia had been noted as directly related to the government's policy of privatisation of what were once regarded as public services. Media academic, Zaharom Naim posits:

> The (deregulation) option is often simplistically assumed to be between state-controlled media and the market, the latter being seen as preferable based on the naive notion that the logic of the market will inevitably lead to plurality of choice, freedom and independence. This, unfortunately, has turned out to be untrue...The government's privatisation policy has undoubtedly resulted in greater commercialisation of television which has resulted in more [of the same] being offered. This has happened not by accident, but as part of the government's strategy...the supposed liberalisation has not really resulted in a loosening of government control over television, contrary to the initial beliefs of many. The reverse in fact has happened. Over the past decade, the main forms of control over the media—legal, political and economic—have certainly been tightened. (Naim 1996:4)

The controlled deregulation of the broadcasting industry in Malaysia has been termed by Malaysian media researchers as 'regulated deregulation' or 're-regulation' (Naim 1993; Khor 1994; Noor 1996). The recent reconfiguration of the structure of the industry has the Ministry of Information revising the Broadcasting Act, allowing for the receipt of direct to user (DTU) broadcast. The Act, which was amended in October 1996, allows Malaysians to subscribe to parabolic satellite dishes and decoder equipment capable of picking up only the digital signals from MEASAT Broadcast's transponders. This means that satellite broadcasters other than ASTRO will be barred from the industry. The political culture that allows the state to dispense patronage through deregulation of broadcasting has been known to benefit politically connected organisations and individuals who dominate the new media infrastructure.

Commercialisation of the media industry has also effectively created a community of infotainment-rich Malaysians in the urban areas, which prompted Mahathir in September 1995 to urge the media to provide equitable access to information for the people, the majority of whom are still living in the rural sectors. Currently, for every 100 Malaysians, there are only 14.7 telephone lines and 23 television sets, compared with 47.3 telephone lines and

38 television sets for every 100 Singaporeans (ITU World Teleconsortium Indicator 1994). Journalists attending a workshop on rural reporting in Kuala Trengganu on 30 May 1996 were also reminded that while they continue to extol the benefits of digital information technology and the internet, they run the risk of neglecting their readers in the villages, some of whom do not even have access to a telephone line or basic electricity supply. Herein lies the paradox of developments in the Malaysian media industry. While the media are accepted as instrumental in fostering 'community and national development', politicians and a privileged group of Bumiputera media executives, through their controlling interests in both the newspapers and television stations, also perceive the communication industry as a politically and economically lucrative enterprise.

In economic terms, as of 1995 the government appears to have its indirect 'control' well targetted in the electronic media industry through a consortium, Cableview Services, of which 40% is owned by STMB and 30% by the Ministry of Finance. Sri Utara, a wholly-owned subsidary of Maika Holdings (an investment arm of the Malaysian Indian Congress, which is part of the coalition government) owns 5% share (according to 1995 figures). As of 1994, the managing director of TV3, the group editor of *New Straits Times* (NST)' and two other investors, through a management buy-out, control half of the equity in TV3 and the NST Press. NST Press in turn has about 25 subsidiary companies ranging from magazine publishing to advertising, communications and insurance. Fleet Group, an investment arm of the ruling United Malay National Organisation (UMNO), holds 30% of Metro Vision. The *Star* is now a public listed company—the major shareholder is Huaren, an investment arm of the Malaysian Chinese Association, a component of the coalition government. The *Sun* is backed financially by the Berjaya Group, which has established investments in digital technology, satellite communications and property development.[10] Tamil newspapers are controlled by private interests affiliated with the Malaysian Indian Congress, part of the ruling coalition party.

---

[10] On 22 October 1994, chief executive of Berjaya Group, Vincent Tan, was awarded RM10 million (US$3.8m) by the High Court in his defamation suit against three journalists, the publisher and the printer of the monthly *Malaysian Industry*. The suit was over four articles in the August and October issues alleging that Tan had used the daily, the *Sun*, which he partly owns, for his own interests. The articles accused Tan of plotting to secretly sell shares of the company Berjaya Textile to another firm. The judge ruled that the articles were written for the express purpose of tarnishing the personal and professional reputation of Tan. As printers are also held responsible for libel under Malaysian law, the judgement has set a hard precedent for investigative reporting and imposed further restraints on printers to accept publications that delve into sensitive issues.

Badaruddin (1996) noted that with the ascent of converging media technology, cable and satellite broadcasting, Malaysian mass media have practically shifted from their traditional role of being a tool of national development and unity to that of a channel for the ruling elites to dispense patronage to politically-connected local entrepreneurs. Also, by rapidly developing nation-based satellite and cable systems and accommodating private political affiliates, the state has maintained an element of indirect control in the national broadcasting systems.

In view of the cross-media ownership demographics, political oppositionists have consistently questioned the ideological balance of the Malaysian media. A study of the media coverage of the Malaysian 1995 general elections by the social reform movement, Aliran, concluded that the opposition parties were severely handicapped in getting their messages across to the public through the media. For instance, the ruling National Front coalition had its manifesto printed in English in full by *New Strait Times*, and in Malay in the national broadsheet, *Berita Harian*. Attempts by the opposition parties to buy advertising space for their manifestoes to be printed in full were not even accepted. Aliran indicated that the National Front had no problem in getting the mainstream dailies to carry full-page advertisements on consecutive pages, ridiculing the opposition and extolling its own leadership.

Hamdan Adnan acknowledges that developments in the current media ownership pattern are 'not proper', but readily points out that the real issue is whether 'the person uses that power or leverage for interest of the public, for one's interest or for his master's interest'[11]. He adds that, ironically, this de facto ownership has led to greater confidence in the media today to openly challenge the official discourse without any harsh legal or financial repercussions. But mechanisms to enable new players to enter the cautiously autonomous, pro-government media industry to nurture an 'informed citizenry through a contest of ideas' remain elusive.

Conclusion

Beyond the subtle controls inherent in the media production process, political and economic forces across cultural boundaries have their own ways of protecting themselves from negative depictions in the media. The business elite, the bureaucrat and the politician in every society will attempt to dominate the media discourse to ensure their own legitimacy and public image. Journalists in any political system will always try to work to appeal to their peers, their readers, their pay masters and the authorities. While 'control' and 'direction' of media contents in the Western world are couched in more

---

[11] (Personal interview, Petaling Jaya, 31 May 1996)

socially and politically acceptable terms, in Malaysia they are articulated more bluntly through the outright cancellation or withholding of publishing and printing permits, and occasional detention of journalists without trials when they are a 'threat to national security'.

Clearly, the forms of control of the media are basically defined by different national, historical and cultural experiences; the level of public expectations, the ability of the media to fulfil these expectations; the leadership's perception of its own legitimacy; and the goals of the dominant ideology. Mahathir has pronounced, since he became Prime Minister in July 1981, that his political leadership is committed to an ideology of social change—thus his 'Malaysia 2020 Vision'. An appendage to this ideology is Mahathir's conviction that the media are the central loci of social change and thus should be used to mobilise the nation towards this vision by 2020. While governments in Western democracy do not overtly engage in directing and controlling the media contents or media ownership, the potential and mechanisms for coercive measures have always existed. The emphasis in the West is on informal restraints and suggestions by appeals to altruistic values or, at the worst, through threats of expensive defamation suits, withholding of critical information, refusal to co-operate, and withdrawal of advertising and funding support. The difference is that political interference in Western media contents is more understated than, for instance, in Malaysia.

The fact is government and media, be they in Australia or Malaysia, will not always see eye to eye on every issue. By nature, democratically elected governments expect their constituents and media to support their policies. However, journalists are by nature harsh critics. Whether democracy is better served by an adversarial press or a 'consensus-driven' press is a matter of cultural perspective. As Mahathir said at the United Nations in New York in 1993:

> Freedom does not mean only to be free to criticise and attack the government, but also freedom to support the government...there is a view that if a newspaper supports the government, it is a sign that it is not free. On the contrary, if a newspaper attacks the government, it is regarded as free, never mind if the attack is made out of fear of forces outside the government, or out of fear that the newspaper might not sell. In fact, such a newspaper is not free. (cited in Maidin 1994:204)

Mahathir sees the media as an information industry, where profits are maximised in the name of freedom and the public interest. If this industry is not regulated, he believes, it will become more influential and powerful than the elected government of the day, and will wield its influence on behalf of a particular group or even on behalf of the editors themselves. Mahathir's long held view is now becoming a reality in the West, where many are beginning to realise that the media have indirect control of the government, and behind them are the press barons, who need not necessarily be citizens of the country. To Mahathir, the age when journalists own newspapers and become heroes in the eyes of the public is over. The open challenge now is whether the government controls the media, or vice versa (Maidin 1994).

Malaysian journalists have never assumed their roles to be necessarily adversarial or co-operative. relationship between the press and government is seen to be in constant flux. Paradoxically, this fluctuating relationship is seen to be ambiguous to reflect its independence—sometimes diplomatically contentious, sometimes critically supportive. The relationship between the Malaysian media and government is clearly prescribed in terms that are born from historical and political necessity. Discrepancies between the Malaysian journalists' ethical codes and their actual behaviour are, thus, not so much a question of media impotence as often perceived by Western critics. It is more a case of Malaysian journalists carrying out their civic responsibilities within the cultural context of dynamic growth in a modernised, multi-racial society.

References

Abdul Razak 1985, *Press laws and systems in ASEAN states*, Jakarta.

A Course Guide in Development Journalism 1983, Asian Institute of Journalism, Manila, (unpublished).

Adnan, Hamdan 1988, 'Communication and the law in Malaysia', background paper for workshop on 'Law for Journalists', Mara Institute of Technology, Shah Alam, Malaysia, 15–17 March.

—— 1989, 'Mass media and reporting of Islamic affairs', *Media Asia*, Vol 16, No 2.

AMCB (Asian Mass Communication Bulletin - Singapore) 1988, Final report on consultation on press systems in ASEAN, No 9, September–October.

Asmah, H O 1985, 'Mass communication and its effect on education and traditional culture in Malaysia', *Media Asia* No 12.

Badarrudin, Noor 1996, 'More market, less State?: Television deregulation, program content and audience in Malaysia', paper delivered at the Communication.

Chalkley, Alan 1979, *Encounters—Journalists meet professionals about the coverage of development and population by the Asian press*, Press Foundations of Asia, Manila.

Chopra, Pran 1980, *Asian news values: A barrier or a bridge?*, UNESCO Paper No 85.

Chu, Godwin 1986, 'In search of an Asian perspective of communication theory', *Media Asia*, Vol 13 No 1.

Dissanayake, W 1986, 'The need for the study of Asian approaches to communication', Media Asia, Vol 13 No 1.

Galtung, Johan and Ruge, Mari 1973, 'Structuring and selecting news' in Cohen, S and Young, J (eds), *The manufacture of news*, Constable, UK.

Idid, Syed Arabi 1993, *Press systems in ASEAN states*, AMIC, Singapore, (2nd ed).

—— 1996, 'Press freedom and responsibility in a developing society', unpublished paper delivered at seminar on Press Freedom and Responsibility, AMIC, Kuala Lumpur, 16–18 May.

Independent 1994, London, 29 February.

Khor, Yoke Lin 1994, 'De-regulation or re-regulation of the Malaysian broadcasting industry?' unpublished paper, annual conference of International Communication Conference, Sydney, July.

Lee, Hsien Loong 1993, quoted in Birch, David, *The Singapore media—communication strategies and practices*, Asian Paper No 1, Longman Cheshire, Melbourne.

Lee, Kuan Yew 1995, 'The price of freedom', *Time*, 7 August.

Lent, John 1990, 'The development of multicultural stability in ASEAN: the role of mass media', *Journal of Asian Pacific Communication*, Vol 1 No 1.

Lim, Kit Siang 1986, 'Press freedom in Malaysia' in *Malaysia: crisis of identity*, Democratic Action Party, Petaling Jaya, Malaysia.

Loo, Eric and Hirst, Martin 1995, 'Recalcitrant or keras kepala: A cross-cultural study of how the Australian and Malaysian press covered the Keating–Mahathir spat', *Media Information Australia* No77, August.

Lowe, Vincent and Kamin, Jaafar 1982, *TV programme management in a plural society*, AMIC, Singapore.

Maidin, Zainuddin 1994, *The other side of Mahathir*, Utusan Publications, Kuala Lumpur.

Masterton, Murray 1992, 'A new approach to what makes news', *Australian Journalism Review*, Vol 14 No 1, January–June.

Merrill, John C 1979, in Lent, John, *Third World mass media: issues, theory and research*, Third World Series.

—— 1974, *The imperative of freedom: a philosophy of journalistic autonomy*, Hastings House, New York.

Naim, Zaharom 1996, 'Commercialisation with a conscience: restoring the credibility of the Malaysian media', *Aliran*, Vol 16 No 2.

Reporters Sans Frontieres 1995 Report (RSF), John Libbey & Co, London.

Sankaran, R 1985, 'The role of communication in a plural society', *Negara*, July.

Sarji, Asiah 1982, 'The historical development of broadcasting in Malaysia and its social and political significance', *Media Asia* No 9.

Sinaga, Edward 1988, *The Pancasila press system*, Bali Booklet.

Sutopo, Ishadi 1983, *Development news in Indonesian dailies*, AMIC Occasional Paper 15, Singapore.

Yeap, Soon Beng 1994, 'The emergence of an Asian-centred perspective: Singapore's media regionalisation strategies', *Media Asia* Vol 21 No 2.

Contemporary Malaysian national culture and foreign relations with Australia

Adam Schofield

Introduction

Australia over the past decade has been involved in a series of incidents with Malaysia that have caused severe diplomatic tensions. These diplomatic ruptures have often seemed intemperate, involving apparently exaggerated responses, and have appeared capable of resulting in large-scale dislocation to other aspects of the relationship between the two countries. By and large, however, these incidents have left unaffected economic and defence ties. Although there has been a great deal of analysis of these incidents by a number of authors, the reasons for Australia's continuing difficulties in relating harmoniously with Malaysia do not appear complete. Kessler, Camroux and particularly Crouch (1991a; 1991b; 1992; 1993; 1994a; 1994b) have written extensively on Malaysian–Australian interaction. Crouch has covered authoritarianism in Malaysia (1992), diplomatic, economic, security and educational relationships (1994a) and industrialisation and political change (1994b). Kessler (1991) considers the 'cultural' difference between Australia and Malaysia, while Camroux (1994) considers Malaysia's recent political history from three different theoretical approaches.

The difficulties in the Australian relationship with Malaysia are quite a new phenomenon:in the 20 year period following Malaysian independence, Australia's leadership communicated easily with Malaysia's British-educated, English-speaking leaders (Crouch 1994a:195; Kessler 1992:149). The Malaysian leaders were committed to the preservation of English institutions, particularly a pluralistic, democratic Westminster system of government, and a world outlook illustrated by its full and active membership of the British Commonwealth (Crouch 1992:21; Andaya and Andaya 1982:266–268; Stubbs 1990:102).

The first important change in government policy occurred after the 1969 election. The indigenous Malays saw a real prospect of losing control of government after this election and a race riot ensued. The government responded by introducing new economic and social policies to secure the Malays' position in Malaysia (Andaya and Andaya 1982:280; Crouch 1994b:15). These changes had no significant effect on Malaysia–Australian relations. The change in these relations over the last decade has coincided with the rise of a new Malaysian leadership. This leadership, which has a pan-Islamic outlook, has severely downgraded its Commonwealth ties, become a leader of the Non-Aligned Movement and has driven the parliamentary institutions of Malaysia to generate a government, bureaucracy and an economy that is strongly biased towards the indigenous Malays to an extent that is out of all proportion to their numbers in the society (Crouch 1991:23; Andaya and Andaya 1982:282; Khoo Kay Jin 1992:50). The new direction in Malaysia is dominated by the personalith of Dr Mahathir bin Mohamad, who became Prime Minister in 1981.[1] Mahathir argued his notion of the 'problem' of the Malays in his book *The Malay Dilemma* (Mahathir 1970). He is widely seen as having made concerted and sustained efforts to develop Malaysia into a modern, industrial exporting economy and to modify its colonial British 'culture' with a Malay-dominated 'culture' (Khoo Kay Jin 1992). Fundamental to this change is the promotion of a 'traditional' Malay 'culture' and 'Islam' at the expense not only of the inherited British 'culture' but also of the 'ethnic culture' of the Chinese and Indians who constitute significant proportions of modern Malaysian society.[2]

The parallel development of a 'Western' modern industrial state with a reconstituted 'traditional' Malay 'culture' during the last decade has led to complex difficulties for the Malaysian leadership. The problem has been to manage the domestic rejection of 'Western business culture' and 'Western' media products while at the same time embracing 'Western' modern industrialisation, education and economic norms. How an understanding of these pressures and their inherent difficulties can illuminate the background to Australia's diplomatic problems with the Malaysian leadership, particularly under Dr Mahathir, is a focus of this article.

As the character and outlook of the Malaysian leadership changed, so did its assessment and representation of Australia. In the years following Malaysian independence, Australia was a fellow member of the Commonwealth, an ally who had provided troops to fight the Communist insurgents in the early 1950s[3] and strongly sided with Malaysia against its closer and bigger Indonesian neighbour during Confrontation in the 1960s (Crouch 1994a:206; Camroux 1994:25). In 1971 Australia (together with New Zealand, the United Kingdom, Singapore and Malaysia) joined as a full member of the Five Power Defence Arrangement contributing two fighter

---

[1] Mahathir bin Mohamad was the first Malaysian prime minister who was not of royal birth. Unlike previous prime ministers his entire education was received on the Malay Peninsular. He began his career as a medical officer in the Malay provinces (Current Biography Yearbook 1988:348).

[2] The population of peninsular Malaysia in 1985 was 59% Malay and indigenous inhabitants, 32% Chinese and 9% Indian (Crouch 1994a:196).

[3] Before this, during the Second World War, two Australian Army divisions helped defend the Malay peninsula from the Japanese.

squadrons stationed at Butterworth in Malaysia.[4] In the 1990's, however, Mahathir's administration has projected quite a different view of Australia:that it is part of a United States 'Western'-dominated 'culture', disseminating values that are opposed to the new Malaysia, and that it is hedonistic, anarchical, anti-Muslim and, worse, that Australian criticism of the structure of the new Malaysian State assumes that 'Western' democracy and a 'free' media are self-evidently the best forms for all countries regardless of their state of development (Camroux 1994). The current Australia–Malaysia relationship is, however, more subtle than this statement would suggest, in that during all the recent diplomatic dislocations, the defence/security relations have been unaffected and in fact have even shown some recent increase in activity.[5] Following former Prime Minister Keating's use of the term 'recalcitrant' to describe Dr Mahathir, the Malaysian Defence Minister, Datuk Najib, stated his long-term commitment to Defence co-operation with Australia (Crouch 1994a:201).

Some concurrent dislocation in the economic relationship between Australia and Malaysia resulting from these diplomatic incidents has taken place, but only to a limited extent, and in each case a diplomatic solution has been found before real damage has occurred (Crouch 1994a; Stubbs 1990). During the deepest and most prolonged incident, over the *Embassy* television series, there is evidence that economic relations were affected only to a minor extent.[6] Overall trade between the two nations has grown rapidly in the past decade.[7] In terms of investment Australia in 1992 was the fourth largest investor in Malaysia (Camroux 1994:44).

---

[4] The Five Power Defence Arrangement grew out of the Anglo–Malaysian Defence Agreement. In 1988, after a successful exercise, Singapore and Malaysia noted that it was an effective regional defence alliance. Earlier, its usefulness and efficiency had been publicly doubted (Methven 1992:114).

[5] In 1993 Australian ships and aircraft contributed to a maritime exercise and Malaysian soldiers exercised together at battalion strength. In addition a P3 Orion aircraft is based at Butterworth with an army rifle company and regular visits of Australian F18 Hornet squadrons are also made to Butterworth (Crouch 1994a).

[6] Gareth Evans, former Australian Minister for Foreign Affairs, has frequently stated that active trade and defence relations between countries provide 'ballast' to the relationship, which helps them ride out diplomatic storms. Evans has noted the steadying effect of trade and defence links in these periods of diplomatic stress with Malaysia (Crouch 1994a).

[7] Australia's exports to Malaysia averaged 14.4% growth per year in the four years after 1989. Malaysia's exports to Australia increased at an average rate of 11% during the same period (Crouch 1994a). Trade between the two countries was AU$2.1 billion in 1993 (*Australian Financial Review* 1993).

The maintenance of defence, economic and associated ties[8] throughout a series of diplomatic incidents stretching over nearly a decade suggests that Mahathir has been careful to keep relations between the two countries that are useful to Malaysia's wellbeing isolated from these disputes. It is proposed here that Mahathir is using his public arguments with Australia, at least in part, for domestic political purposes. In his attacks on Australia he demonstrates to his electorate the worst aspects of 'Western culture', their dominance through the 'international' media and, by implication, reinforces the virtues of 'Malaysian/Malay culture', 'Islamic' virtue and the benefits/necessity of the Mahathir style 'democracy'. 'In Australia, press freedom stretches beyond normal freedom whereby the press are free to come up with all sorts of lies', Mahathir quoted in the *Indonesian Observer*, 29 July 1991.

> Mahathir...dismissing what he considers the decadence of Western civilisation writes:'It is possible for Asia to create a cultural region of unmatched historical greatness...we will never come under European dominance again'. Mahathir attacks Christianity as the basis of the West's 'racist' attitude towards Asia and argues that Islam is a 'tolerant' religion by comparison. (Review of the book *The Asia That Can Say No* by Mahathir et al in *Time* 1994:54)

Mahathir appears to gain in domestic status by standing up to Western nations (such as Australia) and criticising their values from an Asian perspective. 'In the Kampongs the Malays are grinning like Cheshire Cats...they reckon Mahathir has brought the Colonial blighters to their knees' (Kuala Lumpur resident quoted in *Time Magazine*, 5 August 1991 in an article discussing Australia's apology to Mahathir that ended the *Embassy* affair).

The incidents that have led to Australian–Malaysian dislocations cover a wide range of issues. It is important to note that they were all, initiated by Australians (but strongly picked up by Mahathir) and contained a 'moral' or 'cultural' criticism of Malaysia. The first incident in 1986 involved the then Australian Prime Minister Robert Hawke's characterising the act of hanging two Australian drug smugglers as 'barbaric'. Mahathir took this to imply that Australia regarded Malaysian society as 'barbaric' compared with the more developed, 'moral' 'West' (*New Straits Times* 1986; *Age* 1991g; 1991h; 1991j; *Time* 1991a; 1991b; 1991c). The second incident in 1987 concerned the arrest of opposition parliamentarians and activists under the Malaysian

---

[8] A little-realised tie between Australia and Malaysia is that Malaysians form the largest group of Asians living in Australia, as at August 1991 (Shamsul 1992, quoting a Bureau of Immigration Research publication). Another strong link is that over the past twenty years Malaysian students studying in Australia ranged up to 60% of the total number of foreign students in Australia. Currently there are also more than 3,000 Malaysians enrolled in Malaysian campuses of Australia–Malaysia University twinning programs (Healy 1992).

Internal Security Act (Crouch 1992, Camroux 1994:42) which was seen by Australian parliamentarians[9] as a clear divergence from 'Western' democratic principles (*Australian* 1990; 1991; *Age* 1991a; 1991d; 1991f; 1991i; 1992). The next incident involved Australian 'greenies' protesting with other Westerners in Sarawak and advocating economic boycotts against Malaysian logging of rainforest timbers, which, they claimed, caused great ecological damage. Mahathir rejected the moral tone of the criticism, responding that if the 'Western' world wanted to save the rainforest it should be prepared to make economic concessions/contributions to its maintenance.

> It is illogical for them [Western environmentalists] to accuse developing countries such as Indonesia and Malaysia of destroying tropical forests and thus creating environmental damage. On the contrary, fast growing industries in advancing countries are the ones polluting the environment' Malaysia's Minister for Industry, Data Lim Keng Yaik (*Age* 1989).

Camroux (1994:42) quotes Dr Mahathir as saying that the Westerners displayed 'a superiority complex...imperialism is not dead' (*Age* 1989; 1991a; 1991h; 1991l; 1991m; 1992; *Time* 1991c). The longest and deepest problem, however, was caused by the Australian Broadcasting Corporation's (ABC) 1990s series *Embassy*, which was taken by Mahathir as a disguised, distorted, biased but recognisable portrayal of Malaysia. The fact that it was produced by the Australian government-owned and funded television network was taken to show direct involvement by the Australian government (*Age* 1990; 1991b; 1991c; 1991e; 1991g; 1991j; 1991k; 1991l; *Time* 1991b; 1991c). Later, a film made of the novel *Turtle Beach*, which contained similar material, was disowned by the Australian government[10] and subsequently did not become a diplomatic issue (Crouch 1994a; Camroux 1994:43; *Age* 1991l). When former Prime Minister Keating's described Mahathir as 'recalcitrant' for not attending the Seattle Asia Pacific Economic Co-operation (APEC) conference, offence was taken at the dismissive and rude descriptions of Dr Mahathir, with the implication that Australia was again taking a superior stance towards Malaysia (*Age* 1994a; 1994b; 1991e). This dispute had a clear economic basis, with Mahathir advocating an all-Asian economic alliance (East Asian Economic Caucus) against the Australian-promoted APEC, in which the 'West' has a strong presence (see Babbage 1992).

A feature of all these diplomatic incidents has been their public airing in the media rather than the confinement by the two countries of negotiations to

---

[9] Also the report by the International Commission of Jurists, Australian Section (1988).
[10] Camroux (1994:43) states that it had previously been agreed between Hawke and Mahathir at the Commonwealth Heads of Government meeting in Zimbabwe (1991) that the Australian government would in future dissociate itself from Australian media products it deemed to be inaccurate or offensive.

the customary diplomatic channels. Not only have the Australian and Malaysian media acted as a public conduit for the progress of the diplomatic rifts but, in the case of the Australian media, the nature of their reporting and comment on Malaysia and their attitudes also become issues. Mahathir professes to see the Australian media as an organ of the global 'Western' media that criticise Malaysian society in comparison to their own standards: '[Australians feel] that they are superior to us...Australia feels that it is the judge in this region and that it must determine the standard that must be adhered to by all people' (Mahathir quoted in *Age* 1991m).

The Australian press extols its ideals of freedom and tends to promote an ethos of accurate and fearless reporting of the truth—facts that are waiting 'out there' to be discovered. Malaysia employs the argument that the 'Western' media take an unremitting 'Western' perspective that is both prejudiced against Malaysia's administration and sees all events with a mindset that the 'Western' institutions of democracy, individualism and deregulated capitalism are 'superior'.

> Prime Minister Mahathir Mohamad said Saturday that Malaysia could not accept the kind of press freedom practiced in Australia where the media are free to come up with 'all sorts of lies'—Dr Mahathir accused Australia of undermining Malaysia's immage...the Malaysian government ordered all non-essential bilateral projects and contacts suspended last October. Officials said that the Australian media attacks triggered the move. (*Indonesian Observer* 1991)

'Western' leaders have sometimes been quite specific in their assumptions that 'Western' democracy and 'Western' 'human rights' are universally applicable. President Clinton stated that:

> Some have argued that democracy is somehow unsuited for Asia...that human rights are relative and that they simply mask Western culturalism and imperialism. These voices are wrong...It is an insult to the spirit, the hopes, and the dreams of the people who live and struggle in those countries to assert otherwise...we refuse to let repression cloak itself in moral relativism, for democracy and human rights are not occidental yearnings, they are universal yearnings and universal norms' (Clinton 1994).

Mahathir voices offence at the 'Western' media's characterisation of 'Muslim' nations as authoritarian, undemocratic and oppressive of women (Mahathir 1970; the *Age* 2 September 1992 *New Straits Times* reporting Mahathir's speech to the 10th Non-aligned Movement; *Age* 1991n; and Camroux 1994:35). Malaysia portrays a free press as, at best, an anti-productive luxury that a rapidly developing country cannot afford or, at worst, a dangerous agent that can undermine its 'cultural' values.[11] These 'cultural'

---

[11] Malaysia is joined in such an attitude by most ASEAN members (*Indonesian Times* 1991).

values for Malaysia include the 'traditional' family, the intense program of rapid industrialisation and the maintenance of a hierarchy in which everyone knows and accepts their place. It is interesting to note that Mahathir in the past defended feudalism (Mahathir 1970), which he described as a system characterised by a hierarchy of rights and authority. He argues in *The Malay Dilemma* that a feudal society can be dynamic and progressive. One can appreciate that the promulgator of such a perspective may not necessarily view the development of environmental and human rights groups as measures of a society's progress. In his statements Mahathir gauges Malaysia's progress through the attainment of his government's goals:the Gross Domestic Product of an export-oriented, value-added economy and the level of industrialisation.

The dichotomy between the disparate 'cultures' of the Australian and Mahathir's domestic press can help us to understand the Australian–Malaysian conflicts and Mahathir's management of them. For Mahathir, the Malaysian media are agents of nation building and it is therefore desirable that the government has a strong influence on them, bordering on control (Crouch 1992:25). Mahathir appears to be particularly apprehensive about the nature of 'Western' television. Under his administration, radio and television in Malaysia have become virtual government monopolies, with the allegedly private television station being controlled by Mahathir's governing political party, the United Malays National Organisation (UMNO) (Crouch 1992).

The Australian press often promotes its own 'culture' of 'Western liberalism'[12] in quite strident terms:

> If standing up for principles of free speech, for genuine democracy, for preservation of the environment and opposing capital punishment damages a friendship, so be it. Failing to spell out our belief that human rights and democratic principles are universally valid, not only sells Australians short but also does a disservice to courageous Malaysians like Karpal Singh who have paid dearly in fighting for those same values. To suggest that the rights or expectations of Malaysians, or any other nationality might be less than ours is the gravest cultural arrogance of all. (Baker 1991).

It is attitudes such as these that are seen as the 'Western' press's unhelpful contributions to relations between two friendly neighbouring countries. Mahathir clearly fears that Australian and other 'Western' media could have an impact upon his government's 'cultural' program, which emphasises harmony, productivity and loyalty and does not countenance the ideological thrust of the Australian press's 'culture' (with its lifeblood of controversy and its ethos of media as government watchdog). Mahathir therefore contests its

---

[12] Reynolds (1987) conjectures on the origins of Australia's 'cultural' icons and 'cultural' traits from its frontier history and its cultural clash with its Aborigines.

messages, disputes its 'moral' basis and seeks to screen Malaysians from its influence.

After independence, the first ruling elite, led by Prime Minister Tunku Abdul Rahman, came from the English elite school tradition and was generally sympathetic to British traditions and conventions.[13] This ruling class set up and ran a British-style pluralist democracy in which elections took place in a substantially liberal and democratic fashion (Crouch 1992; Stubbs 1990). The initial constitution represented a bargain between the two largest ethnic groups, in which the more numerous Malays would be politically dominant and the Chinese would play the leading role in the economy (Stubbs 1990:102). This phase of development and its underlying social bargain was effectively terminated by the 1969 race riots in Kuala Lumpur. In 1969 the Malay-dominated ruling Coalition failed to secure over half of the vote in its marginal electoral victory against the Opposition parties after divisive electioneering. The Opposition won government in two states, and another two states were marginal. The Malay Alliance (dominated by the United Malays National Organisation—(UMNO) saw the growing electoral success of the Opposition as a potential threat to Malay political dominance. This fear culminated in serious rioting between the different racial groups and the subsequent proclamation of a 'state of emergency', which is yet to be retracted (Crouch 1991). The establishment of the National Operations Council (comprising UMNO figures) saw the detention of vocal Opposition members and the outlawing of the Labor Party, which was held to be a front for the outlawed Chinese-dominated Communist Party (Crouch 1991; Andaya and Andaya 1982).

The riots also saw the end of the acceptance by Malays of the idea of a pluralist society in which the Malays took a leading role in society whilst the Chinese dominated the business sector.[14] UMNO recognised the necessity of a dramatic restructuring of Malaysian society to establish 'Malay culture' as the foundation for the future direction of the country and to increase the state bias towards the Malays. This in practical terms meant an increasing ownership of the economic sphere of Malaysia by the Malays.

After the 1969 riots a young UMNO Executive Committee member, Dr Mahathir bin Mohamad, delineated the indigenous Malays' 'problems' in his book (*The Malay Dilemma*) and proposed 'remedies'. The book was banned (and Mahathir was expelled from UMNO) on the grounds that it exacerbated racial tension. The following excerpt is illustrative:

---

[13] Tunku Abdul Rahman was the President of the Malay Students Society in London in 1925.
[14] It also saw the forced retirement of Prime Minister Rahman.

Deep within them [the Malayo] there is a conviction that no matter what they decide or do, things will continue to slip from their control; that slowly but surely they are becoming the dispossessed in their own land. This is the Malay Dilemma (Mahathir 1970:3).

Mahathir's thesis attributes Malay problems to Malaysia's history of occupation. He argues that the British rule bolstered the socio-economic power of the Chinese and the imported races. He perceived this situation to be exacerbated by intrinsic qualities in the Malay people; complacency, acceptance of exclusion from industry, and politeness (Mahathir 1970:56–57). The book even goes so far as to advocate revolution in order to raise the Malays from their depressed status; this revolution would constitute the urbanisation of Malays, a modification of their attitudes and values while maintaining and promoting Islam (Mahathir 1970). These views of Mahathir are consistent with those of the Malay intelligentsia tradition developed in the vernacular education system.

Although it was banned, the arguments of the book were somewhat vindicated by the New Economic Policy (NEP) instituted by the Malaysian government in 1970. Many see the principles of the NEP coming directly from Mahathir's thesis. The NEP incorporated a Malay bias in business and the affairs of government within the 'pact of domination' (Khoo Kay Jin 1992:49–50). In its preferential treatment of Malays, the policy promoted positive racial discrimination and required a strict, authoritarian administration for its successful implementation.[15] To do this the government armed itself with various legal instruments. One of these was the Internal Security Act,[16] which has been used to detain political challengers/agitators and to censor public debate on racial issues (Crouch 1992).[17] Public criticism by the mass media was restricted through near State monopolisation and a developing network of UMNO ownership and control. Concurrently, in 1971 a national 'cultural' policy was formulated by UMNO on three premises:first, the elevation of indigenous 'Malay culture' to the status of national 'culture'; second, the assimilation of appropriate tropes of other 'cultures' into the national 'culture'; and third, proclaiming the integral role of 'Islam' in this national 'Malay culture' (Tan Sooi Beng 1992:232).

---

[15] Malaysia has always had a strong central government which initially arose from the need to prosecute a widespread Communist guerrilla war between 1948 and 1960 (Stubbs 1990).

[16] The Internal Security Act was adopted originally in 1960, at the end of the Communist insurrection, and is still in force.

[17] Crouch (1992) estimates that 3,000 people were detained between 1960 and 1981 and that the Act was used to arrest members of parliament, which resulted in the objections from Australian parliamentarians noted previously.

The NEP gave the State a powerful role in deciding on areas of expenditure and development, with the private sector providing the capital for the predetermined program. This shift of power answered the demands of the Malay businesspeople and Malay community leaders (many of whom were or became bureaucrats). The overall theme of the NEP was that the State should intervene in favour of the Malays. In the resulting structure the State was dominant and economic, and political power was wielded by technocrats and bureaucrats.[18] The bureaucrats were drawn increasingly from a growing Malay urban middle class and were both the prime generators and beneficiaries of the new Malay national 'culture'. This class was in effect the product of a State-orchestrated racial hegemony who would enjoy both the power of government-controlled private capital and provide the focus for a reconstituted Malay 'cultural' program.

This 'cultural' program was picked up as a central political theme by Mahathir when he came to power in 1981. The purpose of this new 'culture' was to entrench political, economic and bureaucratic power for the Malays and to help define the new industrialised Malaysian State; the 'cultural' production was a means to facilitate the shift from village life to urban, centralised bureaucracy.

The pattern of generating tradition in Malaysia goes back to the colonial era and even earlier (see Kessler 1992:141). Thus to appreciate this promotion of 'Malay' 'culture' it is useful to consider briefly the British cultural production pattern that was used by Mahathir and UMNO for the formation of a new Malay 'culture' (Kessler 1992:141).

The British ruled the Malay States indirectly through local princes (Andaya and Andaya 1982:171) and involved the Malay Courts, which exercised power over the Malay population and also set standards for the Malay religion and customs. Both the British and Malay princes gained power and prestige from the exercise, and thus added to and elaborated the rituals and regalia that had originated in the ancient courts. The princes gained stature through the control of the Malay religion and 'culture' and administered their subjects under British 'advice' while Britain retained genuine executive rule through the princes (Kessler 1980; Roff 1967). As the high status princes deferred to the British on all matters of administrative substance they enhanced perceived British power and prestige. In this process of constructing tradition the British repeated, and the Malay princes emulated, the model used for the British royal ceremonies that were under active

---

[18] Such central state control was necessary in order to achieve the drastic redistribution of ownership foreshadowed in the NEP. In 1970 foreign interests owned 60% of corporate assets and the aim was by 1990 for foreign interests to be reduced to 30% and Malays to own 30% with non-Malay Malaysians owning the remaining 30% (Stubbs 1990:117).

invention in the late 19th and early 20th century.[19] This method of generating tradition was active in Malaysia from independence to 1969 (Kessler 1992:143)[20] but after 1970 the NEP required a significant change in the Malays' role in the social structure, and consequently the 'invention' of tradition became a central, very active, political program for the government. The new 'culture' was focussed on the character, identity and social positioning of the new middle-class Malays.

Current cultural generation in Malaysia often involves activities of ancient courts and villages that are being resurrected and actively promoted by middle-class urban dwellers as 'traditional Malay culture'. In the contemporary Malaysian countryside, however, rural Malay peasants are more likely to be watching Western television series and show little interest in traditional activities being promoted to urban Malays as their 'traditional culture' (Kahn 1992:164–165). State-funded 'cultural' festivals 'recreating' 'traditional' Malay life are becoming more common and elaborate. As Kahn (1992:163) puts it 'Malaysia is currently awash with the symbolism of "traditional Malay culture"'.

While traditional values are used, they are often put in new forms. For instance, a central trait of obedience to the raja is recycled as loyalty to Malaysia (and UMNO) in the 'Loyalty Song' written for UMNO before an election. A detailed analysis of the song and its cultural impact is given by Kessler (1992:149); suffice to say it became extremely popular to the extent of Malay public servants 'lining up outside their offices...for a ceremonial singing' (Kahn 1992:154).

Since the 1950s there has been a growing official policy to have Malay as the primary language of instruction (Tan Liok Ee 1992:189; Tan Sooi Beng 1992:283) at the expense of Chinese and English. The fact that English is the international language of business and that Mahathir wants Malaysia to become an industrial trading nation shows how important culture is seen in building the new Malaysia, in that a decrease in the usage of highly useful 'international' English for 'cultural' Malay is promoted. Related to the use of Malay in education is the rhetorical use (especially by Mahathir) of Malay words such as *bumiputra* (the Malay sons of the soil who have the special political and economic consideration in the new Malaysia) (see Khoo 1992:50–53).

---

[19] See Carradine (1983), quoted in Kessler (1992).

[20] The system of an elected monarch as the Head of State in Malaysia was invented. These rulers' powers came from a cultural and religious tradition that was not reliant on the Malaysian Constitution. Ceremonies of the monarchy, new titles and honours, further levels of status and rank for Malays, were developed in this period (Kessler 1991).

Mahathir's cultural realignment has taken new directions, however, in his non-British, 'Eastern' stance. In the early 1980s he exhorted Malaysians to 'look East' to Japan and South Korea as economic and cultural models for the future. During the same period Mahathir initiated the 'Buy British last' policy, in which all public sector contracts with British companies had to be cleared through his office (Stubbs 1990:119). Recently he has advocated looking to China, in a dramatic reversal of earlier anti-Chinese positionings.

The notion of nationwide 'cultural' values and symbols across class, power and gender boundaries within a politically defined country is highly problematic in an Asian nation such as Malaysia. For instance, there has been continuous significant interchange over the past two centuries between Indonesia and Malaya (Andaya and Andaya 1982)[21] and these processes were accelerated and overlaid by colonial trade, which in turn imposed administrative boundaries and disrupted local trade. In the modern world the international trade has fed into Asian cultures 'Western' symbols and their material embodiment. The culture of modern Malaysia is therefore a mixture of strongly developed regional Malay culture and elements of an industrialised modern economy. Malaysia is, however, at paints to have only those parts essential to industrial economic growth and exclude unwanted aspects of 'Western culture'. This process is clearly evident in modern Malaysia, where transnational capital, industrial practices and Western technical education are adopted with little modification whereas other norms, of press freedom, popular culture, independence of the judiciary, human rights and the Westminster system of government, are significantly modified and married with the newly-invented 'traditional' Malaysian culture.[22]

Mahathir has moved to contain the 'Western' media and its unwanted 'Western' messages, described by Said (1991) and Ahmed (1992). It is important for him to do so as many of these 'Western' messages run counter to his vision for Malaysia, which encompasses a faith in modernity, industrialisation, central control and working as part of a family or group and obeying the leader. His Malaysian federal government is to be seen as having the plans and answers and to function as a co-ordinated unit. In Mahathir's scheme, every Malaysian has his/her place in the hierarchy respecting the

---

[21] Malaysian Islamic politicians and theorists in particular have had strong links with Indonesia over the last century (Kessler 1980).
[22] This, of course, applies also to non-'Western' transnational movements such as fundamentalist religions. Fundamentalist Muslim movements in Malaysia have quite a different character in their interaction with state policies from those in Pakistan, Saudi Arabia or Iran (Grewal and Kaplan 1994:chapter1; Kessler 1980).

person above him or her,[23] the family is held as sacrosanct and religion is revered as a central part of life. Mahathir's construction of 'Malay culture' emphasises village life, religion, kindness and compassion (Ong 1987; Kessler 1992). Rock concerts and performances by Western rock stars are effectively prohibited.[24] The UMNO-dominated media use highly orchestrated images of state Ministers building the country, and state-funded public religious festivals are finely tuned political rituals.[25] These elaborate 'cultural' rituals play an important role in distracting the 'Islamic' activists within Malaysian society from the Mahathir Government's increasing power. The Islamic movement is given great symbolic reverence but no real share of executive control.

Within Mahathir's doctrine of modernity and industrialisation there exists an inherent dilemma. He wishes to use 'Western' science, technology, technical understanding and training to build a modern industrialised state and to participate fully in global capital flows. However, the 'Western' intellectual property and technical education needed for modernisation contain social and political messages. It is increasingly difficult for him to quarantine these messages and prevent 'Western' cultural ingress through the current explosion in information and communications technology carried by international computer connections and satellite delivery of video. To maintain control of Western messages reaching the Malaysian population Mahathir has attempted to bring down 'cultural screens' (Tan Sooi Beng 1992; Crouch 1992).[26] These screens have taken the form of an UMNO monopolisation, whether through indirect UMNO patronage or direct UMNO ownership, of radio, television and newspapers, with a consequent control or at least strong influence over content. Foreign newspapers are deliberately delayed by Customs officials to decrease their saleability by making them old news (Crouch 1992:25; Camroux 1994:20). Most Malaysians are prohibited from owning television

---

[23] A survey carried out in Malaysian universities showed that 40% of those interviewed looked upon politicians as their role models (*New Straits Times* 1994). This would be an unlikely statistical result in Australia.

[24] In 1986 the Ministry of Home Affairs declared a ban on all open-air rock concerts and ordered the policy not to issue permits for such concerts throughout the country (Tan Sooi Beng 1992:286).

[25] UMNO-controlled television broadcasts employ long editing sequences, in direct contrast to the 'Western' television concatenation of rapid, discordant images. This is perhaps a subtle way of communicating the Islamic-Malay ideal of measured pace.

[26] At the 1994 UMNO Youth/Wanita conference a delegate, Sharifah Mohomed, urged the Information Ministry 'to review the role of television because many of the programs had a bad influence on the viewers, especially the youth' (*New Straits Times* 1994a).

satellite dishes that may receive 'Western' media.[27] Film and television are subjected to a considerable degree of censorship (Tan Sooi Beng 1992:287), which can be for the protection of Mahathir's constructed 'family values' or alternatively a political censorship in order to preserve international Islamic ties—exemplified by the banning of the film *Schindler's List* (Camroux 1994:21).

Mahathir's intense program of 'Western' industrialisation has generated a number of problems and social tensions resulting from his integration of industrial goals with a renewed focus on 'Islam' and 'traditional' Malay life. The Malaysian government realised early that social change would be a consequence of the NEP. In 1979 the Malaysian Home Affairs Minister stated that 'urban drift' was a 'deliberate' 'societal engineering strategy', as 'the only major reservoir' of labour left for 'economic modernisation' was in the countryside (*Sunday Mail* 2 December 1979 in Ong 1987:145). The dilemma for the government is that the economy cannot as yet provide much welfare support for its people and has to rely (and encourage) the moral responsibility of the family to do so (Stivens 1987). At the same time it is driving an economic policy that encourages individualism and materialism (Stivens 1987). The State expected these policies to produce nuclear families:'The emergence of the nuclear family system in place of the extended family will further increase pressures on the projected supply of housing during the Plan period' ('Third Malaysia Plan 1976–1980' in Stivens 1987).

The changes now underway in Malaysia are causing family structures and relationships to be remodelled, some even reversed. The largest changes centre around the situation of young women, many of whom now work in factories remote from their familial home, living in a company dormitory with other young workers.[28] While nearly all remit money to their parents, many control their own savings. Marriage is being delayed by these women, many of whom see migration to a city as a means of escaping male kin control over their lives. The wages of the women give them some increased autonomy and in many cases make their parents—or their diminished extended families—dependent on them (Stivens 1987 Ong 1987:179). Migrant women workers are now 'dating' and many select their own husbands. Mandatory factory night shifts see the young women out at nights by themselves.[29] This

---

[27] 'Last week Mr Mohamad (the Malaysian Information Minister) announced that Malaysia would not allow private use of satellite dishes to receive foreign television broadcasts' (*Age* 1991o).

[28] In the ten years from 1970 to 1980 the manufacturing work force nearly doubled (8.7% to 16%) and more than doubled in the retail trade (11.4% to 23.5%) (Ong 1987:144).

[29] The National Unity and Social Development Minister, Datuk Napsiah Omar, called for curfew hours for youth and was supported at the recent UMNO youth/wanita conference (*New Straits Times* 1994).

is something that would not be condoned in village life. Factory work requires rigid time keeping and intense manual activity and engenders consumerism, of Western clothes, despite the 'Islamic ideals' of the primacy of the spiritual life and mandatory modest dressing. This factory life drives other changes in gender relations:supervisors need to be firm, authoritative and demanding, whereas traditional 'Islamic' culture preaches harmony and co-operation in the workplace. Urban people with factory jobs have less time for ceremonies and some matrilineal extended kinship practices are in decay.

These developments have provided fertile ground for the growth of fundamentalist Islamic groups.[30] It is not only 'Islamic' fundamentalists who are concerned about social changes:the Malaysian State has been highly interventionist and prescriptive in family matters since 1970.[31] Concern about changes to the structure of the Malay family is evidenced by a constant stream of family-related legislation, articles in the government-sympathetic media and speeches by prominent UMNO and government leaders. At the 1994 UMNO General Assembly a motion was passed for steps to be taken to strengthen the family institution and to emphasise the role of parents in instilling moral and religious values. In putting the motion, Kamilia Ibrahim stated that:'the Government must provide suitable infrastructure for family development as it is vital in creating a resilient and disciplined young generation with high moral values' (New Straits Times 1994b). The next day it was announced that the 'Employment Act (1955) would be amended to encourage more women to work part-time, make working hours and wages more flexible' (New Straits Times 1994c).

Embassy and other Malaysian diplomatic incidents with Australia

The development of an augmented national culture in Malaysia over the last decade or two and Mahathir's domestic political agenda can illuminate the political discourse surrounding diplomatic incidents between Australia and Malaysia. Many of Mahathir's responses to diplomatic issues with Australia over the past decade are, from this perspective, predictable.

The Australian television soap opera, *Embassy* was set in the fictitious Southeast Asian country of 'Ragaan' and deals with contentious issues that have confronted the Australian–Malaysia relationship. There were a number

---

[30] Particularly the Dakwah (meaning proselytising) group of ABIM, who have called for Islamic Malaysian women to refrain from drinking alcohol, driving cars and watching television and films, which are seen as a conduit of undesirable foreign values (see Kessler 1980).

[31] At the 1994 UMNO Youth/Wanita General Assembly, delegate Khalijah Mohamed Amin said that 'the present social ills could only be overcome with strong religious education' (*New Straits Times* 1994).

of stylistic and visual cues that step playfully on the periphery of the geographic, demographic and national nomenclature of the country:for instance, a flag that could be associated with many Muslim countries. Although the leader of Ragaan, 'General Mamoud', was a strong and charismatic ruler who was preoccupied with moral issues, his supporting advisers had a much darker profile. They exude a sense of expediency, collaboration and scheming, with the preservation of the public image and the sovereignty of the government their motivations.

Mahathir condemned the series *Embassy* as an Australian satirical assault on his country. The series contains a range of ingredients at which Mahathir could take genuine offence, as well as material offering an opportunity for him to reinforce both his promotion of a national culture and his characterisation of the 'Western' media for domestic political use.

In one episode of *Embassy*, a Ragaani general viewing Asian boat-people approaching the Ragaani shore said to the media 'We will shoot them', which he later modified to 'We will shoo them'. The Australian diplomats were shown as responding with explosive hilarity to this crude attempt to deceive people. The events depicted were uncomfortably close to an incident involving Mahathir (Crouch 1991a) in Malaysia viewing Vietnamese boat-people, including the alleged modification of the statement. In another episode, Mahmoud had an affair with a white woman—not the behaviour of a respectable Islamic leader. In this incident Mahmoud's behaviour carried with it implications that he was anti-family, deceitful and impious.

Mahathir professed to see *Embassy* as a semi-authorised Australian government product, and if it was not government sanctioned it was at least made by the Australian government-owned broadcasting corporation; as three separate series[32] were produced, surely the Australian government could influence their ABC if they wanted to. UMNO effectively owns all Malaysian television, monitoring and shaping its cultural productions for Malaysians. It is perhaps not an easy concept for a non-British-educated prime minister to believe that the Australian government provides all funding for the ABC, appoints the members of its governing body, can get ready access to air time to present important messages to the Australian electorate and yet cannot influence, even informally, the broadcasting to its citizens of a cultural production clearly offensive to one of its neighbours.[33] Earlier British-

---

[32] The ABC produced three 13 episode series of *Embassy*.

[33] In an article by Austin (*Sydney Morning Herald* 1991) Mahathir was quoted as saying, at a press conference in Nadi, Fiji: 'The Australian Government could also influence the ABC with regard to Malaysia'. Crouch in the *Age* (1991c) wrote 'it is inconceivable to Dr Mahathir that a government-owned television station should show a program mocking him without the connivance of the Australian Prime Minister'. The *Indonesian Observer* (1991) stated 'Dr

educated Malaysian prime ministers, with their knowledge of the British Broadcasting Corporation, may have been able to see the position of the Australian government more easily. Alternatively, Mahathir may not have wanted to see the Australian government's problem. *Embassy* presented him with an excellent opportunity to attack, over an extended period of time, 'Western' media imperialism.

There are grounds, however, for thinking that the involvement of the ABC was important to his attitude. When we consider the subsequent *Turtle Beach*[34] incident involving a media product that was clearly not produced by an Australian government agency, the public rejection of its content by Australian government ministers defused the matter, in spite of the fact that it contained similar 'biased' material about what was in this case explicitly Malaysia.[35]

Mahathir's response to the Australian government's refusal to disown or apologise for *Embassy* was interesting. Mahathir instructed[36] the Malaysian media to run only negative stories about Australia, focussing particularly on Australia's poor treatment of Aborigines. In 1991 Malaysian television station, TV3, which was controlled by UMNO, produced a four-part series entitled 'The Ugly Face of Australia', focussing on Australia's treatment of Aborigines and Asian migrants (Camroux 1994:43). The Aborigine target was accurately chosen, as it was at a time of awakening in the Australian popular consciousness of ill treatment of Aborigines by white Australians and coincided with political controversy surrounding Aboriginal deaths in custody. Mahathir chose an attack that highlighted Australian's racist nature, using his government-owned media. It is perhaps of note that, to discredit Australia, he was using 'corrupt Western' tactics similar to those that he had accused Australia of employing.

Mahathir said during a visit to Fiji that Australian leaders had lied in claiming that they had no influence over the ABC's television series because Canberra had influenced ABC's coverage of the Gulf War'.

[34] *Turtle Beach* was a film adaptation of the novel by an Australian journalist Blanche D'Alpuget. The film involved fictionalised accounts of incidents in Malaysia including the landing of boat-people.

[35] Camroux (1994) states that this approach to handling such incidents was agreed by Prime Ministers Hawke and Mahathir at the Commonwealth Heads of Government Meeting in Zimbabwe in 1991 in the aftermath of the resolution of the *Embassy* affair.

[36] McGregor (1991) claimed that he obtained secret Malaysian government documents that direct the Malaysian media to run stories that reflect badly on Australia. In part, the Cabinet directive said 'Any stories which will reflect negatively on Australia should be used in our news bulletins' and 'Specific issues such as bad treatment given to Australian Aborigines and Australia's discriminatory immigration regulations should be exaggerated and emphasized'.

There was a precursor to the *Embassy* incident that probably sensitised Mahathir to the representation of Malaysia/Ragaan as cruel and authoritarian in *Embassy*. This was Former Prime Minister Bob Hawke's characterisation as 'barbaric' of the 1986 hanging in Malaysia of two convicted drug smugglers, who were Australian nationals, and his description as 'grotesque and improper' of their hanging before all legal options were exhausted (Camroux 1994:41). According to Lindsay Murdoch (*Age* 1991h), Hawke's 'criticism was taken as a personal insult by Malaysia's Prime Minister, Dr Mahathir Mohamad, who has repeatedly referred to it while leading an aggressive anti-Australian campaign'.[37]

Many of the forces working on Mahathir can be seen in the incident in which former Prime Minister Keating referred to Mahathir as 'recalcitrant'. This work was perhaps intentionally translated by some of the Malaysian Parliament (see Crouch 1994a) and the media into Malaysian words that were far more insulting.[38] The incident was presented to Malaysia as Mahathir being described by a 'Western' leader as stupid and someone who can be satirised and not taken seriously. The incident arose at the APEC meeting in Seattle in which eminent 'Western' leaders, among them Paul Keating and Bill Clinton, were working to draw most of the Southeast Asian nations into a loose economic union that Mahathir speculated would be dominated by the 'West' (US, Canada, Japan, Australia). Mahathir had been a prime mover in establishing an Asian only club, EAEC (East Asian Economic Caucus) and did not attend the meeting, turning his absence into a political point. To attend and co-operate with these 'Western' nations would contravene his 'Look East' policy (Camroux 1994:44). Furthermore, if APEC developed into an economic unit it would necessarily entail Malaysia's trading more co-operatively with 'Western' nations,[39] making it perhaps harder for Mahathir to maintain his 'cultural screens'. It would also give the appearance that associations of 'Eastern' newly industrialised countries can't produce the goods and growth Malaysia aspires to and that a 'Western'-led association can better attain Mahathir's goals (Camroux 1994:6). It would also be a set-back to Mahathir's pan-Islamic initiatives and co-operation (see Camroux 1994:19). As this incident was played out, Mahathir showed himself to be an adroit operator in an international 'cultural' contest by again initiating

[37] See also Murdoch (*Age* 1991j) and Mellor (*Time* 1991c).
[38] Translations of the term 'recalcitrant' were *keras kepala* (stubborn or hard-headed) or *kurang ajar*, which 'reflects seriously on one's background and family, implying that one's parents did not bring them up properly' (Camroux 1994:5).
[39] Babbage (1992:27) notes that small Asian nations like Malaysia do not welcome the development of large trading blocs, as they are in 'no position to contemplate retaliatory economic measures' if these blocs develop policies against their interests (see also Camroux 1994).

disruption to Australia–Malaysia ties, threatening trade. The rejection of an initial letter of apology from Paul Keating seemed to improve Mahathir's position at least in the media's coverage of the issue. Before the recalcitrant remark, Mahathir was the only invited leader not attending APEC, looking somewhat left out of a promising advance in regional trade relations. At the conclusion of the affair the two countries (Australia and Malaysia) were focussed on attempts by Paul Keating's attempts to deliver an acceptable apology. To an extent, the positions had been reversed and Mahathir had shown his domestic constituency a 'Western' leader who was (again) impolite, intemperate and unable to deal properly with an 'Eastern' nation like Malaysia (Camroux 1994:47).

The manner in which these 'insults' to Malaysia have been handled appear significant. The normal diplomatic routes of calling in high commissioners to express displeasure and formal diplomatic notes of protest were not reported unlike the very public statements through the media and the publicly announced carriage of personal letters (of apology) by Australia's Minister for Foreign Affairs and Trade. The incidents had a strong public relations aura to them (for domestic Malaysian political consumption) rather than that of a serious diplomatic discourse. There is other evidence for believing that Malaysia is engaged in public relations designed not to harm any of the useful (to Malaysia) ballast in the Australia–Malaysia relationship. The Five Power Defence Agreement (FPDA) was largely unaffected through all the incidents, and yet this relationship is a colonial leftover with strong paternalistic overtones. Negotiated in the late 1960s, in the wake of the Indonesian Confrontation, the FPDA is a treaty in which the United Kingdom, Australia and New Zealand guarantee to defend Malaysia and Singapore (Stubbs 1990:104; Methven 1992).[40] It is quite an active and vigorous interaction with regular multinational military exercises and military training for Malaysian officers in the United Kingdom and Australia. However, through the deepest and longest of the diplomatic rifts (the *Embassy* affair) defence interaction was barely affected,[41] with the Malaysian Minister for Defence reaffirming his support for the arrangement.

There are some claims that economic relations between the two countries were affected by these diplomatic incidents. Economic sanctions, however,

---

[40] Because of its size and geography, neutralism as a security stance has never been an option for Malaysia. The Malaysian view of its security future (as part of Mahathir's Vision 2020) is given in Nathan (1992).

[41] Malaysia did cancel some visits by defence officials to Australia (*Age* 1991n). The Malaysian Defence Minister, Datuk Najib Abdul Razak, however, maintained a dialogue with Australian Defence Minister Ray during the 'recalcitrant' incident, acting as a conciliator (Camroux 1994:45).

have been decidedly marginal: during the recalcitrant affair the UMNO youth
league resolved that in future Malaysian students should not go to Australia
for tertiary training; Australian films and television products were removed
from Malaysian outlets for the duration of the affair and many bureaucrats and
businessman voiced solidarity for Mahathir, resulting in non-Australian
foreign companies gaining an advantage in bidding for Malaysian clients. At
the cessation of the incidents, trade relations returned quickly to normal and
have shown long-term growth.

Conclusion

The development of a revitalised and augmented national culture and its
defence are central, high-profile components of Mahathir's plan to rapidly
develop a modern industrial Malaysia. The new national culture is running
counter to many aspects of the historical and cultural legacy of British
colonialism. It has been suggested that Mahathir in effect has been actively
promoting a recreation of Malay 'traditional culture' in much of his policy-
making in recent years. He has deployed an essentialist reified understanding
of culture for his rhetorical claims for the *Bumiputra*.

The idea of Malay/Malaysian 'culture' is also a cardinal element in
Mahathir's foreign relations stance. In order to industrialise and trade
internationally, Malaysia must import 'Western' intellectual property and
methods and must negotiate with the 'West'. These necessities have
implications for Mahathir's domestic culture industry. The theory that
'culture' is defined in the area of contestation between groups or nations
seems to work well when we look at the 'cultural' definition of a series of
diplomatic incidents and the associated exchanges in the media surrounding
the Malaysian–Australian relationship. That these diplomatic incidents are
driven primarily by 'cultural' and domestic political concerns is supported by
the fact that economic and military ties during the incidents appear to have
been largely unaffected. The domestic political agenda that Mahathir is
pursuing is one of enhancing national self-respect, electoral support, domestic
multicultural cohesion, socio-economic restructuring and keeping domestic
'Islamic' forces supportive of his party while excluding them from the
executive sphere of government.

However, Mahathir's concurrent programs of rapid industrialisation and
'cultural' production result in inherent conflicts. First, the importation of
'Western' industrial 'culture' brings with it undesirable 'Western' popular
'culture' that Mahathir and his government see as undermining the new
Malaysia. Mahathir's response has been to construct 'cultural' screens to try
to quarantine Malaysia from the 'worst' aspects of the international 'Western'
media. Mahathir has also attacked the 'West' as decadent and immoral and

the 'Western' press as judgemental, biased and prone to adopt a superior tone. Second, the industrial 'culture' required to service a modern industrial state, such as the need for a mobile, disciplined labour force, including young women, is at odds with such aspects of 'traditional' 'Islamic' 'Malay' 'culture'. This produces difficulty for the Malay government because it needs this 'traditional village' 'culture' for welfare services the State cannot as yet provide.

The dialogue between Mahathir, the Australian government and the Australian press uses cliches rooted in their respective cultures. These cliches form a sub-text to the public discourse in the diplomatic incidents between Mahathir and Australia. A series of such incidents when analysed shows Mahathir to be using them to advance his own domestic and foreign political agenda, and the points at issue are predictable given the history of Malaysia, Mahathir's current domestic situation and his aspirations for his country, his government and himself.

References

Age 1994a, 9 November.

—— 1994b, 10 November.

—— 1992, 22 September.

—— 1991a, 18 April.

—— 1991b, 20 April.

—— 1991c, 21 April.

—— 1991d, 3 May.

—— 1991e, 2 June.

—— 1991f, 19 July.

—— 1991g, 22 July.

—— 1991h, 23 July.

—— 1991i, 24 July.

—— 1991j, 25 July.

—— 1991k, 26 July.

—— 1991l, 27 July.

—— 1991m, 28 July.

—— 1991n, 29 July.

—— 1990, 20 November.

—— 1989, 13 September.

Ahmed, Akbar S 1992, *Post Modernism and Islam:Predicament and Promise*, Routledge, London.

Aitkin, S 1994, 'Unrocking Malaysian relations', *Canberra Times*, 28 September.

Andaya, Barbara Watson and Andaya, Leonard Y 1982, *A History of Malaysia*, Macmillan Education Ltd, Houndsmills, Basingstoke and London.

Australian 1990, 20 November.

—— 1991, 7 January.

Australian Financial Review 1993, 6 December.

Babbage, Ross 1992, 'The Changing Global Strategic Environment', *Asian Defence Journal*, 1.

Baker, Mark 1991, 'Our political fiction harms Malaysia', *Age*, 3 May.

Camroux, David 1994, *Looking East and Inwards: Internal Factors in Malaysian Foreign Relations during the Mahathir Era, 1981–1994*, Centre for the Study of Australia Asia Relations, Australia–Asia Papers No. 72.

Clinton, W 1994, '1994 "National Security" Strategy Report', released 21 July.

Crouch, Harold 1994a, 'Malaysia', in Trood, Russell and McNamara, Deborah (eds), *The Asia–Australia Survey 1994*, Centre for Australia–Asia Relations, Melbourne.

—— 1994b, 'Industrialisation and Political Change' in Brookfield, Harold (ed), *Transformation with Industrialisation in Peninsular Malaysia*, Oxford University Press, Kuala Lumpur.

—— 1993, 'Malaysia: Neither Authoritarian nor Democratic', in Hewison, K, Robison, R and Rodan, G (eds), *Southeast Asia in the 1990s: Authoritarianism, Democracy and Capitalism*, Allen and Unwin, St Leonards.

—— 1992, 'Authoritarian Trends, the UMNO Split and the Limits to State Power' in Kahn, Joel S and Loh, Kok Wah Francis (eds), *Fragmented Vision: Culture and Politics in Contemporary Malaysia*, Asian Studies Association of Australia and Allen and Unwin, St Leonards.

—— 1991a, 'Did we really have to apologise to this man?', *Sunday Age*, 28 July.

—— 1991b, 'Poor relations between Malaysia and Australia relate to differing perceptions of the role of the media', transcript of the *Morning Show*, ABC Radio, 31 July.

Current Biography Yearbook 1988, Mahathir

Indonesian Observer 1991, 29 July

Indonesian Times, 3 August 1991

International Commission of Jurists, Australian Section 1988, 'Arrests in Malaysia: Internal Security Act, October–November 1987', Report of the International Commission of Jurists Australian Section, Mission to Observe Habeas Corpus Applications by Detainees, March.

Jomo, K S and Cheek,Ahmad Shabery 1992, *Malaysia's Islamic Movements*, in Kahn, Joel S and Loh, Kok Wah Francis (eds), *Fragmented Vision: Culture and Politics in Contemporary Malaysia*, Asian Studies Association of Australia and Allen and Unwin, St Leonards.

Kahn, Joel S 1992, 'Class, Ethnicity and Diversity: Some Remarks on Malay Culture in Malaysia', in Kahn, Joel S and Loh, Kok Wah Francis (eds), *Fragmented Vision: Culture and Politics in Contemporary Malaysia*, Asian Studies Association of Australia and Allen and Unwin, St Leonards.

Kessler, Clive S 1992, 'Archaism and Modernity: Contemporary Malay Political Culture', in Kahn, Joel S and Loh, Kok Wah Francis (eds), *Fragmented Vision: Culture and Politics in Contemporary Malaysia*, Asian Studies Association of Australia and Allen and Unwin, St Leonards.

——— 1991, 'Negotiating Cultural Difference: On Seeking, Not Always Successfully, to Share the World with Others—or, in Defence of "Embassy"', *Asian Studies Review*, Vol 15 No 2.

——— 1980, 'Malaysia: Islamic Revivalism and Political Disaffection in a Divided Society', *South East Asia Chronicle*, 75.

Khoo Kay Jin 1992, 'The Grand Vision: Mahathir and Modernisation', in Kahn, Joel S and Loh, Kok Wah Francis (eds), *Fragmented Vision: Culture and Politics in Contemporary Malaysia*, Asian Studies Association of Australia and Allen and Unwin, St Leonards.

Mahathir bin Mohamad 1970, *The Malay Dilemma*, Asia Pacific Press, Singapore.

McGregor, Richard 1991, 'Malaysian government tries to spread unfavourable information about Australia after some conflict over ABC program', *AM*, ABC radio, 19 February.

McPhail, Thomas L 1981, *Electronic Colonialism: The Future of International Broadcasting and Communication*, Sage Publications, Beverly Hills.

Methven, Philip 1992, 'The Five Power Defence Arrangements and Military Co-operation among the ASEAN States', Canberra Papers on Strategy and Defence No 92, Strategic and Defence Studies Centre, Australian National University, Canberra.

New Straits Times 1994a, 18 November.

—— 1994b, 21 November

—— 1994c, 22 November

—— 1986, 10 July.

Ong, Aihwa 1987, *Spirits of Resistance and Capitalist Discipline: Factory Women in Malaysia*, State University of New York Press, Albany.

Putnis, Peter 1990, 'Press Freedom in Southeast Asia', *Media Information Australia* No 57, August.

Roff, William 1967, *The Origins of Malay Nationalism*, Yale University Press.

Said, Edward W 1991 [1978], *Orientalism*, Penguin Books, Harmondsworth.

Shaheen, Jack 1984, *The TV Arab*, Bowling Green State University Popular Press.

Shamsul, A B 1993, 'Australia–Malaysia Relations: "The Negotiation of Cultural Difference: Where to From Here?"', *Asian Studies Review*, Vol 16 No 3.

Stivens, Maila K 1992, 'Perspectives on Gender: Problems in Writing About Women in Malaysia', in Kahn, Joel S and Loh, Kok Wah Francis (eds), *Fragmented Vision: Culture and Politics in Contemporary Malaysia*, Asian Studies Association of Australia and Allen and Unwin, St Leonards.

—— 1987, 'Family, State and Industrialisation: The Case of Rembau, Negeri Sembilan, Malaysia' in Afshar, H (ed), *Women, State and Ideology*, Macmillan, London.

Stubbs, Richard 1990, 'The Foreign Policy of Malaysia' in Wurfel, David and Burton, Bruce (eds), *The Political Economy of Foreign Policy in Southeast Asia*, Macmillan, Basingstoke.

Sydney Morning Herald 1991, 6 July.

Tan Liok Ee 1992, 'Dongjiaozong and the Challenge to Cultural Hegemony 1951–1987', in Kahn, Joel S and Loh, Kok Wah Francis (eds), *Fragmented Vision: Culture and Politics in Contemporary Malaysia*, Asian Studies Association of Australia and Allen and Unwin, St Leonards.

Tan Sooi Beng 1992, 'Counterpoints in the Performing Arts of Malaysia', in Kahn, Joel S and Loh, Kok Wah Francis (eds), *Fragmented Vision: Culture and Politics in Contemporary Malaysia*, Asian Studies Association of Australia and Allen and Unwin, St Leonards.

Time Magazine 1991a, 7 January.

—— 1991b, 6 May.

—— 1991c, 5 August.

—— 1994, 21 November.

Obstacles to openness: international television services and authoritarian states in East Asia

William Atkins

Introduction

The global growth of 'satellite broadcasting' during the final decade of the 20th century has prompted many bold assertions in relation to the new media in East Asia. At the beginning of the 1990s a frequently used headline in English-language newspapers, business magazines and academic journals of the Asian region was 'The Sky's the Limit'. Invariably, reference was being made to satellites, implying that the economic opportunities and consumer choice that satellites would deliver knew no bounds. For some the phrase alluded to a new era of unimpeded information, including political information.

There was a sense that a new television information order would develop that was largely outside state control—a situation welcomed by some international media proprietors and those who opposed television censorship but received with caution by those who supported continued regulation of television content. Authors such as Pool, Toffler and Dizard argued that the new information technologies would lead to more information (and entertainment) reaching more people, 'thus stimulating a more democratic environment' (Wasko 1993:164). The 'borderless television' scenario was anticipated by the liberal press of East Asia. The *Far Eastern Economic Review* noted in 1991 that a direct-to-home (DTH) satellite service 'defies the tradition that national sovereignty includes state control over television within a nation's borders' (Scott 1991:32).

But the initial predictions have not been borne out by experience. Even after half a decade of frantic expansion, East Asia's television industry, is far from borderless. And while the telecommunications companies and DTH network operators may feel their profits are—or will be heading skyward, the mechanisms that limit the social and political activity via satellite and other new media are still very much grounded through complex relationships between economics, politics and culture. States have been able to maintain significant influence in the styles and genres of programming that their citizens are able to watch.

East Asia contains some of the most information-sensitive governments in the world. Countries including China, Malaysia, Indonesia, Burma and Singapore remain restrictive towards reporting about their internal affairs and most have severe limitations on ownership and use of satellite dishes. A BBC correspondent in Singapore observed in 1996:

> Governments in this region are very worried about losing control. Whether that loss of control comes through global satellite broadcasters or the internet or alternative political parties within their own country, governments want to cling on to power. The idea of single party states and single party rule is not dead in Southeast Asia by any means. (Simpson 1996)

But the new television technology has marched into East Asia whether governments are ready or not. Since 1990 an array of terrestrial, cable and satellite broadcasters has mushroomed due to technology and to broader economic deregulation. In some cases the new satellite television services were made possible by the existence of government satellite systems. For instance, Indonesia's Palapa system not only allowed a rapid penetration of government-endorsed programming to the distant corners of the country, but was later the platform for the introduction of international services including CNN, Australia Television and ESPN throughout Southeast Asia. Palapa had become a 20th century electronic wooden horse of Troy. With more than one million private satellite dishes in Indonesia, the government realised it could not hope to restrict the international services, so officially adopted an 'open skies' policy. While this experience perhaps reflects an unintended consequence of technological development, other governments in Asia have been quick to emulate Indonesia by establishing competing national satellite systems. In part it is an opportunity to take profits from the communications revolution, but it also represents an attempt to regain some semblance of sovereign control over television.

One associated strategy has been the rapid development of private—but politically supportive—local networks, which have circumvented demand for expensive private DTH subscriptions from foreign broadcasters. The governments allow the programming from transnational media corporations on to these local private services on the basis of the programming being politically acceptable to the state. Thus the international television industry in parts of East Asia largely marginalises programming dealing with domestic politics and discourses that challenge dominant economic groups or cultures. This chapter will outline the dynamic that has developed between authoritarian states and transnational media corporations—to the detriment of international public broadcasters and groups in civil society that have sought to develop broadcasting structures premised on greater openness and political transparency. Primarily, these latter groups—most commonly non-governmental organisations (NGOs)—have looked to western European public service broadcasting models as a starting point, with a view to integrating characteristics sensitive to local social structures. A core component is liberal information programming, including independent news and current affairs. The concept has received minimal attention. Instead, the international services that have flourished in the region have either ignored news and current affairs programming from the start, excised it from their schedules or restricted 'news' to stock market and other financial information.

'Commercial forces'—a phrase that marries market operations with the realpolitik of government relations—have become the chief mediator of the development of television in the authoritarian states of East Asia in the 1990s.

The public and private spheres in East Asian television

The communications-oriented NGOs in countries including the Philippines, Thailand, Malaysia and Indonesia have been pressing their case for public service broadcasting models at a time when internationally the genre is at a low ebb. The phrase 'public service broadcasting crisis' has become something of a 1990s global truism. In the past decade national public service broadcasting organisations the world over have been rationalised, corporatised, privatised and/or marginalised. The confluence of technological, ideological and economic forces has washed across national borders—challenging long-standing media structures and notions of broadcasting monopoly, spectrum scarcity and regulation. For many scholars and advocates of public service broadcasting, a key challenge has been to formulate strategies to ensure the development and endurance of the institutions in the face of commercial competition and pressures. This has been advocated in the interests of representative democracy, which allows and encourages reflection and examination of opinions and experiences of society. So far the majority of the work has focussed on European institutions, with authors such as Denis McQuail, Anthony Smith and Michael Tracey emphasising the value of public service broadcasting. More recently, Sreberny-Mohammadi has sought to refine the relationship between the state and society in the new communications environment. She suggested to a pan-Asian audience in 1996:

> [N]ational cultural hegemony can be regressive and repressive...The role of states needs to shift from 'control' to 'steerage', prompting a dynamic cultural environment not through negative controls but through the active support of human and cultural rights and the nurturing of civil society. (Sreberny-Mohammadi 1996:1)

It is a concept gaining increasing voice and organised force, with intellectuals, NGOs and media unions across Asia arguing for more diverse and critical broadcasting services. Delegates at a conference in Jakarta in July 1996—a gathering backed by the Geneva-based International Federation of Journalists—sought greater political and economic support for an independent public broadcasting sector in the region. The title of the conference was 'Open Skies, Towards an Open Society: The challenge for Asian Public Service Broadcasting'—rather cheekily borrowing the Indonesian government's own 'open skies' satellite broadcasting policy slogan. However, the precariousness of the conference organisers' mission was reflected by the Indonesian government's decision to deny visas to some international delegates and to discourage participation by state officials. As well, conference organisers connected to the unrecognised journalists trade union—the Alliance of Independent Journalists (AJI)—were questioned by security intelligence officials at the conclusion of the conference and their computers were siezed. The absence of delegates from Singapore and Malaysia also reflects the rather jaundiced view the governments of those countries take towards such gatherings. Nontheless, the Jakarta gathering reflected the growing desire of sections of societies of the Asia—Pacific to confront the issue of broadcasting structures in a rapidly changing economic and political environment.

It is a challenge not without parallel. The political change that swept eastern Europe in the wake of the collapse of Soviet communism sparked a stimulating discourse about appropriate media structures in the transition to democracy. When communications scholars from eastern and western Europe met to compare scholarship in 1991, they found there were fundamental differences in the mass communications prescriptions: western scholars urging a move away from commercial structures that maintained their 'position in the political and economic system of the capitalist society' towards a greater state role in regulation. Perhaps not surprisingly, those from the former Soviet bloc rejected this direction, urging instead market mechanisms and 'civil structures' to engender and maintain diversity (Manaev and Pryliuk 1993:viii). Their experience of state control of media (and other elements of socio-political life) meant they would not trust the state in the new 'democratic' era. In this context, Splichal makes a telling point about the dynamic relationship between democracy and mass media.

> Democratic communications are the basis of any democratic culture and political system, or 'general democracy'; however, a democratic environment is also necessary for democratisation of communications themselves. (Splichal 1993:3)

In East Asia, the presence of television services belonging to transnational media corporations such as Rupert Murdoch's News Corporation, Turner International and Dow Jones underlines the remarkable shift in the politico-media landscape in the region since the turn of the decade. Known for its social and political conservatism, adherence to governmental political imperatives and exclusion of government network competition, the television industry in the region has undergone significant structural change. From a narrow base of terrestrial, usually state, broadcasters, there is now an array of terrestrial, cable and satellite broadcasters—funded by subscription, advertising and government. This new environment has been shaped by the convergence of distinctive ideological, technological and commercial forces. Essentially, these forces at work in East Asia represent an extension of trends that underpinned the radical reshaping of broadcasting in the West during the 1980s. The intellectual force behind this change was the revival of ideas that are less egalitarian and more individualistic: those of John Stuart Mill and the utilitarian philosophers. During the 1980s, under the Reagan and Thatcher administrations, neo-classical market-place philosophies gained ascendancy, displacing notions of 'public good' in broadcasting in favour of 'public choice', thereby challenging 'all those who wish to treat broadcasting as a cultural property with ideals and ambition' (Negrine and Papathanassopoulos 1990:11). The convergence of the telecommunications, broadcasting and computing industries has added complexity to the 'new media' environment. The dismantling of the long-established telecommunications regime in the United States that occurred with the divestiture of AT&T, for instance, was to place competitive pressures on other sectors, often in other countries...a so-called 'ripple effect' (Teske 1990:128; Negrine and Papathanassopoulos 1990:9).

The ripples quickly reached the shores of those East Asian nations that were adopting liberalised trading practices and broad deregulation, under pressure from multilateral bodies such as the General Agreement on Tariffs and Trade (GATT). The removal of trade barriers in the communications sector was to be encouraged with even more vigour by GATT's repleacement—the World Trade Organisation (WTO)—and the Asia Pacific Economic Co-operation (APEC) forum. When the first meeting of the WTO was held in Singapore in December 1996, the most critical achievement in the eyes of participants was the winding back of trade barriers in the communications sector.

Today the region's telecommunications sector—which provides the satellite, cable and wireless transmission infrastructure for the television industry—is an extremely complex web of corporate and government relationships in which Asian, European and American companies hold stakes. Australian companies, especially Telstra, are active in this environment. As a consequence, the content side, which is delivered via these internationalised systems, is less able to be regulated by governments. Particularly in the states of the Association of South East Asin Nations (ASEAN), the economically liberal ideology behind the internationalisation of the communications hardware has come into conflict with the long-established position of 'broadcasting sovereignty' held by most regional governments. In these circumstances the 'closed political system is in at least some tension with the socio-economic forces towards openness' (Tiffen 1994). This has manifested itself in the form of divergent goals between those elements of the state charged with development of the communications infrastructure and those responsible for the flow of information content. Most commonly the ministries and departments involved in this problematic relationship are information and telecommunication. To varying degrees, the information ministries tend to be nation-centric and more inclined to develop policy with historic perspectives of post-colonial identity, nation-building and media imperialism. East Asia's telecommunications ministries and agencies are, with the exception of North Korea, Vietnam and China, international in orientation, aggressively seeking international capital for development both at home and abroad, and tend to publicly express support for modernisation. These separate arms of the state are working to quite different agendas—most notably in the case of Indonesia, but also in Malaysia and Thailand. Singapore too has grappled with this tension, but the differences are less public.

In this environment, distinctive characteristics have emerged in the new media broadcasting sector. First, the political culture affects the way transnational media corporations find a role in the region's broadcasting sector. The deregulation or 'reregulation' of broadcasting in the region has enabled state political élites to dispense patronage (Lim 1994). In several countries, politically connected organisations controlling the new media infrastructure are key partners with international broadcasting players: thus transnational media corporations establish links with local 'mini-moguls'. It is unlikely that this was the original intention of the governments, which hurriedly approved the setting up of the private networks to counter the tide of foreign programming around the beginning of the decade. Second, the public broadcasting structures historically have evolved less as tools for discourse and inquiry than for nation-building and state reinforcement. State ideology is historically rooted in experience of anti-colonial struggle and the challenge of uniting diverse peoples in colonially constructed borders. Against this background, there is little support—and more often open hostility—by regional government leaders towards the public sector broadcasting principles of organisations such as the BBC and the Australian Broadcasting Corporation. This antipathy is also central to the arrangements that are evolving between authoritarian states and international media organisations, which see Western public sector broadcasters, and the values they promote, marginalised.

The culture of the broadcasting market in the region is reflected by the mushrooming television trade press. Titles such as *Television Asia, Asia Image, Satellite and Cable Asia* and *Broadcasting Asia* represent the prevailing mood about the industry with their glossy paper, fat monthly issues, high advertising ratios and networks of correspondents. They challenge the collegiate institutional publications that have been around far longer: *AMIC Bulletin*, *Media Asia*, *Asian Journal of Communication* and *ABU (Asia–Pacific Broadcasting Union) News*. These latter publications link media practitioners via contests of ideas, values and knowledge. The new genre of publications adds the links of markets, sales, ratings, strategies and economic opportunities.

Broadly, the changes in the foundations of broadcasting have led to a greater commodification of television programming in the region. The social utility of the medium is diminished in favour of the commercial imperatives. Hoover, Venturelli and Wagner (1993:103) have assessed the implications of the shift in the conception of 'public' sphere as a community of free citizens to one of 'public' as individual consumers.

> [C]urrent Asian trends converting communication into a commodity run counter to the possibilities for rational and autonomous public communication necessary to the practice of liberal democracy. A headlong rush to a global economic market as the definer of communications processes has forced governments to share power with national and multi-national private commercial interest, thereby radically altering the very structure of institutions shaping communication policy and practice.

Transnational media corporations in East Asia

The transnational media companies operating successfully in China and the ASEAN states have two distinct operational characteristics. First, they are working in collaboration with well-connected local elites; second, they countenance and engage in arrangements, often informal, with governments regarding their programming. A key political strategy—most notably but not exclusively used by Rupert Murdoch's News Corporation—has been to engage in pro-active government relations, in which unorthodox and sometimes illiberal broadcasting management practices have been offered and adopted in an effort to receive favourable treatment from governments. While the political history of broadcasting throughout the world is littered with examples of media moguls extracting favours from governments by taking particular editorial or programming stances, recent dealings by Murdoch's News Corporation and Ted Turner's CNN with governments in Asia have been notable because, in some cases, the arrangements have resulted in the winding back of the gains made by the more vigorous and open information programming that first came to the region with satellite television in the late 1980s and early 1990s. Most notable is Murdoch's attempt to ingratiate News Co-operation's Star TV with the Chinese government by dumping BBC

World Service Television from the network beamed to China and other parts of Northeast Asia.

The strategy is even more remarkable when juxtaposed with Murdoch and Turner's anti-state rhetoric centred on liberty and choice. Murdoch effectively used these views to erode public and government confidence in public service broadcasting, most notably in Britain in the 1980s. Having initially failed to realise that these attacks on state control of broadcasting would be counterproductive to their commercial ambitions in Asia, Murdoch and Turner (and their senior managers) have subsequently engaged in regular meetings with government leaders. Shortly after coming under attack from regional government leaders for its purchase of a majority stake in Star TV in 1993, News Corporation issued a statement in Hong Kong that said the network would be a 'service which governments in the region would find both friendly and useful' (*Straits Times* 1993b).

Star TV here is pivotal to the way the television industry is developing, not only in Southeast Asia but throughout the region. It is ironic for one so publicly contemptuous of governments that Murdoch's purchase of Star TV in July 1993 was born in part from the political nervousness of a Hong Kong tycoon. Li Ka Shing, a property developer with close connects to Beijing, had set up Star TV three years earlier. Importantly, a key channel on this free-to-air service was BBC World Service Television (BBCWST), now known as BBC World. Li Ka Shing's executives, including his son Richard Li, regularly voiced the rhetoric about freedom of choice and challenges to authoritarian governments. But, behind the liberal sentiment, Li's control of Star TV led to a deterioration in his relationship with China, where he had significant non-media business interests. A Singapore newspaper suggested at the time of the sale: 'He probably did not enjoy getting phone calls from a Beijing high official every time Star beamed an offensive news or movie item' (Ong 1993). Into this environment, Murdoch stepped forward with a $US525 million offer for a controlling stake in Star TV. (In 1995 News Corporation bought the remaining stake for $US300 million.) While not a single territory under the Star TV footprint had a regulatory structure to accommodate the network, the determination by Murdoch to engage in business in the region was not out of character. More than once News Corporation has manoeuvred itself into a position of commercial advantage by pre-empting (or simply ignoring) regulations. 'The technology is galloping over the old regulatory machinery, and in many cases making it obsolete,' said Murdoch in 1993 (*Business Times* 1993).

The weeks after the purchase of Star TV were to be a defining period for Murdoch's Asian strategy. His political tactics and public statements underscored his failure to make the conceptual adjustment to the stark differences in the political landscapes of Europe and Asia. His corporate empire clearly struggled to adjust to planting a foot in each camp. On one hand, the governments of Asia were being told there was nothing to fear. Star TV 'would not become a vehicle for outside interference in Asian affairs...News Corporation intended to make Star TV a service which Asian families could enjoy in their homes' (*Straits Times* 1993b). But just days later, an audience of the British political and media establishment at the Banqueting House in London were being told by Murdoch that the Orwellian spectre of state information control had been circumvented by new technology.

> Advances in the technology of telecommunications have proved an unambiguous threat to totalitarian regimes everywhere. Fax machines enable dissidents to bypass state-controlled print media; direct dial telephone makes it difficult for a state to control interpersonal voice communications; and satellite broadcasting makes it possible for information-hungry societies to bypass state-controlled television channels...The Bosnian Serbs can't hide their atrocities from the probing eyes of BBC, CNN and Sky News cameras...the extraordinary living standards produced by free-enterprise capitalism cannot be kept secret. (*Business Times* 1993)

The very technology he was lauding beamed Murdoch's presentation live to a Hong Kong breakfast program, where, in all likelihood, Chinese government officials were watching. While Murdoch's rhetoric was consistent with the economic rationalist broadcasting policies that had been adopted by governments in the United States and much of Europe, it was clearly at odds with messages News Corporation was sending to Asian governments. Today's atrocities by Bosnian Serbs could be tomorrow's intercommunal rioting or labour unrest in Southeast Asia or student unrest in Chinese universities. The Chinese authorities had already experienced the threat of satellite television to political control, when coverage of the 1989 Tiananmen Square demonstrations by CNN and other Western broadcasters led to a 'global feedback loop', whereby information and images from Beijing were filtered through the Atlanta and other metropolitan headquarters and back to Beijing via satellite, thus feeding into the unfolding events (Wark 1990:9). A similar difficulty faced the Thai military government of General Suchinda Kraprayoon in May 1992, when BBCWST reports of the Bangkok civil uprising and military crackdown were received by satellite in private homes in Bangkok and videotaped and distributed to the government's opponents. The BBC reports were to discredit both the government military action and its manipulation of events on state-controlled television and radio, as well as embolden the demonstrators (Atkins 1995:50–60). Then in June 1996 news images of political violence on the streets of Jakarta surrounding the struggle for power in the Indonesia Democracy Party (PDI) were only accessible to Indonesians via the international satellite services. None of the domestic services ran the story, nor would they co-operate with international news agencies attempting to transmit footage out of Indonesia. The international news organisations transported videotapes of the footage by air to Singapore, from where it was filed via satellite to their newsrooms (Simpson 1996).

The concerns by governments of Asia regarding satellite television are not only connected to global feedback loops during times of crisis, important though these phenomena are. Issues of education, materialist value systems, race relations, sexuality and religion feature among the reasons given by government for the need to circumvent Western programming (Lent 1989). A recent—although not especially important—casualty of this complex environment was Porky Pig, a cartoon that was dropped from Turner Broadcasting system's TNT & Cartoon channel because of the risk of offending Muslim viewers in Asia (*Eastern Express* 1995). In contrast, the channel in 1995 ran a festival of movies and other programs about 'making money' to coincide with the Lunar New Year—squarely aimed at Asia's Chinese viewers. Topping the bill in the cartoon programs was Richie Rich (Blennerhassett 1995).

China: Star's elusive prize

Rupert Murdoch's Banqueting House pronouncement about the new media being a threat to 'totalitarian regimes everywhere' drew immediate retribution from Beijing. While the government had been irritated by BBC reportage on Star TV under Li (prompting it in February 1993 to ask 'why the BBC hates China so much as to regard China as its enemy') (*Straits Times* 1993a), Murdoch's rhetoric clearly raised the Chinese authorities' concerns to new heights. Individuals and businesses in China were banned from setting up or using parabolic antennae without government approval. Unauthorised manufacturers and retailers were to be closed down. The order signed by the Prime Minister, Li Peng, in October 1993, said the regulations were designed to 'promote the construction of a socialist spiritual civilisation' (Lam 1993). The ruling represented a very serious setback for Star TV's commercial plans. China was considered the plum of the Asian television market. Despite its developing industrial status, China is the biggest single television market in the world, with an estimated 186 million television households. Because of the country's size and regional nature, the television industry is extremely fragmented. Historically the state broadcaster—China Central Television (CCTV)—has dominated the country's television industry, alongside government-controlled regional stations. Unable to officially reach the vast audiences by DTH or cable, Murdoch began a campaign designed to ingratiate News Corporation with Beijing, jettisoning many of his stated liberal principles in the process.

While Murdoch controlled the Star TV network, he had no say in the programming on BBCWST. The BBC further infuriated Chinese authorities by airing pictures of the 1989 violence in Tiananmen Square and producing and airing on its domestic service in Britain a documentary on Mao Zedong which referred to his sexual activity with young women. In February Guo Baoxing of China's Ministry of Radio, Film and Television told Star TV to remove the BBCWST (Harris 1994). About the same time, while visiting India, Murdoch floated the notion of dropping BBC WST from Star TV unless it addressed accusations of bias against China and India. 'There has been some sensitivity, particularly about beaming foreign news into China...We certainly intend to do everything we can to resolve certain difficulties with the Government of China' (Finlay 1994). In another gesture to Beijing, News Corporation sold most of its half share in the Hong Kong newspaper the *South China Morning Post*. In its editorial pages, the publication was supportive of the colony's Governor, Chris Patten, an adversary of the Chinese political leadership (*Australian* 1994b:20).

When BBCWST was axed in March 1994 to be replaced by Mandarin language films (only on the AsiaSat satellite system's northern footprint covering China, not on the southern footprint covering India and the Middle East), it was stated that it was for 'purely commercial reasons'. Star TV's chief executive, Gary Davey, told a news conference that the move had nothing to do with political sensitivity of beaming BBC news into China (*Asian Wall Street Journal* 1994:5). Three months later Murdoch revealed that this defence was untrue. He told his biographer, William Shawcross, that BBCWST had been pulled in the hope of soothing bad relations with Beijing. 'I was well aware that the freedom fighters of the world would abuse me for it' (*Australian Financial Review* 1994:27). The openness and transparency of world affairs promised by the new liberalised and instantaneous telecommunications environment at Murdoch's Banqueting Hall speech was to have its limitations. A telling explanation subsequently came from Davey in a 1995 Channel 4 documentary, which revealed the fragility of the commitment to news and current affairs programming at the network.

> Davey: It (the removal of BBC World Service Television from Star TV over China) suited very important business imperatives.
>
> Question: But it also suited a political imperative?
>
> Davey: That is part of our business. (*Satellite Wars* 1995)

Several strategies designed to improve relations with Beijing were adopted by Star TV in 1995: commercial sponsorship of activities for the family of China's paramount leader, Deng Xiaoping; commercial ventures with government media services; and logistical and broadcasting support for Chinese sport. Murdoch moderated a news conference in New York for Deng

Rong, the Chinese leader's eldest daughter. Through its publishing subsidiary Harper Collins, News Corporation had secured the rights for the English translation of her 1993 book *My Father, Deng Xiaoping*. As well Murdoch offered to pay for a visit to Australia and New Zealand by Deng Rong's brother Deng Pufang, who was to lead a tour by disabled Chinese athletes (*Sun-Herald* 1995:10). News Corporation announced a joint venture to build four television studios in Tianjin at a cost of $US12 million and in June a $US5.4 million, venture to develop on-line information services with the *People's Daily* (*South China Morning Post* 1995). Sport, considered politically safe television programming, has also gained Murdoch's attention, resulting in the setting up of a management company, Sportscorp. Focussed on China, its function is to stage large sporting events such as tennis, golf and basketball. It has also staged badminton competitions in Malaysia and Indonesia. The competitions may well end up on Star TV's Prime Sports channel (Ellis 1995). As well, Prime has acquired the broadcasting rights to games from the Chinese Football Association.

While it is convenient to single out Murdoch as the mogul-villain, deeper attention needs to be paid to the underlying conflict between the ethical and commercial imperatives of broadcasting organisations seeking to penetrate into a market such as China. This conflict lies at the heart of the perplexing and often-illiberal broadcasting structures born of political and business alliances, unfettered by the ethics of public service broadcasting principles. When Murdoch seeks an entrée into a market such as China, he is required to engage in a bidding process with rivals. Not only are host governments—via their agencies or business allies—being offered financial rewards from collaborative partnerships, they are also being offered new levels of sycophantic support from broadcasting organisations. Consider Hong Kong-based China Entertainment Television Broadcasts (CETV), which won rights from Beijing for a cable and terrestrial distribution network covering 35% of China's television homes, including all major cities. One time Playboy-style channel operator Robert Chua is chairman of CETV. The network proclaims 'no sex, no violence, no news'. While the slogan fits neatly with the commercial tenor of 1990s television, it is perhaps worth reflecting on the value of a broadcasting system where news and current affairs information is rated with the same level of disdain as murder, rape and pornography. Chua told a Pan-Asia Television conference in 1994 that CETV would devote itself to 'government-friendly, family entertainment' (*Straits Times* 1994). The pitch has been successful, with take-up on government-endorsed cable systems in China, Malaysia, Taiwan and Singapore. CETV claims an audience of 28 million in China alone, although that figure has not been independently verified (Heim 1995).

In the international broadcast news Industry, the trend is the same, although somewhat less crass in its articulation and less overtly collaborative in its execution. Ted Turner, the chairman of CNN's parent company, Turner Broadcasting, found it necessary to proclaim after Murdoch's run-in with Beijing: 'I personally don't believe that any country is in a position to tell any other country what to do. I'm a great believer in live and let live.' (Turner 1994). In 1994 Turner concluded an agreement with CCTV for CNN to be rebroadcast throughout China. CNN's reports on the fifth anniversary of the Tiananmen Square demonstrations and killings were cut by Chinese censors (O'Neill 1994:64). More recently CNN was singled out for mention for apparently compromising its coverage in an effort to conclude rebroadcasting agreements with the authorities in Pyongyang.

> CNN generally tries to avoid political confrontation. If you look at its recent coverage of North Korea, they sent a crew to North Korea and it was well-known that they were looking at various commercial deals in North Korea and their coverage of the country was unrecognisable compared to anybody else's coverage...Their stories came out just before the news of the famine broke. (Simpson 1996)

Turner Broadcasting executives say that with the more competitive environment in Southeast Asia since the arrival of Star TV, they are paying more attention to government relations. 'We need to have contact with people at the top, to get their blessing' (Private interview, CNN executive, 16 March 1995). Thus there are regular meetings with ministers.

In 1994 Star TV announced it was seeking partnerships in all Asian countries, and the services would not pose political problems. At a presentation for governments and industry leaders in Hong Kong, Gary Davey suggested there would be massive returns for Asian governments that worked with, rather than against, the network (Lee 1994). As far as one can generalise about the experiences among the diverse nation-states of East Asia, the trend has been for Murdoch to achieve agreement at an elite political level, then execute logistical arrangements through broadcasting organisations, which invariably are either arms of state broadcasting or private companies with close affiliations to the government. Under these arrangements, there will be potential for all the cable or national satellite operators to censor material on the Star TV service. However, under News Corporation's carefully developed 'glocalisation' (global company/local programming) plans, the local language programming is likely to have been carefully scrutinised in a process of self-censorship, notwithstanding the anodyne nature of the programming.

Plans announced in 1995 by Murdoch for a News Corporation global 24-hour news channel to rival CNN now appear to exclude the Asian sphere. When Murdoch revealed the global news channel proposal in November, he explained that it was needed to restore balance, as Ted Turner and CNN were shifting 'further and further and further to the left' (*Sydney Morning Herald* 1995:22). However, eight months later a Star TV executive emphatically denied the network would be part of the global news services. Television news, it seemed, was not appropriate programming for Asia. Star TV had 'four key entertainment categories: sport, music, movies and general entertainment—versioned for local markets' (Gautier 1996:1).

A growth area in international broadcasting in the region is 'business' television. Asia Business News (ABN), based in Singapore, was set up in 1994 by Dow Jones, Tele-Communications Inc and Television New Zealand. An investment arm of the Singapore government—Singapore International Media, which also controls all of the country's 'corporatised' free-to-air television services holds 10% of ABN. The channel reports data from global financial markets, interviews with business leaders and soft news. A second satellite-delivered channel, CNBC, began the following year, an offshoot of the NBC network of the US, owned by General Electric. Political comment or opposition perspectives are avoided on both channels.

> They tend to avoid any kind of critical comment on the governments. It's quite notable that they'll talk about the economy and criticism of the economy and criticism of business, but they really steer clear of any critical comment of regional governments. (Simpson 1996)

In Malaysia in late 1994, Prime Minister Mahathir Mohamad announced that government officials would study Rupert Murdoch's global television networks before deciding whether Star TV would be allowed to be officially broadcast in Malaysia. It was revealed for the first time that the Prime Minister had secretly met Murdoch two weeks earlier in Kuala Lumpur to discuss the proposal. 'He [Murdoch] assured me that we can switch the programmes on and off. If we don't like a particular programme, we can switch it off,' said Mahathir (*New Straits Times* 1994). This reported agreement between Murdoch and Mahathir represented the ultimate realpolitik approach to broadcasting regulation—an agreement between the heads of a government and a transnational media corporation for a state 'master switch' able to black out unwanted media product.

The meeting between Murdoch and Mahathir—and their agreement on the rather unique broadcasting principles—seemed unimaginable one year earlier, when they were perceived as international adversaries: the media imperialist versus the anti-Western nationalist. Their media values and ambitions for control collided in full international gaze. It is still uncertain; Star TV appears set to be distributed there on government-endorsed satellite and terrestrial pay television systems, both of which are controlled by commercial groups with close links to UMNO, the ruling party.

In Indonesia, the terrestrial television industry has also grown rapidly, from the single state broadcaster TVRI (Televisi Republik Indonesia) to an additional five commercial networks, the majority controlled by members of the Suharto family or close business associates. Bambang Trihatmodjo, ex-President Suharto's second son, heads the huge Bimantara Citra group. In 1993 Bambang declared Bimantara would 'become the real telecommunications King' in Indonesia. In addition to effective control of Satelit Palapa Indonesia (Satelindo), Bambang controls the most successful television network in the country, RCTI, and the sole direct-top-home (DTH) pay-television company, Malincak.

In 1994 Malincak was awarded, by ministerial decree, the exclusive right to deliver international DTH programming. A partner company, Satelindo, has been handed exclusive development rights for the Palapa system. Initially the large US programmers, including Turner Broadcasting, Home Box Office (HBO) and ESPN Sports, entered a joint project—Indovision—with Malincak. However, after a poor subscription take-up, Star TV effectively replaced the other international broadcasters in the venture to form Star Indo Entertainment. News Corporation has been made the international gatekeeper of the exclusive satellite delivery platform to Indonesia for encrypted programming, requiring its competitors such as Turner Broadcasting and HBO to lease transponder time. Star plans to bring a number of subscription channels to Indonesia via this service, although news will not be part of the schedule. Star TV has based its Southeast Asian operations in Jakarta and will employ about 400 local people to run the service. Star TV's Southeast Asia director, David Dennis, said at the commencement of operations in Jakarta in 1995: 'We try to be as non-political as possible' (Soh 1995).

Singapore has most successfully resisted intrusion of DTH services, achieving 100% compliance with its ban on private dishes, unlike in China and Malaysia, where the regulations are widely flouted. It has, however, commissioned an optical fibre cable network, including 35 television channels, that was planned to reach all 750,000 homes in Singapore by 2000. The venture, Singapore CableVision, is controlled by two state-owned companies, Singapore Press Holdings (owner of the *Straits Times* which effectively is an arm of the state) and the third largest United States cable operator, Continental Cablevision. One of the channels will be BBC World News (Karp 1995:81). Singapore's approach to news is uncertain. CNN has set a precedent, however. It alerts SCV of any material it considers may upset the Singaporean authorities, for instance coverage of the caning of a US teenager found guilty of vandalising cars in Singapore.[1]

Thus far, the BBC has been unyielding in its insistence that the news must be run in its entirety or not at all, arguing that censorship by governments undermines the credibility of its brand name. This was most clearly demonstrated in 1994, when the BBC withdrew from an arrangement with Malaysia's RTM to rebroadcast its world news bulletin. RTM had edited out a bulletin's lead item featuring labour protests on the Indonesian island of Sumatra, involving tens of thousands of workers. The segment showed the lynching of an ethnic Chinese businessman and vandalism of Chinese-owned shops by factory workers demanding more money. The parliamentary secretary for the Ministry of Information, Fauzi Rahman, said the footage was damaging to Malaysia's good relations with Indonesia, but also harmful to the racial harmony of Malaysia. Fauzi said Malaysia did not mind losing screening rights to BBC news as it could turn to other services such as CNN or Britain's ITN (*Australian* 1994a). After the BBC incident, a US diplomat in Kuala Lumpur declared: 'CNN has stayed in good favour by tolerating editing of its material.' (private interview).

In April 1996 BBC World disappeared from many screens across Southeast and South Asia, when Star TV decided not to renew its delivery contract with the BBC on the AsiaSat system. News Corporation's decision banishes BBC World to a less accessible satellite system, PanAmSat, which requires an expensive decoder in Southeast Asia (Waltham 1996). The BBC is now looking to cable redistribution to rebuild its audience. Star TV has replaced BBC World with a Hindi movie channel.

Conclusion

The engagement of well-connected local partners—which often share the paternalistic values of the government—helps eliminate political distractions for transnational media corporations. These arrangements provide conduits for their programming through cable and domestic DTH systems. Ironically, while these government-sanctioned processes evolve, in the West Murdoch continues to belittle regulation. He said on Australia's *60 Minutes* program in 1995: 'We don't like licences from governments. We don't even like dealing with governments.' (*60 Minutes* 1995). The fact is that for the time being, the transnational media companies needs governments in East Asia. The state is not withering away in the area of electronic information control; instead elements of the state are forming links with accommodating private sector

---

[1] Interview with SCV official, Singapore, November 1994. In this case, the Singapore authorities raised no objections to the item; however, they asked to be given a right of reply.

partners in order to preserve elements of the broadcasting systems most essential to power.

Contrary to Rupert Murdoch's claim that the new media are an 'unambiguous threat to totalitarian régimes everywhere', the systematic collaboration of transnational media corporations with regional governments has the potential to retard the development of more challenging and dynamic television, especially in information programs. News Corporation's decision to remove BBCWST from Star TV, and CNN's agreement to modify its news coverage to placate political sensibilities are symptomatic of the dangers of an internationalised television environment where programming choices pass through filters forged from commercial and political collaboration rather than through filters developed by careful analysis of social goals and principles. The evolution of 'business-only' news channels, without balancing services to investigate social and political forces in Asia, limits the scope for wider pluralism and political openness in the region. It serves to legitimise the authority of market systems and logic of economic imperatives in the framing of government policy. CETV's 'no sex, no violence, no news' formula—embraced by Chinese and Singaporean authorities—is a striking example of the privatised, political-moral authoritarianism that can evolve from such alliances. Clearly, the 'liberalisation' of the media marketplace does not necessarily give rise to the liberalisation of the marketplace of ideas.

References

Asian Wall Street Journal 1994, 'Star TV Plans to Implement New Strategy', 23 March.

Atkins, William 1995, *Satellite Television and State Power in Southeast Asia: New Issues of Discourse and Control*, Centre for Asian Communication, Media and Cultural Studies, Edith Cowan University, Perth.

Australian 1994a, 'Malaysia will defy BBC news order', May.

—— 1994b (Business Asia section), 'Beijing "influenced STAR"', 22 June–5 July.

Australian Financial Review 1994, 'Murdoch axed BBC to appease Chinese', 15 June.

Blennerhassett, Jane 1995, 'One man's meat is another's taboo', *Business Times*, Singapore, 19 January.

Business Times 1993, 'Dawn of the convergent, interactive era', 17 September.

Eastern Express 1995, 'No sex (or pigs) please, it's Asia', Hong Kong, 19 January.

Ellis, Eric 1995, 'Murdoch's new tactic: A sporting invasion of Asia', *The Australian Financial Review*, 4 April.

Finlay, Victoria 1994, 'Murdoch threat to drop BBC', *South China Morning Post International Weekly*, 19–20 February.

Gautier, Douglas 1996, 'Thinking Globally and Acting Locally: The Art of Accommodation', paper presented to 25th Annual Conference of Asian Mass Communication Research and Information Centre (AMIC), Singapore, 1–3 June.

Harris, Margaret 1994, 'Murdoch star struggles to shine', *Sun-Herald*, Sydney, 20 March.

Heim, Kristi 1995, 'CETV Attracts Three Foreign Partners', *Asian Wall Street Journal*, 1–2 December.

Hoover, Stewart M, Venturelli, Shalini Singh and Wagner, Douglas K 1993, 'Trends in Global Communication Policy-making: Lessons from the Asian Case', *Asian Journal of Communication*, Vol 3, No 1.

Karp, Jonathan 1995, 'Star Burst: Satellite Broadcaster gets into Singapore', *Far Eastern Economic Review*, 6 April.

Lam, Willy Wo-Lap 1993, 'PM issues ban to halt spread of influence from satellite TV', *South China Morning Post International Weekly*, 16–17 October.

Lee Han Shih 1994, 'Murdoch offers Asian govts package to help turn around Star TV', *Business Times*, 23 March.

Lent, John 1989, 'Mass Communication in Asia and the Pacific: Recent Trends and Development', *Media Asia: An Asian Mass Communications Quarterly*, Vol 16, No 1.

Lim, Khor Yoke 1994, 'Deregulation or Reregulation of the Malaysian Broadcasting Industry?', Annual Conference of the International Communications Association, Sydney, 1994.

Manaev, Oleg and Pryliuk, Yuri 1993, 'Introduction', in Manaev, Oleg and Pryliuk, Yuri (eds), *Media in Transition: From Totalitarianism to Democracy*, ABRIS, Kiev.

Negrine, R and Papathanassopoulos, S 1990, *The Internationalisation of Television*, Pinter, London.

New Straits Times 1994, 'KL to take closer look at Murdoch's Sky TV', 14 November.

Ong, Catherine 1993, 'Why is Li Ka-shing reducing stake just when Star TV is getting its act together?', *Business Times*, 28 July.

O'Neill, John 1994, 'The Great Stonewall of China', *The Independent Monthly*, Sydney, September.

Satellite Wars 1995, Channel 4 and Brook Productions, London.

Simpson, Iain 1996, BBC World Service Correspondent (Singapore), private interview with the author, Jakarta, 26 June.

60 Minutes 1995, Nine Network Australia, 26 March.

South China Morning Post International Weekly 1995, 'Murdoch's rising STAR', 12 August.

Soh, Felix 1995, 'Star TV tailors shows to woo region's viewers', *Straits Times*, 25 August.

Splichal, Slavko 1993, 'Searching for New Paradigms: An Introduction' in Splichal, Slavko and Wasko, Janet (eds), *Communication and Democracy*, Ablex, Norwood.

Sreberny-Mohammadi, Annabelle 1996, 'Whither National Sovereignty: Cultural Identities in a Global Context', paper presented to 25th Annual Conference of Asian Mass Communication Research and Information Centre (AMIC), Singapore, 1–3 June.

Straits Times 1993a, 'High anxiety in China over 'subversion' by satellite TV and fax', 9 February.

—— 1993b, 'Murdoch firm reassures Asians over Star TV buy: Network won't become vehicle for interference, it says', 6 August.

—— 1994, 'Beijing urged to resist open-sky television policy', 22 September.

Sun-Herald 1995, 'Murdoch woos China', 5 February.

Sydney Morning Herald 1995, 'Turner to 'squash' Murdoch', 12 December.

Teske, Paul Eric 1990, *After Divestiture: The Political Economy of State Telecommunications Regulation*, State University of New York Press, Albany.

Tiffen, Rodney, 'International News and Political Agendas in the Asia-Pacific Region', paper presented to the Australia–Japan Symposium, University of Tokyo.

Turner, Ted 1994, 'The Mission Thing', speech delivered to the 1994 Pan Asia Cable and Satellite Television Conference, Hong Kong, March, reproduced in *Index on Censorship*, Vol 23, No 4–5.

Waltham, Tony 1996, 'Costly Devices needed to pick up BBC Again', *Bangkok Post*, 4 April.

Wark, McKenzie 1990, 'Vectors of Memory...Seeds of Fire: The Western Media and the Beijing Demonstrations', *New Formations*, No 10.

Wasko, Janet 1993, 'Introduction: Studies in Communication Democracy', in Splichal, Slavko and Wasko, Janet (eds), *Communication and Democracy*, Ablex, Norwood.

Notes on the contributors

Dr William Atkins is a private-sector media consultant in London, specialising in broadcasting, satellite and Asia–Pacific media issues. In 1999 he was awarded a PhD by the University of Sydney, his thesis focussing on the political economy of media in ASEAN in the 1990s. From 1996 to 1998 he was chief researcher in communications at the Sydney-based Research Institute for Asia and the Pacific. During the 1980s, William worked as a journalist for the BBC and ITN in London and the ABC and West Australian Newspapers in Australia.

Dr Damien Kingsbury, a former journalist, is Executive Officer of the Monash Asia Institute. He is co-author of *Media Realities: the News Media and Power in Australian Society* (1996 Addison Wesley Longman) and author of *Culture and Politics: Australian Journalism on Indonesia* (1996 CSAAR) and *The Politics of Indonesia* (1998 OUP).

Dr Philip Kitley is Senior Lecturer in the Department of Humanities and International Studies, University of Southern Queensland. He is the author of *Television, Nation and Culture in Indonesia* (2000 Ohio University Press). Philip Kitley was First Secretary (Cultural) at the Australian Embassy in Jakarta, 1986–89. His chapter in this volume was originally published in the *University of Technology Sydney Review* (1998 Vol 4 No 2).

Professor Alan Knight is Chair of Journalism and Media Studies at Central Queensland University. An Honorary Research Fellow at Hong Kong University's Centre of Asian Studies, Dr Knight has been researching how foreign correspondents cover Asia. With Dr Yoshiko Nakano, he co-authored *Reporting Hong Kong: the Foreign Press and the Handover* (1999 Curzon, London). He was formerly a journalist at the Australian Broadcasting Corporation.

Glen Lewis is Associate Professor in the Faculty of Communications at the University of Canberra; Professor of the Graduate School, University of Bangkok, Thailand; and Adjunct Professor at the UNITEC Institute of Technology, Auckland, New Zealand. He is co-author of *Communication Traditions in 20th Century Australia* (1995 OUP).

Dr Eric Loo is Head of the Graduate School of Journalism at the University of Wollongong. He has worked as a journalist in Malaysia, the Philippines and Australia. He has also conducted journalism workshops in Laos and Malaysia. His research interests are comparative media studies, and the internet's impact on conventional journalistic practice. He is founding editor of the *AsiaPacific Media Educator*.

Barry Lowe is an Associate Professor in the Department of English at the City University of Hong Kong, where he teaches journalism and multimedia authoring. He also does media training throughout the Asian region and runs a video production studio in Hong Kong. He has worked for a number of print and broadcast outlets in Australia and abroad. His main research interest is in reporting conflict.

Dr John Marston is Professor and Researcher at the Centro de Estudios de Asia y Africa, Colegio de México. In the early 1980s he worked in refugee camps in Thailand and the Philippines, and he has been going to Cambodia regularly since 1989. He worked for the UN in Cambodia at the time of the 1993 elections. He completed a doctorate in anthropology at University of Washington in 1997.

Warwick Mules teaches and researches in cultural studies at the School of Humanities, Central Queensland University. He has co-authored a successful book, *Tools for Cultural Studies* (1994 Macmillan Education Australia), and has written articles on media and the transnational public sphere, the technology of visual culture, television and film. His current research project involves an historical analysis of the technology of visual print media.

Dr Patricia Payne is a Research Associate with the School of Professional Communication, University of Canberra, and works with the Australian Biography of Senators Unit at Parliament House. Her PhD, from Sydney University, examined the role of the press in reporting major policy decisions during Australia's participation in the Vietnam War. She is author of *The Canberra Press Gallery and the Backbench of the 38th Parliament 1996–98* (1999 Department of the Parliamentary Library, Canberra).

Angela Romano has recently completed doctoral research into the professional cultures and practices of journalists in Indonesia, winning the 1998 Cultural and Media Policy Research Prize and the 1999 AMIC Asian Print Media Write Award for articles resulting from her thesis. She writes for *Business Asia* and has worked as a print and radio journalist in Australia and Jakarta.

Adam Schofield holds a Bachelor of Arts (Honours) from Monash University and a Masters Degree in Political Science from the University of Melbourne. Adam worked with the first Howard Government as a Ministerial Adviser, liaising with trade missions from various Asian countries. He is currently the Manager of Government Affairs at Cable & Wireless Optus, whose parent company is active throughout Asia. Adam has an abiding interest in Australia's political engagement with Southeast Asia and in particular Australia's relationship with Malaysia.

John Tobbutt is completing a cultural history of Australian foreign correspondents with a focus on Asia. He has worked as a radio correspondent in the Philippines, and led a study tour of Australian journalists there in 1991. He is currently teaching journalism at Monash University. Previous publications include 'Corresponding Affairs: media and foreign policy' in Craik, Jennifer, Moran, Albert and James Bailey, Julie (eds) 1995, *Public Voices, Private Interests*, Allen and Unwin. He is an editor for the journal *AsiaPacific Media Educator*, including, with Angela Romano, a 1999 edition on foreign correspondents.

Dr Rodney Tiffen is Associate Professor in the Department of Government, University of Sydney. He is the author of *Scandals: Media, Politics and Corruption in Contemporary Australia* (1999 UNSW Press), *News and Power* (1989 Allen and Unwin) and *The News from Southeast Asia: the Sociology of Newsmaking* (1978 Institute of Southeast Asian Studies, Singapore).

Also published by the Monash Asia Institute

To be free: stories from Asia's struggle against oppression
Chee Soon Juan.
1998, $24.95. ISBN 0 7326 1173 3

This popular and controversial book tells the personal and political stories of people who have been persecuted because they stood up for freedom and democracy in Asia: Chia Thye Poh in Singapore, Aung San Suu Khi in Burma, Pramoedya Ananta Toer in Indonesia, Benigno Aquino in the Philippines, Kim Dae Jung in South Korea and Shih Ming-teh in Taiwan. Chee Soon Juan challenges the myth that 'Asian values' should deny human rights and democracy in Asia and prevent the international community from being concerned about these issues.

The last days of President Suharto
edited by Arief Budiman, Barbara Hatley and Damien Kingsbury
1999, $24.95. ISBN 0 7326 1179 2

This collection of analytical articles from the international media details the financial crisis and public pressure that led to the resignation of President Suharto, including detailed information about the student protests, para-military activities and the people currently competing for power in Indonesia.

Regionalism, Subregionalism and APEC
edited by John Ingleson
1997, $24.95. ISBN 0 7326 1167 9

Can Asia Pacific Economic Co-operation become a successful umbrella organisation across such a diverse group of countries? Can it help in the development of an Asian-Pacific community? How is it viewed by the United States, Japan, Korea and Australia? The contributors to this book come from a variety of disciplines, universities and countries. Together they have produced an assessment of APEC in its wider regional and global context.